William Roscoe Burgess

Notes, Chiefly Critical and Philological, on the Hebrew Psalms

Vol. II

William Roscoe Burgess

Notes, Chiefly Critical and Philological, on the Hebrew Psalms
Vol. II

ISBN/EAN: 9783744779746

Printed in Europe, USA, Canada, Australia, Japan

Cover: Foto ©Thomas Meinert / pixelio.de

More available books at **www.hansebooks.com**

NOTES,

CHIEFLY CRITICAL AND PHILOLOGICAL,

ON THE

HEBREW PSALMS,

BY

WILLIAM ROSCOE BURGESS, M.A.,

VICAR OF HOLLOWELL.

VOL. II.

WILLIAMS AND NORGATE,
14, HENRIETTA STREET, COVENT GARDEN, LONDON,
AND 20, SOUTH FREDERICK STREET, EDINBURGH.
1881.

WADDINGTON:
PRINTED BY GEORGE POWLSON, ADVERTISER OFFICE,
MARKET GATE.

NOTES

ON THE

HEBREW PSALMS.

Psalm LXIX.

v. 5. This verse presents many difficulties. By adopting the reading which the Syriac translator seems to have found, not only do these difficulties vanish, but a remarkably beautiful and symmetrical meaning appears. The Syr. read מעצמותי instead of מצמיתי. The meaning thus is:—*They that hate me without a cause are more numerous than the hairs of my head: They that are deceitfully adverse to me are stronger than my bones;*—with a play upon the Hebrew words for *strong* and *bone.*

The authority of the LXX. is, however, totally opposed to this. They give οἱ ἐχθροί μου, οἱ ἐκδιώκοντές με ἀδίκως. Now the Hiph. of צמת is rendered by ἐκδιώκω also in Ps. ci. 5. And ἐχθρός is the constant rendering of איב. It seems certain, therefore, that the LXX. read

איבי מצמיתי instead of the inverse order, which is the order of the present Hebrew text. This inverted order, however, is in favour of the existing text, since it suits the reading מצמיתי, but is quite incompatible with מעצמותי. So that, against the Syriac reading, as given above, may be adduced, not only the Septuagint rendering of the words in question, but also the order in which the LXX. appear to have found them.

id. *When I never robbed, then I restored. O God Thou knowest.* Comp. Ps. xl. 10.

This disjoining of ידעת from לאולתי obviates the objection that ידע is not elsewhere followed by ל. The next verse will now begin with לאולתי, thus—

v. 6. *As for my thoughtlessness and my open transgressions, they are not hid from Thee.* For this use of ל see Gesenius. See also my note on Ps. xvii. 3, 4.

From the frequent use of אולה in the Book of Proverbs we may gather that it denoted a sin of thoughtlessness, or a condition of thoughtlessness. The word אשמה, however, denotes something much more serious, viz. sin that amounts to a breach of the covenant.

v. 7. Such sin would both give occasion to the enemies of the Lord to blaspheme, and would also be a scandal to the faithful. This latter result of his offence is here deprecated by the Psalmist.

v. 8. In this view it is impossible to take עליך as meaning *For Thy sake*. The reproach under which the Psalmist lay was the penalty of his sin,—not, as it were, a burden borne for God. Yet although the expression cannot mean, in this sense, *For Thy sake*, it may well mean *Because of Thee*. It is thus a continuation of the thought of the preceding verse, as if the writer should say, I care little for the reproach of men: it is on God's account that I feel the shame and disgrace of my sin,—lest I should bring reproach upon Him and upon His people.

Perhaps the nearest rendering will be,— *It is in consideration of Thee* that I have borne reproach. Reproach has been to me reproach, chiefly in this light and with this consideration.

v. 9. Still dependent upon the עליך of v. 8.

It is in consideration of Thee that I am estranged, &c.

v. 10. קנאת ביתך, *Jealous anxiety for Thy household.** *It is because a jealous anxiety consumes me*, viz. lest they that wait upon God should be put to shame through my sin.

id. *The reproaches of them that reproach Thee are fallen upon me,*—Why? Because if I had not sinned they would have had no occasion of reproaching Thee. The reproach falls upon me the more heavily because I have involved *Thee* in the same reproach.

v. 11. The mention, in this verse and the next, of the Psalmist's weeping, fasting, and putting on of sackcloth, shews him as a penitent on account of some grievous sin. It is of importance to observe this, because the usual interpretation of this Psalm shews the writer rather as a man who, though conscious of integrity, is yet willing to suffer shame for God's sake.

id. ואבכה בצום נפשי. *And I bewailed my soul with fasting.* בכה is followed by an

---

* For this meaning of ביתך see Ps. cxxii. 8 and 9, where the Psalmist identifies his brethren and companions with the house of the Lord his God.

accusative of the person bewailed in Gen. xxiii. 2, xxxvii. 35, and l. 3. The expression, *to bewail one's soul*, may be compared with the blessing or congratulating of one's soul, as in Ps. xlix. 19.

v. 14. It is clear from this verse that the Psalmist, however by his sin he had forfeited covenant privileges, had been restored to those privileges in consequence of his penitence, and in consequence no doubt of such ceremonial observances as were ordained in such cases. In my note on Ps. xxxii. 6, I have compared the expression עת מצא there with עת רצון here; adding that "in this latter place the covenant relationship is certainly assumed, because God's faithfulness (אמת ישעך) is pleaded."

The enemies of the Psalmist desire that he may not be so restored, and represent him as unworthy of such restitution. With respect to him, and others who endure God's chastisement, they pray, not that their iniquity may be forgiven, but that God will add to it, and so on, as in verses 28 and 29.

v. 27. יספרו *They speak*. What they speak is given in the next two verses. But both the LXX. and the Syriac read יספו or יוספו instead of יספרו.

vv. 28 and 29. My reason for putting these two verses into the mouth of the adversaries is, not that the language is too strong for the Psalmist to use towards them, but because it is far more appropriate as used by them towards him. The effect of the Psalmist's sin, unless repented of and forgiven, would be precisely the effect of their imprecation. He would not have returned to the state of righteousness, (בצדקתך) which is God's righteousness; for which see notes on Ps. xl. 10, and li. 21. He would have been blotted out of God's Book, in accordance with that which is written in Exod. xxxii. 32,—*Whosoever hath sinned against me, him will I blot out of my book.* He would not have been written among the righteous, because of his persistence in iniquity. These are the opposites of those things that the Psalmist hoped for, upon his repentance; and they therefore are the theme of his opponents' imprecation.

Again, it does not appear that these opponents cared about God's favour, or covenant privileges, or anything of the kind; and therefore the imprecation is without point if put into the Psalmist's mouth.

Moreover, the Psalmist seems to end his imprecation in v. 26, since in v. 27 he proceeds to give a reason and a justification of it. It would be strange if, after this, he should resume the imprecation. It is therefore reasonable, on this ground, to make verses 28 and 29 a part of his justification, viz. a recital of the expressed desire of the enemies.

I have here identified *the book of the living* of this Psalm with the *book of God* mentioned in Exod. xxxii. 32. Delitzsch, however, takes the expression of the text to mean " struck out of the list of the living, that is, of the living in this present world." But this can hardly be, since the expression is so immediately amplified by the mention of those who are written among the righteous. Much better is the following from Dr. Perowne, who, however, takes the imprecation as uttered by the Psalmist. He says, —" The figure is borrowed from the civil lists or register in which the names of citizens were enrolled. To be blotted out of this denotes exclusion from all the blessings and privileges of the theocracy."

v. 30. *However poor and however miserable, of myself, yet Thy Salvation, O God, lifts me up.*

"For Thy sweet love remembered such wealth brings
That then I scorn to change my state with kings."

v. 31. And hereupon comes that which is the peculiar privilege of God's people, viz. the *Tehillah*.

So shall I boast (אהללה) *the Name of God.*

v. 32. The *song (Shir)* of the preceding verse, will be more acceptable than *an ox (Shor)*. The alliteration seems to be intentional; and, if so, the mention of the horns and hoofs of the ox will merely serve the purpose of explaining the play upon the words.

v. 33. Compare ראו ענוים ישמחו דרשי אלחים ויחי לבבכם יאכלו ענוים וישבעו יהללו יהוה דרשיו יחי לבבכם לעד in Ps. xxii. 27.

In this 33rd verse the LXX. read דרשו (imperative) instead of דרשי. They also read ויחי (imperative) instead of ויחי; and in their reading לבבכם was wanting. Perhaps we ought to take all the verbs as imperatives, thus:—*Be-*

hold ye poor and rejoice : seek God and live, or, *let your heart revive.*

The Syriac reads לבבכם, but omits the words דרשי אלהים.

Psalm LXX.

This Psalm is identical (excepting a few variations) with the latter part of the 40th Psalm. The important variations are these :—

Ps. XL.	Ps. LXX.
14. רצה יהוה להצילני יהוה לעזרתי חושה	2. אלהים להצילני יהוה לעזרתי חושה
15. יבשו ויחפרו יחד מבקשי נפשי לספותה	3. Omits יחד and לספותה
16. ישמו.	4. ישובו
17. יהוה תשועתך.	5. אלהים ישועתך
18. אדני יחשב לי עזרתי אלהי	6. אלהים חושה לי עזרי יהוה

Since the 40th Psalm would plainly be imperfect if deprived of those verses which we find repeated here, we must conclude that this 70th

Psalm is only a detached portion of the former:—detached, probably, as being of more general application than the whole of the Psalm. The variations noted above shew that it must have existed as a separate Psalm for a considerable time previous to the present arrangement of the Psalter. The words Jehovah and Elohim seem to be used indifferently.*

---

* Ewald says of the indifferent use of these words here, and in the Psalter generally, that "it has nothing in common with the interchange of the same Divine names in the Pentateuch." He supposes it to arise from the greater or less degree of scrupulosity, on the part of copyists, as to the use of the sacred name Jehovah. In like manner, Kuenen, after reciting the general principles of distinction between these names, says:—"Ceci toutefois n'empêche pas que très-souvent aussi aucun motif général ne détermine le choix, et qu'un auteur ne se serve d'un nom plutôt que de l'autre pour des raisons toutes subjectives. . . . . . Ainsi, dans les livres plus récents de l'Ancien Testament, (comme dans l'Ecclesiaste), on évite le nom de Jéhovah : dans plusieurs psaumes, on rencontre le nom d'Elohim avec le même sens où, dans le recueil de ces cantiques et ailleurs, on trouve employé le nom de Jéhovah." In illustration, he compares Ps. xiv. with Ps. liii.; and Judges v 4, 6, with Ps. xlviii. 8, 9. He might have added the comparison of this seventieth Psalm with the fortieth.

v. 2. The verb רצה, of Ps. lxx, is omitted here. Yet the construction, with this omission, is not unexampled, as Delitzch supposes. See Ps. xxxv. 23.

Psalm LXXI.

v. 3. *Be Thou to me a fortress-home, to which I may always resort.*

Thou hast decreed my salvation. See the same expression in Ps. xliv. 5. See also Ps. xlii. 9.

v. 6. גוזי is to be interpreted by reference to Ps. xxii. 10, אתה גחי מבטן, where it is to be observed that גח is quite the proper word to be used in this connection.

There is a phenomenon of popular language that has been frequently observed and noted, viz. that when an unfamiliar word occurs, with, however, some glimpse of its meaning,—a more familiar word, approximate in meaning and sound, is substituted.

It is by means of this popular habit that I would explain the גוזי of the text. The writer had Ps. xxii. 10, in mind. The word גחי was unfamiliar to him,—perhaps as being an antiquated word—perhaps for provincial reasons. He therefore substitutes for it the nearest word in sound and in sense that he can think of, viz. בורי.

The LXX. knew not what to make of this word בו. They render it by σκεπαστής; and, since they give σκέπη for מעוז in Isaiah xxx. 3, it is not unlikely that they supposed the word to be equivalent to עו.

It has been thought that בורי means "my benefactor"; because the root, meaning primarily *to divide*, may also mean *to distribute*, thence *to reward*, &c. &c. The chief objection is, that, for such reasons, the word may mean, not only this, but anything else.

v. 7. *As a monster*, or, *As an evil omen.* The antithesis of the second clause—*But Thou art my strong confidence*,—requires that this word in the first clause should be understood in an evil sense.

id. מחסי עו. The LXX. probably read מחסה, in stat. constr. with עו. The construction, as the text stands, is unexampled.

v. 8. Observe the same construction in

this verse and in v. 15. Comp. also v. 18 and v. 22.

v. 16. *I will come* (sc. into God's presence) *in the strength of the Lord Jehovah.* That is, I will appear before God on the grounds of the righteousness and salvation mentioned in the preceding verse. For גבורות here must be taken as equivalent to גבורות ישע in Ps. xx. 7; and indeed the word is almost always used of God's power as exercised in behalf of His people. The result of this power thus exercised is the *salvation* and *righteousness* to which reference is here made.

For צדק and ישע, denoting equally *states of blessedness*, see note on Ps. lxv. 6.

v. 18. לדור לכל יבוא. For the omission of the relative after כל, compare כל הרע אויב in Ps. lxxiv. 3, and כל הכינותי in 1 Chron. xxix. 3.

Such omissions are not to be regarded as of later and more careless and colloquial origin. The use of the relative form of the demonstrative is really later than its disuse.

v. 23. *My lips shall shout for joy when I play upon the harp to Thee.* The meaning is very obvious, viz. that the Psalmist will accompany his *instrumental* with *vocal* praise.

v. 24. See note on Psalm xcii. 4.

Psalm LXXII.

According to Ewald, this Psalm was composed on the accession of some king of the house of David: "not Solomon, but some later successor, perhaps Josiah, or one still later."

vv. 1 and 2. Observe the order of the words, *judgment, righteousness,—righteousness, judgment,* and see note on Ps. lxviii. 21.

Comp. Isaiah xxxii. 1, *Behold a king shall reign in righteousness, and princes shall rule in judgment.* Comp. also Isaiah xi. 4.

v. 3. This is also to be explained by reference to Isaiah xxxii., where, in the 17th verse, it is said that *The work of righteousness shall be peace.* In this place it is *through righteousness* that the mountains and hills shall bear *peace* for God's people.

There are examples, in sufficient number, of נשא used in the sense of bearing fruit.

The LXX. took בצדקה into the next verse,

in connection with ישפט. For many reasons this arrangement is plausible. Against it, we consider that this third verse would so be left incomplete in form and in meaning.

v. 4. Between this and the fifth verse Ewald supposes a two-membered verse to have fallen out.

v. 5. *With the sun* means *coævally with the sun*.

id. לפני ירח. The same expression is used with regard to the *sun* in v. 17.

In Job viii. 16, the same expression seems to mean— *So long as the sun shines:*—a meaning very suitable here. *As long as the moon shines*, will thus mean *As long as the world lasts*.

v. 6. *He shall come down like rain upon hay-grass.* The word may mean either *grass for mowing* or else *mown grass*, i.e. *hay*. The latter meaning is obviously inappropriate in this place. It is, however, possible that the word is intended to denote the bare field that *has been mown*. Rain upon this would make the grass sprout again.

vv. 14, 15. Comp. Ps. xlix. 9, 10, where

A

the same expression and the same construction are found. There is, however, this difference, that, whereas *that* place refers to *eternal* redemption accomplished by God, *this* refers to *temporal* redemption, accomplished by man.

The meaning of this place is

v. 14. *He shall redeem their life from fraud and violence, and the ransom of their blood shall be a precious thing in his sight:—*

v. 15. *So precious and so effectual that the ransomed one shall live, and shall give &c.*

id. ויתפלל בעדו, *And shall pray for him,—* that is, the redeemed shall pray for the redeemer. See the same expression in Deut. ix. 20, and 1 Sam. vii. 5.

v. 16. *Let him be* (as it were) *an abundance of corn in the earth.* So the Syriac.

The usual derivation of פסה from פסס, i.q. בשא, to *spread,* is satisfactory.

id. *Let His fruit be abundant, on the top of the hills, like* (the cedars of) *Lebanon.*

So in Ps. xcii. 13 : *He shall increase* (so. in number.—ישגה) *like the Cedars in Lebanon.* So also Hosea xiv. 5.

The word used in the text (רעש) denotes *(a) manifold motion,* as of the waves of the sea, ears of corn, tree-tops in a wood, crowds of men, &c.; *(b) tremulous motion.* In the kindred word רגש, which denotes tumultuous crowding, sc. of men, the idea of *multiplicity* seems slightly to outweigh that of *motion.* So with regard to רעש in the text:—whilst the intention is only to express multitude (*i.e.* abundance) of fruit, the figure chosen, (viz. that of the waving crests of innumerable trees), requires a verb that combines an idea of motion with that of multitude. In translating, we are at liberty to give prominence to the latter, as I have done above, and as is done by the Syriac translator, who uses here the same word by which elsewhere (*e.g.* in Ps. xcii. 8, 13), he renders the Heb. כרה.

It is easy to see how the idea of manifold motion passes on to that of trembling.

id. *And let the offspring of his bowels be* (numerous) *as the grass of the earth.*

In this last clause, instead of ויציצו מעיר, I propose the reading ויצאאי מעיו, as in Isaiah xlviii. 19, a passage which is entirely parallel with this. For as it is there said,

Thy seed had been as the sand, and the offspring of thy bowels (צאצאי מעיך) *as the gravel thereof: his name should not have been cut off &c.—* so here we shall find, *The offspring of his bowels shall be as the grass of the earth: his name shall endure for ever.*

Compare also my proposed reading
וצאצאי מעיו כעשב הארץ
with Job v. 25, וצאצאיך · · · · · כעשב הארץ, bearing in mind that, as Gesenius observes, מעים, or some such word, must always be understood, if not expressed, in connection with צאצאים.

It is to be observed, also, that the Syriac read some form of יצא where we now read ויציצו.

The whole verse will thus express, by three similitudes, the increase of the posterity of him who is the subject of the Psalm. This posterity shall be numerous (1) as the abundant corn, (2) as the crests of the cedars that wave on the heights of Lebanon, (3) as the grass of the earth.

In the first similitude, the sign of comparison is supplied in the Syriac. It is easily understood in the Hebrew.

In the third,—it is sufficient to discredit the received reading, יציצו ••• כעשב, to observe that עשב is precisely the word that would *not* be chosen for such a purpose. See note on Ps. xcii. 8.

v. 17. *May his name endure for ever.*

As long as the sun lasts may his name prevail.

May all nations be blessed in him, and call him blessed.

Whether we read יבין or יכון, the idea of the word is that of *increase, prevalence, multiplication.*

v. 19. The use of את before a nominative is unusual, but not unexampled.

Psalm LXXIII.

v. 1. *Behold, God is good to Israel, &c.* For this general meaning of אך, see note on Ps. lxii. 2.

To them that are of a clean heart. This moral qualification is the complement of God's calling of Israel. See note on Ps. xxiv. 4. The meaning is this,—that God's goodness is assured to those whom He has called, who walk worthily of their calling.

v. 2. We here find נטה used as equivalent to שפך. There is no more difficulty attending the use of the one verb than of the other. See my notes on Ps. xvii. 11, and foot-note on p. 415 of Vol. I. Both words have an unusual appearance, perhaps, in this connection. But since the idea of *strength, firmness, &c.,* is in Hebrew almost always expressed by some word that denotes *binding,* we may expect just what we find here, viz. that *weakness* is expressed by words that denote *pouring out, relaxation, dissolution, &c.*

The meaning is that the Psalmist was in danger of falling away from trust in God.

נטוי is to be taken in connection with רגלי, as a noun singular.

v. 3. *I was jealous of the exulting ones : I envied the prosperity of the ungodly.*

The verb ראה, *to see*, or *look at*, frequently implies an ethical idea. So in the expression *Mine eye hath looked upon mine enemies*, sc. with rejoicing over their fall. See note on Ps. liv. 9. So God is said to *look* (sc. with favour or pity) upon His people. See note on Ps. xxv. 18, 19. So here, *video = invideo*, i.e. to *look upon* that which is another's with covetousness or with jealousy.*

For other examples of a future in the latter clause corresponding with, and continuing, a preterite in the former, see v. 6 of this Psalm. See also Ps. lxix. 27; cii. 15. If in these places it should be assumed that the *vau* which introduces the latter clause acts with conversive power upon the following verb, even though other words intervene,—then, to obviate such an objection, I adduce Ps. xxxix. 4, חם לבי . . . .

---

* "Ambiguum nomen *invidiæ*, quod verbum ductum est a nimis iutuendo fortunam alterius." *Cic. Tusc. Disp.* iii. 9.

אֵשׁ תְּבְעַר ; Ps. xl. 10. לֹא אֲכַלָּא ... בִּשַּׂרְתִּי ; and Ps. cxiv. 3, הַיָּם רָאָה ... הַיַּרְדֵּן יִסֹּב. Many other examples will occur to the reader.

v. 4. The usual rendering of this place, *They have no bands in their death*, has been rejected very generally, and I think for good reasons. For לְמוֹתָם does not mean *in their death*. The preposition ל is quite inappropriate for the expression of this meaning. Then the mention of the *death* of the ungodly is out of place in a passage which is concerned with the godless enjoyment of *life*. Moreover it was by no means the intention of the Psalmist to represent the wicked as unaffected by the terrors of death. On the contrary, he represents them in v. 20 as ending a life of sensuous ease by a death of overwhelming terror.

Let it further be considered that here, as very often elsewhere, the sensual nature is described in terms appropriate to brute animal nature. So perfectly does the Psalmist identify the sensual man with the beast that perisheth, that he acknowledges that he was himself as a *beast* (v. 22, בַּעַר and בְּהֵמוֹת) in God's sight, so long as he envied the brutish pleasures of the ungodly.

Consistently with this idea, we find in this verse the ungodly represented as *fattened*, by a term exclusively appropriate to fed beasts. The characteristics of such men are arrogance, insolence, insubordination. Those whom Jeremiah describes as fed horses, full of lust (v. 8) are in the same chapter (*v.* 5) represented as breaking the yoke and bursting the bonds. In the same way in Deut. xxxii. 15, *Jesurun waxed fat and kicked.* So *fatness* is connected with *kicking*, that is with restlessness under the yoke, in 1 Sam. ii. 29. It would therefore not be surprising if, in this 4th verse of Ps. lxxiii., we should find mention of the *libido effrenata et indomita* which characterises well-fed beasts and sensual men.

This, I think, we do find. Since the necessity of some textual emendation is very generally acknowledged, I propose to read למוטם instead of למותם. The meaning will thus be, —*There are no bands to their yoke.*

It is unnecessary to remind the reader how frequently the *bands of the yoke* are mentioned, as shewing that the restraining power of the yoke resided in the *bands*. But it is remarkable that in the only other place in which this word חרצבות occurs, viz. in Isaiah lviii. 6, it is used in connection with, and apparently as equivalent to, the expression אגדות מוטה, *the bands of the yoke.*

Ewald, Olshausen, Delitzsch, and others, have adopted this division :—

כי אין חרצבות למו
תם ובריא אולם

i.e. *they have no pangs: firm and fat is their belly.* Against this, Dean Perowne's objection is sufficient, viz. that "תם is no-where used of physical, but always of moral, soundness."

The meaning of אול is doubtful, and the ancient versions throw no light upon it. The most probable opinion, from the kindred איל *a ram,* and from other words derived from the same root, is that it denotes *animal strength.* The import of the words will thus be,—*their animal strength is well nourished.*

v. 5. It is not absolutely necessary to observe the distinction between אנוש and אדם. In such a balanced sentence the one subject is expressed under various names, perhaps only for the sake of variety.

v. 6. The two verbs in this verse are denominatives,—the first from ענק, *a necklace*; —the second being a compound of the verb עטף and the noun שית. Ordinarily this verb would take this noun after it in such close connection as to make the two appear as one word. That is to say, יעטף־שית would mean, *he covereth with a cloak.* It is easy to see how in such a case the two words are combined to form the one denominative verb, just as in the former case the one word, with the two combined meanings of noun and verb, assumes what is called the denominative form. The peculiarity of these cases may be represented in English thus,— only that it is *not* English—

Pride necklaceth them: Violence cloak-covereth them.

It is likely that an idea of self-asserted *enfranchisement* is implied in the former verb, ענקתמו,—for which see my note on Ps. xiv. p. 117 of Vol. I.

v. 7. The sentiment of this verse may be unfolded by a reference to Jer. xxii. 17, "Thine *eyes* and thy *heart* are not but for thy covetousness." So here, the meaning is, *Their greedy eye wandereth forth beyond satiety : they surpass the desires of the heart.* The latter clause is well rendered in E.V. *They have more than heart could wish.* The former clause is to much the same effect. Their eye wanders for food just as if they were famishing, whereas they are fat already. We might render מחלב *on account of fatness,* but for the consideration suggested by Delitzsch, that fatness does not cause one's eyes to *stand out,* but rather to seem more deeply set in. On the other hand, I do not take these words to mean *from fatness*, as if the eyes were represented as looking out from a pair of fat cheeks;—but I take the preposition מ- to denote *beyond,* so that *the going forth beyond* (יצא מ-) of the former clause will correspond with the *surpassing* (עבר) of the latter.

v. 8. *They talk of wickedness mockingly: they talk of oppression haughtily.*

In the first clause the literal rendering is *they mock, they talk.* That this Hebraism is correctly Englished as above will not be questioned. The verb (ידברו) which is followed by ב in the first clause, takes the accusative in the second. Both constructions are found elsewhere. Perhaps the ב was used in the first case to avoid an ambiguity:—there being no need of such precaution in the other case.

The verb מיק is found only here. There seems no doubt as to its meaning. The LXX. and the Syriac translator had a totally different reading.

v. 10. The first clause of this verse stands thus:—לכן ישיב עמו הלום.

In trying to find out its meaning, we must first show what meanings, however plausible, it cannot bear.

(*a*). The subject of the verb (ישיב) is not God; because this subject has not hitherto appeared. If it should now for the first time be introduced, surely it would be expressed.

(*b*). The subject is not the prosperous ungodly, because all through the Psalm these are spoken of in the plural number.

Excluding these hypotheses, we are almost compelled to take עם (whether עמו as in the text, or עמי as the LXX. and Syr. read) as the subject of the proposition.

Let us now consider what the context may

lead us to expect in this verse. We shall find that as the ease and complacency of v. 5 result (לכן) in the haughtiness expressed in v. 6, so the ostentatious parade of v. 9 may be expected to result in popularity in v. 10, which is also introduced by לכן, *therefore*.

This we do find. It might have seemed conjectural to understand the expression ישוב עם of *popularity*, if it had not happened that a popular warrior of David's time took his name, Jashobeam, ישבעם, from this very phrase:— the name being interpreted by Gesenius as " *To-whom-the-people-turn.*"

It seems therefore that, whatever becomes of the other words, these two, ישוב עם, must constitute the body of the proposition, and must bear the meaning of *popularity*, as presumed from the context.

This is the most important result; and, if this be established, it matters little to the general meaning how we deal with the word הלם. Taking it as it stands, we may render it *hither, so far*, as a sort of limitation to the unworthy popularity of the ungodly. But the balancing of the two parts of the verse seems to require the substitution of either להם or למו. This question I do not pretend to decide, since it hardly admits of such a satisfactory determination as does that which we have considered above.*

The general meaning of these two verses (9 and 10) may be given thus:—

Their profession vaunts itself to heaven, and their self-trumpeted fame goes through the world. Therefore they are popular, so far,— (or, *therefore do the people turn to them*)—*and the waters of a full cup* (sc. of applause) *are sucked out by them.*

The sentiment is one that is universally recognised, viz. that self-glorification is the surest road to popularity.

---

* I put in a foot-note a conjecture that I do not care to hazard in the text,—viz. that ישיבעמו may be taken as one word, a denominative verb formed like the denominatives in v. 6. Such a use would be warranted by the fact that the two words are found actually concreted into one *nomen*, viz. the proper name *Jashobeam* mentioned in the text. Since any *nomen* may constitute the basis of a denominative verb, it is not inconceivable that this compound may be so used in this place. The meaning will be the same,—*Therefore are they popular.*

v. 13. *Behold in vain have I cleansed my heart, &c.*

v. 14. *Since I am plagued all the day, &c.* That is, he takes his chastisement as a token of God's wrath. His efforts to walk uprightly before God are surely in vain, if, notwithstanding these efforts, he is afflicted, whilst the ungodly are prosperous.

In the latter verse לבקרים means *until the morning.* The expression *all the day and until the morning* is a poetical method of saying *all day and all night.* See note on Ps. xlix. 15.

v. 15. כמו does not mean "*thus.*" In order to express such a meaning it must be followed by a demonstrative. We are therefore almost compelled to take the following word as the requisite demonstrative. The words כמו הנה will thus mean "*things like these,*" and are only a fuller form of כהנה, as this word appears in 2 Sam. xii. 8, and Job xxiii. 14.

With regard to אמרתי, at the beginning of the verse, it has been objected that "not the forming the purpose to speak so, but the speaking so itself," would have constituted the sin. To this it may be answered that the Psalmist did not actually adopt such language as his own:—it only occurred to him as an evil suggestion. So that we may give the sense of the words thus,—*If it occurred to my mind to say such things as these.* The literal rendering, of course, is, *If I have said, I will talk in this way.* But this does not give the precise shade of meaning. Compare Ps. cxxxix. 11, *If I say, Surely darkness shall cover me,* i.e. *if it should occur to my mind that darkness will cover me.*

The whole verse may be represented thus: —*If ever I have seriously purposed such talk as this, then I have betrayed the generation of Thy children.*

We are traitors to our sonship if ever we allow ourselves to forget that whom the Lord loveth He chasteneth, and that He dealeth with us as with sons when He scourgeth us. This the Psalmist was tempted to forget, when he said, or thought of saying, *It is in vain that I try to stand on the ground of covenant-relationship with God,* (sc. by cleanness of hands and purity of heart, as in Ps. xxiv. 4, and xxvi. 6) *if I am scourged all the day, &c.* This was the suggestion of the Evil One to our Saviour Himself, Surely you poor hungry fainting man cannot be the Son of God ? *If Thou be the Son of God, command that these stones be made bread,* &c.

v. 16. *And however I tried to get to the knowledge of this, it was still a vexation to me.* For חשׁב denotes mental effort in scheming, contriving, devising, &c. See note on Ps. xl. 18.

v. 20. *As one upon awakening despiseth his dream, so, O Lord, when Thou awakest* (the expression purposely and poetically varied) *Thou wilt despise their vain shadow.*

In the light of eternity, the weak things of the world appear as eternal realities; whilst

"The glories of our blood and state
Are shadows, not substantial things."

v. 22. *I was, as it were, a beast with Thee,* i.e. *in Thy sight.* See the same expression in Ps. l. 11, *The beasts of the field are with me.*

v. 23. *Yet am I always with Thee,* &c. Since this is the meaning of עמך in these two verses, we are hardly warranted in putting another meaning upon the same expression in v. 25.

v. 24. The LXX. give μετὰ δόξης, apparently for the words אחר כבוד, though this is not the meaning of the Hebrew. The preposition μετά does indeed very often represent the Heb. אחר, but only with the meaning of *after*, when of course it would be followed by the accusative. However this may be, it is certain that אחר is very frequently used in the sense of *afterwards*, in which sense the word seems to be used here. The usual and obvious rendering of this verse appears to be the right one, viz. *Thou shalt guide me with Thy counsel, and afterwards Thou wilt receive me with glory.* The connection with the preceding verses seems to be this:—*guided by my own feelings of envy towards men and distrust towards God, I was in Thy sight as brutish as those whom I envied. But, guided by Thy counsel, I shall be no more degraded in Thy sight, but shall be received by Thee with glory.*

v. 25. עמך must, I think, mean *with Thee* here, as in the 22nd and 23rd verses. This verse may therefore be rendered thus:— *Whom have I in heaven?*, a rhetorical question that needs no expressed answer,—*And so* long as *I am with Thee I desire nothing upon earth.*

It was not always so. Once he did desire and covet earthly things, and was unmindful of the treasure laid up for him in heaven.

vv. 27 and 28. The beautiful antithesis of רחק and קרב must not be overlooked. *They that are far from Thee shall perish.* ... *But nearness to God is good for me.*

The last words of v. 28 do not mean *That I may declare Thy works;* but rather, *That I may deliver Thy messages:*—*That I may declare the things that Thou hast commissioned me to declare.*

This observation is due, not merely to pedantic accuracy, but to the complete meaning of the passage. In v. 15 we find the Psalmist, in distrust of God, tempted to declare (אספרה) the dictates of that distrust, viz. that the service of God is without reward. Here we find him brought near to God, recovering his trust in God, and in that trust ready to declare, What? —Not the dictates of the evil one:—not the suggestions of his own narrow experience:—

not the selfish maxims of mere worldly wisdom;
—but that which he had learned in the Sanctuary of God (v. 17), the message of peace to his own soul, the message which God had put into his mouth for others' welfare,—yes, for *ours.*

The change of address, in this 28th verse, creates a difficulty. This the Syriac translator either did not find, or, finding, sought to obviate. For שתי-ב he read שמך. It is also observable that the expression שתי ‑ ‑ ‑ מחסי is found nowhere else. The reading of the LXX. was much the same as ours; but at the end of the verse they add ἐν ταῖς πύλαις τῆς θυγατρὸς Σιών,—*in the gates of the daughter of Sion.*

Psalm LXXIV.

The occasion of the composition of this Psalm and of the 79th has been a matter of much controversy. I offer no opinion, since it consists more with my general purpose to dig out materials for the determination of such questions than to attempt their direct solution.

It is not improbable that the words which the LXX. place at the end of the preceding Psalm may have been really a title of this Psalm. They read בשערי בת ציון; but we may conjecture that the true reading was בשוררי, &c., *Against the adversaries of the daughter of Zion,*—a title very appropriate to this Psalm.

v. 2. זה, the demonstrative with relative power, according to the earliest usage in all languages.

v. 3. *Lift up Thy feet for everlasting destruction (for) all the evil that the enemy hath done in (Thy) sanctuary.* For משאות see the preceding Psalm, v. 18, where the word (which in this form occurs only in these two places) denotes the destruction that God brings on ungodly men.

vv. 4 and 5. *Primâ facie* grounds for the interpretation of these two verses may be found in these considerations, viz.

(*a*) שׂום אתות does not mean to *set up* signs, *quasi* ensigns, but to exhibit, or show, signs. See Exod. x. 2, and Ps. lxxviii. 43.

(*b*) הביא אתות means, to bring such signs to pass, to fulfil them.

In consideration of (*a*) we are led to disconnect the final אתות from v. 4, and to take it into v. 5 in connection with יודע, which, with the LXX., we may perhaps read יודעו, in the plural. The meaning so far will be, *They have shown their signs : Let (their) signs be known, or understood;* with which we may compare Ps. lxxix. 10, יודע נקמת דם

In this latter place it happens also, as in the former, that the gender of the nominative noun is not observed in the verb.

In consideration of (*b*) we are led to take the meaning of כמביא, in v. 5, to be—*When Thou bringest to pass* (sc. the signs). Such use of כ with the participle is rare; but an example occurs in Gen. xxxviii. 29.

The idea seems to be that in the very place where God's people were accustomed to see the signs of His presence, the enemies were now dealing forth devastation. This is spoken of as *showing their signs*,—a figure of speech which might seem far-fetched and incongruous but for this consideration. Having adopted the figure, the Psalmist continues it awhile in the next verse,—*Let it be known what these signs mean when Thou fulfillest them loftily*, i.e. when Thou liftest up Thy feet for their eternal destruction, as in v. 3.

To בכבד, in v. 5, the LXX. prefixed כ,— ὡς ἐν δρυμῷ. They also took into this verse the first word of the next, which now stands as ועת. They read it as some plural verb, with the meaning of *cutting*; and to this meaning the consonants ערו readily lend themselves. It is not permissible, however, to take such liberties with the Hebrew text as to assimilate it to the Greek in such a case as this. Their reading of כבכבד is more allowable, and I propose its adoption. Other emendations obviously suggest themselves; but I refrain even from indicating them, through fear of bringing discredit upon the main line of interpretation which I propose independently of such emendations. The interpretation will be somewhat as follows:—

v. 4. *Thine adversaries roar in the midst of Thy congregation: they have wrought their signs.*

v. 5. *Let it be known what these signs mean; when Thou fulfillest them on high;* (i.e. when Thou on high fulfillest them. Comp. the אות למעלה that God proposed to Ahaz, Isaiah vii. 11). *As in a thicket of trees men smite with hatchets,*

v. 6. *So now the carved work thereof do they smite down with axes and hammers.*

The simile is very appropriate, since the carved work (פתוחים), with which Solomon adorned the temple, is said (1 Kings vi. 29) to have represented palm-trees and flowers. Yet this remark is itself appropriate only on the supposition that the destruction of the first temple is the subject of the Psalm.

The fem. form of the suffix points to some foregoing word that does not appear in the existing text.

v. 7. The expression שלח באש seems to be a poetical inversion of שלח אש ב. It is very delusive to compare the French *mettre à feu*, or the English *set on fire*, as if there were some common account to be given of these idiomatic expressions.

id. " *Ils ont profané à terre ton sanctuaire* est bien plus vif, mais moins logique que, *Ils ont profané ton sanctuaire en le renversant à terre.* Toutes les langues offrent des exemples de ces sortes de constructions; mais je doute qu'aucune en présente d'aussi fréquents et d'aussi caractérisés que l'hebreu." *Renan: Langues Sem.* The same expression occurs in Ps. lxxxix. 40.

v. 8. Since, both before and after, God is addressed in the second person, it seems strange to find this abrupt mention of Him in the third person, viz. in the expression " they have burned up all the houses of God in the land," שרפו כל מועדי אל בארץ. This difficulty is obviated by the reading of the LXX. and the Syriac, where the second verb, as well as the first, is in the first person plural, viz. *let us burn up*, &c. The whole verse is thus put into the enemy's mouth.

The plural form מוֹעֲדֵי אֵל does not of itself denote more buildings than the one, viz. the temple, as if synagogues were meant. But, taken in connection with בָאָרֶץ, this meaning must certainly be intended. It is remarkable, however, that the LXX. and the Syr. read מֵאֶרֶץ instead of בָאָרֶץ. If this rendering be admitted, then there is nothing in this verse that is not applicable to the one building of the first temple.* Since there is some doubt as to the prefix of the word אֶרֶץ, it is allowable to suppose that it ought to be neither ב nor מ, but ל. The meaning then will be, *They have burned* (or, *let us burn*) *all the temple of God to the ground.*

v. 9. The words that stand at the end of this verse cannot, I think, mean *There is none that knoweth how long;* though this meaning is now very generally accepted. For עד־מה is certainly an interrogative:—the instances of the

---

* *We* do not speak of burning a thing *from* the land. But neither do we use such an expression, for example, as the Latin *ex vinculis causam dicere.* Such a difference of idiom creates no difficulty; and this same use of the preposition מִן is found elsewhere, *e.g.* in 2 Chron. xxxi. 1.

relative use of מה being too few and too archaic to be adduced here. We are not warranted in taking עד־מה as in all respects equivalent to *quousque.* This Latin expression may mean either *the time until which,* or *unto what time?* But a Hebrew writer, who wished to say that he did not know the time when a calamity would end, or a blessing be bestowed, would not, in the first place, use an interrogative form, nor, in the second, would he use a relative form like *quousque,* with ellipsis of the antecedent. The antecedent is just what he would express in this case. He would say that he did not know the times or seasons (when &c.) : the relative part of the expression being omitted.

I therefore suppose that עד־מה ought to be taken into the next verse, as a reduplication of the impassioned cry, *How long!* The participle יודע will thus be left as used absolutely, as often elsewhere : *There is no longer a prophet, nor is there with us any that knoweth.*

v. 11. According to the existing Hebrew text, the Prayer Book version of this place is adequate :—*Why withdrawest Thou Thy hand? Why pluckest Thou not Thy right hand out of*

Thy bosom to consume the enemy? Even so, we are almost compelled to read לכלה. The imperative כלה suits the context before almost as ill as behind. Though the Septuagint reading is inadmissible, it can be accounted for on the supposition that this last word of the verse had an initial ל.

v. 12-17. These verses have retrospective reference to God's dealings (*a*) with Israel, and (*b*) with the whole world. According to *our* method we should probably, in such a retrospection, adopt the historical order; taking the creation of the world, &c. first, and God's dealings with Israel next. But it is quite in accordance with Hebrew usage to mention first that which stands nearest in respect of time.

The same subjects appear in the same order in Ps. lxxxix. 10-14.

vv. 13, 14. The sea-monsters here mentioned appear to be representative of Egypt. And a comparison of the latter part of v. 14 with Ezekiel xxix. 3, 4, 5, can leave no doubt that the meaning is, *Thou hast given Egypt* (perhaps the *corpses* of the Egyptians) *as food to the beasts of the desert, jackals, &c.*

v. 18. *Remember this.* The LXX. expand and expound the expression thus:—μνήσθητι ταύτης τῆς κτίσεώς σου.

id. *How the enemy have reviled, O Lord, and the foolish people have scorned Thy name.* This seems preferable to taking יהוה as the accusative, whereby an awkward change of address is necessitated. We need not regard חרף as used absolutely (though this would be a smaller difficulty), but as governing שמך.

v. 19. Accepting the reading of the received text, it might seem unquestionable that the same meaning ought to be put upon the word חית in the latter as in the former clause of this verse. But this is not absolutely necessary. Hebrew writers were very fond of what we call *punning*, and frequently vary an expression slightly when they purpose an important variation of meaning. We may have recourse to this consideration when, as in this case, the common-sense method of interpretation fails. I therefore suppose that חית (for חיה) in the former clause denotes *prey*, sc. of living creatures. The same word seems to be used in Ps. lxviii. 10, to denote the *quails* which were a prey to the Israelites in the wilderness. So the Syriac translator understood it in this place, representing it by the same word which in Ps. vii. 3, and elsewhere, represents טרף.

With the expression thus arrived at, *Give not up for a prey,* Compare that in v. 14 of this Psalm, *Thou gavest him for food.*

The verse may now be rendered thus :—
Give not the life of Thy dove for a prey : forget not the congregation of Thy lowly ones for ever.

v. 20. If we compare the מלאו ··· ארץ ··· חמס here with the oft-repeated formula מלאה הארץ חמס, as in Gen. vi. 13, &c., we can hardly avoid taking this formula as the groundwork of our interpretation of this verse, thus :— *They have filled the land with violence.* But the two words מחשכי and נאות have to be woven into the proposition. With regard to the latter, which means always *quiet resting-places,* and almost always the resting-places of God or of God's people, I am prevented by this usage from coupling it with חמס, as if it meant *the dwellings of violence.* The idea of the one word is so diametrically opposed to that of the other, that we can hardly associate them in this manner. But the very inconsistency of the two ideas is suitable to the Psalmist's theme:—the quiet dwellings of God (sc. His temple) and of God's people being filled with violence. It occurs therefore to render the whole verse thus:—*Look upon the covenant, for they have filled (Thy) land with darkness: (Thy) quiet dwellings with violence.* The only textual alteration required for this meaning is the reading of מחשכים instead of מחשכי.

The Psalmist seems to revert to the state of the world before the flood, *when the earth was filled with violence,* and then to God's covenant with the world, and His promise that cold and heat, summer and winter (קיץ וחרף, as in v. 17 of this Psalm), and day and night, should not cease (Gen. viii. 22). It is this covenant that is called to mind, though not perhaps to the exclusion of the more special one made with Abraham and his seed. As if the state of things contemplated and lamented by the Psalmist required a deprecation of God's wrath, lest it should burst out in devastation as in the days of Noah.

It is perhaps unnecessary to remark that the omission of the article before ארץ and נאות is quite in accordance with poetical usage; as is also the inverse order of the words in the two clauses,—*They have filled with darkness the land: the dwellings with violence.* For another example of this order see Ps. cv. 43,—*He brought forth His people with gladness: with rejoicing His chosen.* The reader will readily call to mind many other examples, which really come under the law of sequence stated in my note on Ps. lxviii. 21.

Psalm LXXV.

v. 2. *We praise Thee, O God, we praise Thee, and Thy wonders wrought in our behalf declare that Thy Name is near to us.*

For the word נפלאות is appropriated almost exclusively to the manifestations of God's power in behalf of Israel. And God's presence amongst His people, of which they were assured by such manifestations, is constantly described as the result of His putting His Name amongst them, and upon them.

The opening sentiment of this Psalm is

therefore in strong contrast with that which pervades the preceding one. There God's presence was not manifested amongst His people by prophets, by signs, or by wonders. That His Name was near, even in their midst, was a matter of doubt, when the enemy had profaned *the dwelling-place of His Name* to the earth (lxxiv. 7).

In any conjecture, therefore, as to the date and the occasion of this Psalm, it must be assumed that it was written at a time when God's presence amongst His people was still manifested by נפלאות.

For קרוב שמך the LXX. read some shortened form of נקרא, followed by בשמך, *We praise Thee and call upon Thy Name.* They also read אספרה, *I will declare,* instead of ספרו. These readings would bring the text into complete conformity with Ps. cv. 1,—*Praise the Lord; call upon His Name: make known His doings among the people.*

v. 3. *For I appoint a set time,* (wherein) *I shall judge in righteousness.*

Comp. St. Paul's words as recorded in Acts xvii. 31,—*Because He hath appointed a day, in the which* He *will judge the world in righteousness.*

If in this place we should find אתן instead of אקח, the meaning which I have assigned to it would be unquestioned, since the verb נתן is constantly used in the sense of *appointing*. I have elsewhere pointed out that the ideas of *giving* and of *taking* are only modifications of the one common idea of *bearing;* and that a word that denotes simply *bearing* may become appropriated to denote either giving or taking. With this consideration in view we need feel no hesitation in taking the word אקח in the text as equivalent to אתן. Some slight difference there is, undoubtedly. Whereas אתן מועד would mean, *I appoint to others a fixed time*, the expression of the text, אקח מועד, means *I appoint to myself the time wherein &c.* God does not make known to others the time of judgment. Of these times knoweth no man, nor even the angels in heaven.*

The expression of 2 Cor. vi. 2, καιρὸς δεκτός, might be taken as illustrating the usage

---

* To the same effect Ewald gives, *For I choose a fixed time.*

of the text, but for the consideration that it is a rendering of a totally different Hebrew expression.

v. 4. *The earth and the inhabitants thereof are moved: It is I that (first) settled the pillars of it.*

It is reasonable that the earth should tremble at the presence of Him who first fixed its foundations. The expression of the nominative by the pronoun אנכי, and the position of this pronoun, require that it should be marked emphatically. And this emphasis is note-worthy, as apparently intended to rebut the heathenish notion that the limits of the people of Israel were the limits of Jehovah's dominion, and that the earth's stability was something to be set against Jehovah's claims. I have elsewhere observed that the existence of such notions amongst the heathen, and perhaps amongst the faithless members of the Israelitish nation, is to be inferred from such counter-assertions as that in the text. See notes on Ps. xciii. 1, 2; and xcvi. 10.

The emphatic assertion of the text is applicable to the sceptical thought of the present day. If the permanence of Nature's materials and forces is urged against the claims of a God of providence and of grace, Christians must take God at His word when He says,—*It is I that established them all;* and must acknowledge that *it is according to His ordinance that they continue to this day.*

The Hebrew תכן seems to denote primarily *to settle*, as the materials of a road, or the foundations of a building. It is represented in Syriac by תקן, and this again represents the Heb. יסד, or כון. It is certain that the idea of making even or level, or of weighing, cannot be the primary idea. Whereas it is easy to see how the idea of *weighing* (which certainly belongs to this root) is connected with that of *settling,* sc. of the arms of the balance.

v. 7. *For not from the East, nor from the West, nor yet from the South, (cometh) exaltation.*

I cannot imagine how any one can take הרים here to mean *mountains* (which is the rendering of the LXX.), in view of תרימו in v. 5, and again in v. 6, and of ירים in v. 8.

There seems to be no doubt that the South is here denoted by ממדבר, whether the desert of

Arabia is intended, **or,** as is more probable, some intervening pasture land. Comp. Acts viii. 26, κατὰ μεσημβρίαν . . . . . αὕτη ἐστὶν ἔρημος.

What may we infer from the omission of the *North* in this enumeration? Nothing necessarily. The Hebrews were quite regardless of scientific accuracy in their divisions, whether of time, of space, or of number. If the Psalmist's intention was to express help from God only, to the exclusion of all other sources of help, these sources would be as completely enumerated by the naming of two or three as by the naming of four. He had no more inducement to name four than six or seven.

v. 9. In order to unfold the meaning of this verse, the following considerations ought to be regarded.

(*a*) The cup in the Lord's hand is not necessarily a cup of unmixed wrath. In two preceding Psalms the ungodly are said to have a share, and the godly a share, of this cup. (Ps. xi. 6, and xvi. 5, מנת in both cases).

(*b*) The varied distribution of the contents of this cup, may be presupposed from the context. In the preceding verse, God humbles *this* (זה) and exalts *this* (זה). We may therefore assume that the מזה of this 9th verse serves to denote the same distributive meaning. In order to this, it ought to be repeated, מזה ּ ּ מזה. Standing alone, the מזה of the text is not easily to be accounted for. Now this repetition *is* found with a slight variation both in the Septuagint and in the Syriac,— ἐκ τούτου εἰς τοῦτο.

I suggest this meaning, if not this reading.

The מן of מזה will thus correspond, in form and meaning, with the מנת כוס of Ps. xi. 6, and xvi. 5.

(*c*) The word מסך occurs no-where else as a noun substantive. It is therefore allowable to take it here in its usual state, viz. as a verb, corresponding with מלא, which I also propose to read as a verb. Now it has been generally admitted by modern Hebraists that מסך, which usually means *to mix*, has an antecedent meaning of *pouring out:* that it is, in fact, both akin and equivalent to נסך. In at least one place, viz. Isaiah xix. 14, the only suitable meaning seems to be that of *pouring*. Moreover, the Syriac מזג, which is the constant representative of Heb. מסך, means *to pour out*, as well as *to mix*. יין חמר means simply *wine*.

We thus arrive at this meaning,—

In the Lord's hand there is a cup, and He hath filled it (or, it is filled) with wine (יין חמר).

Then comes the proposed reading

מסך מזה ויגר מזה.

He hath poured out to some such a share: and He hath shed forth to others such a share. But the dregs of it, the ungodly of the earth shall drink and wring out to the very last drop.

The meaning, in other words, would seem to be, that while the life of the godly is a mingled cup of good and evil, the evil alone is reserved for the ungodly.

It may be added, that, in strict grammatical accuracy, we ought to find מזאת, rather than מזה, if the word is intended to refer to כוס, since this is a feminine noun. But it would be pedantic to insist upon this, since such irregularities are of frequent occurrence. A more important consideration is this, that if the meaning were intended, *He poureth out of it*, sc. out of the cup, the word would surely have been ממנו, or ממנה.

If, as I suppose, the מזה ought to be repeated, so as to correspond with the repeated זו of the preceding verse, we may perhaps account for the omission of the former מזה from its resemblance in form and sound to the preceding word מסך. Such a word as this, especially if pronounced according to the form מזג (for which see Cant. vii. 3), might easily be confounded with, and then supplant, the word מזה. Or the reduplication itself may account for the omission. A scribe who had written the word once might easily forget to write it a second time. However this may be, I have adduced sufficient warrant for the reduplication.

The LXX. render the words יין חמר, οἴνου ἀκράτου, though they seem to stultify their rendering by proceeding to speak of the same cup as πλῆρες κεράσμενος. They at least recognise the difficulty which I have tried to remove. It seems probable that the words in Rev. xiv. 10, are echoed from the Septuagint Version of this Psalm:—ἐκ τοῦ οἴνου τοῦ θυμοῦ τοῦ Θεοῦ, τοῦ κεκερασμένου ἀκράτου ἐν τῷ ποτηρίῳ τῆς ὀργῆς αὐτοῦ.

It would seem, also, that יין חמר here has

been confounded with the יין חמה which is often elsewhere spoken of.

One cannot, without appearing arbitrary, even attempt to subordinate all the details of the text to the general meaning which I have sketched out. I have been contented here, as often elsewhere, simply to indicate " that unbodied figure of the thought that gave it surmised shape."

v. 10. For אגיד the LXX. read אגיל, ἀγαλλιάσομαι. This might at first sight seem preferable, since the Hiphil of נגד is never elsewhere used so absolutely. It is found elsewhere with omission of the thing declared, or with omission of the person to whom a thing is declared. Here there is omission of both: *I will declare for ever*, which at first sight seems to convey no meaning. But the word is so constantly used to denote a sort of exulting assertion of God's wonders as manifested in behalf of His people, and this meaning is so suitable here, that it cannot be rejected. It is here connected with אזמרה, and in the same connection it occurs in Ps. ix. 12, and in Ps. xcii. 2, 3.

Psalm LXXVI.

It has been very commonly assumed, as if it were unquestionable, that this Psalm celebrates the extraordinary overthrow of Sennacherib's invading army. This is not at all unlikely, but I must confess that it would by no means be suggested to my mind by the internal evidence. The allusions of the Psalm throughout point distinctly and emphatically to that great event which seems to have been ever present to the Jewish mind, the deliverance at the Red Sea. Not that this event is necessarily the subject of the Psalm. But the resources of Hebrew poetry seem to have been so far exhausted by the triumphal songs of that occasion, that the language appropriate to that occasion is constantly re-echoed whenever in after times a similar strain of triumph is required. The Song of Deborah and the Sixty-Eighth Psalm are so mixed up with references to the Exodus that the special occasion of these compositions, or rather compilations, barely appears in either. We can easily account for this. The records of that primary deliverance became in the course of time sacred language, and this language became sacred especially to the purpose of recording all later manifestations of God's favour and championship. How difficult it is to emancipate oneself from such a habit may be acknowledged by ourselves, who, in returning thanks for a bountiful harvest, never think of mentioning our wheat and barley and peas and beans &c., but fall back invariably upon the sacred language in which vineyards and olives and figs are mentioned.

It thus happens that the special occasion of a composition may sometimes be quite put out of sight; and to my mind this appears to be the case with this 76th Psalm. It may have been written πρὸς τὸν Ἀσσύριον, but I should believe this rather on the authority of the LXX. than upon the internal evidence.

v. 2. The mention of Judah and Israel in this verse is to the same effect (and to nothing further) as in Ps. cxiv. 2, *When Israel came out of Egypt. . . Judah was His sanctuary, and Israel His dominion.* In both places, the reference seems to be to the deliverance from Egypt.

v. 4. If we take שמה to mean strictly *there*,

it is not necessarily referable to either Salem or Sion. It may point back to the great event on the shores of the Red Sea. Or, which is most likely, it is simply a demonstrative of interjectional power:—*Behold! He hath broken, &c.* See Pss. xiv. 5, cxxxii. 17, and my note on xxxvi. 13.

id. *He hath broken the deadly missiles of the bow.* This of course denotes *arrows.* But the word (רשף) is always elsewhere used of *pestilence;* and never of *lightning,* as is commonly assumed. It is associated with דבר in Hab. iii. 5, and also, as I think, in Ps. lxxviii. 48. It certainly denotes *pestilence* in Deut. xxxii. 24.

That the attacks of pestilence were usually likened to a discharge of arrows appears from Ps. xci. 5, 6, where *the arrow that flieth by day* is associated with *the pestilence that walketh in darkness.* Then one cannot but call to mind the Homeric description of pestilence on man and beast, when "fierce and deadly twanged the silver bow: First on the mules and dogs, on man the last." רשף קשת is thus merely *lethalis arundo.*

He hath broken . . . . *the battle.* See the same expression in Hosea ii. 20. It is pedantic to suppose an ellipsis of כלי before מלחמה, as if it were meant *the weapons of war.* The expression of the text, without any such expletive, is thoroughly Hebrew.

v 5. *Thou* (comest with) *splendour and majesty from the mountains of prey.* Comp. Deut. xxxiii. 2,—*The* Lord *came from Sinai, and rose up from Seir unto them, He shined forth from mount Paran.*

It seems probable that the same occasion of shining forth, and the same mountains, are described in both places. It is likely enough that the mountainous region of Seir might be described as the hills of the robbers. Yet we can hardly help seeing that *God* is the spoiler here spoken of. His *cave* and His *lair,* סכו ומעונתו in v. 3, are terms appropriate to this representation of Him as a roaring lion. The reader will easily call to mind other examples of this metaphor.

vv. 6 and 7. That the original reference of these verses is to the destruction of the

Egyptian host at the Red Sea, is suggested by almost every word.

(a) אבירי לב, *bull-hearted*. See my note on Ps. lxviii. 31, Vol. I. p. 434, to which I now add the following observation from Brugsch-Bey, as shewing the propriety of the epithet to the princes of Egypt :—

From several inscriptions on the obelisks and fragments of ruins at Tanis, we derive incidentally much information of an historical and mythological character. One of these describes the king as *Warrior of the goddess Antha : Bull of the god Sutekh*. Another calls him *the bull in the land of Ruten*.*

(b) אנשי חיל. See the accounts of the delivrance at the Red Sea, *passim*.

(c) מנערתך. See again my note on Ps. lxviii, 31.

(d) רכב וסוס. See the triumphal songs upon the same occasion.

v. 6. To say that the men of might *did not find their hands* is to use an expression to which it is certainly possible to assign a meaning of some sort, but to which nothing analogous is found in Hebrew usage.

---

* Hist. of Egypt. Vol. II. p. 95.

On the other hand, to say that *one's hand findeth*, or doth not find, *anything*, is to use an expression of very common occurrence in Hebrew, with the meaning that one does, or does not, find occasion for anything. The special meaning here would thus be that *the men of might had nothing to do :—had no opportunity of displaying their prowess.*

In this view, ידיהם, *their hands*, is the nominative instead of the accusative. It is the subject of the verb מצאו. But if this be so, we might expect to find ידי אנשי חיל. But such an accumulation of nouns in the construct state was always regarded as objectionable, and was usually avoided by the adoption of other syntactical contrivances. The contrivance of the text is an obvious one, and the reader will easily call to mind another example such as that of Ps. xviii. 31, האל תמים דרכו, for דרך אל תמים.

I suppose *The men of might, their hands did not find, &c.* to stand for *The hands of the men of might did not &c.*

The order of the Syriac favours this rendering, which is further confirmed by the Syriac fem. form of the verb, which requires that *their hands* should be taken as the nominative.

v. 8. מאז אפך. *When Thou art angry.* See the same construction in Ruth ii. 7,—מאז הבקר. It almost seems as if the simple demonstrative אז had assumed the functions of a noun substantive in these places. The Greek usage, sc. ἐκ τότε, εἰς τότε, ἐν τῷ τότε, is not qu:te parallel, though the analogy serves to throw light upon the Hebrew usage. The LXX. give simply ἀπο τῆς ὀργῆς σου, whence it seems probable that for מאז they read מאת.

v. 9. *The earth feared and cowered down* (שקטה). The Syriac render the last word by דחל, which in the Aramaic dialects denotes a timid cringing quietness. In this place the context teaches that the stillness intended is that produced by fear.

v. 11. *The fury of man acknowledgeth Thee: they who escape from that fury celebrate a festival to Thee.* The allusion is to the Israelites escaping from the rage of the Egyptians. The purpose of the Exodus is expressly declared over and over again to have been that the Israelites might hold a festival (חג) to Jehovah.

That the expression שארית חמה means *that which escapes from fury*, and not, as is usually supposed, *the remainder of fury*, can hardly be denied.*

The apparent impossibility of making any meaning out of the reading of the Hebrew text, תחגר, induces me, with Ewald, to adopt that of the LXX., תחגך, ἑορτάσει σοι. This will stand for the more usual form תחג לך, corresponding with ויחגו לי in Exod. v. 1, (LXX. ἵνα μοι ἑορτάσωσιν). But this alternative construction is so perfectly according to rule that it presents no difficulty here.

v. 12. *Vow and pay* (i.e. *pay your vows*)

---

* This meaning being so very obvious, it is disappointing to find Ewald contenting himself with what he calls a "very lofty conception," as follows:—" Jahve judges and punishes to this end alone, that the ungodly even who are most raging and furious in their senselessness may at last come to the knowledge and therewith to the praise of Jahve. And although many fall under punishment, at least the remainder, instructed by such powerful experiences, will yet be saved."

to the Lord your God. This is, of course, addressed to the Israelites.

Bring tribute to the dreadful One, ye that are round about Him. This seems to be addressed to the heathen nations. Their tribute is such as is imposed upon vanquished enemies. To the Israelites, the discharge of their own vows was a blessed privilege.

Psalm LXXVII.

v. 2. For the construction, see note on v. 11.

v. 3. ידי ‏· · · נגרה ולא תפוג.

עיני נגרה · · · מאין הפגות, Comp. Lam. iii. 49, See also Lam. ii. 18. The expressions seem more appropriate to the *eye* than to the *hand*. For נגרה the LXX. read נגדו. With this reading of theirs, לילה נגדו, comp. lxxxviii. 2,— בלילה נגדך.

The expression אדני דרשתי, if it means *I sought the Lord*, is unexampled, and unwarrantable. The verb requires יהוה, or at least אלהים as its object. In many MSS. יהוה is supplied.

I suspect an irremediable corruption of the text.

v. 4. I would divide the verse thus :—

אזכרה אלהים ואהם
יה אשׂיחה ותתעטף רוחי

*Do I call God to mind, then am I disquieted :
Do I contemplate Jehovah, then my spirit fainteth.*

It will be observed that the Psalmist, in failure of his purposed contemplation of God Himself, succeeds and finds comfort in the contemplation of God's *works*, especially His dealings with His people. This seems certainly to be the contrast intended between v. 4 &c. and v. 12, &c.

v. 5. *Thou hast closed my eyelids: I am struck dumb, and cannot speak.* This was the result of his attempted contemplation of the Deity, wherein " angels tremble as they gaze," and man is " blasted with excess of light."

For אחז in this sense, comp. the Syriac usage.

For נפעמתי, let it be considered that the word occurs as a verb only in these places, viz.

(*a*) in Gen. xli. 8, where Pharaoh's spirit " is troubled," (E.V.), on account of a dream which he is unable to expound :—

(b) in Judges xiii. 25, of Samson's initiation as a prophet:—

(c) in Dan. ii. 1 and 3, of Nebuchadnezzar's spirit being "troubled" (E. V.) on account of a dream which he could not expound.

(d) in this place (Ps. lxxvii. 5) in connection with the *restraint of speech*.

Although it is not necessary to assume such a common meaning of the root פעם as may be modified to accord with the requirements of these four occasions, yet it seems obvious that פעם is in all these places equivalent to פאם, of which Gesenius says that "it is one of the roots ending in *m* which express sounds uttered with the mouth shut." I therefore assume the common idea of *dumbness*.

For (a) and (c), it would appear that as the expounding of a dream &c. is usually spoken of as the *opening* of the dream, &c., so the lack of such exposition is expressed in terms that denote *closing*, whether of the mouth or of the mind.

With regard to the usage of (b), Samson's initiation as a prophet,—let it be considered that those who were subjected to such divine influences seem to have been usually bereft of their own natural faculties and natural senses;' and, in particular, that those who were commissioned to declare the Word of God seem to have been precluded from the privilege of speaking their own words. Till the Word of God came to them they were dumb. The reader will easily call to mind illustrations of this assertion. For the present I cite only Ezek. iii. 15, *I remained dumb seven days*, sc. till the Word of the Lord came, v. 16. See vv. 26, 27, of the same chapter; also and especially xxxiii. 22.

It will thus appear how a man called to exercise the prophetic office is properly described as *struck dumb*, mutus quoad verba sua, eloquens quoad verbum Dei. We may compare the analogous notion of the Roman haruspices, as expressed by the Grammarian Pompeius Festus,—" muta exta dicuntur, quibus nihil divinationis aut deorum responsi inesse animadvertunt." The Chaldee word for a *magician* is חרשא, *dumb*. And it seems highly probable that the name *(Elymas)* of Simon Magus is connected with אלם *(to be dumb)* rather than with עלם, as has usually been assumed. In confirmation of this supposition it may be mentioned that the Syriac form of the word Elymas has an initial א. It is perhaps also worthy of notice, that when Zacharias was struck dumb for a season (Luke i. 20-22) the people at once concluded that "he had seen a vision," i.e. that he had received some divine communication. Upon the general subject, viz. of the suspension of bodily power and sense in subjection to a divine impulse, see my notes on Ps. lxiii. 2, 3.

I therefore suppose the literal rendering of Judges xiii. 25 to be this: *And the Spirit of the Lord began to silence him,* sc. Samson,—that is to make him a vehicle of God's purposes rather than of his own.

In this place (Ps. lxxvii. 5) the technical meaning of *prophetic dumbness* is inadmissible. I assume only the ordinary meaning of *closing,* sc. the mouth.

v. 7. ויחפש רוחי, *And my spirit inquired.* The subjects of the inquiry are mentioned in the next three verses.

v. 11. *Then I said, Herein is my disease: I will make mention of the years of the right hand of the Most High.* As if he should say,

—" That was my *delirium:* Now, with the practical effort of a sound mind, I will not think of what God is, but will declare what He has done."

It will be observed that I disconnect the word אזכיר from the next verse, and add it to this.

The sentiment of חלותי היא, *that is sheer delirium*, may be paralleled and illustrated by that of *King Lear*, " O, that way madness lies."

v. 12. Putting back the word אזכיר into the preceding verse, the construction of this verse will be the same as that of the second verse of this Psalm, and of Ps. cxviii. 10, 11, and 12. See also cxxviii. 2.

v. 14. *O God, Thy way is with Thy saints.* This meaning might seem far-fetched if it were not warranted by other examples. See my note on Ps. lxviii. 18, and 25. The meaning is very appropriate here, where the Psalmist turns from the fruitless attempt to contemplate God's Being to the contemplation of *His way with His saints*. This, in the next verse, is spoken of as made known amongst the nations; just as in Ps. lxvii. 3, *That Thy way may be known in the earth,* &c. Observe also the mention of this way, or progress, of God, in the 20th verse of this Psalm, still in connection with the great deliverance from Egypt. See moreover Ps. cxiv. 2 :--*Judah was* לקדשו.

With regard to the usual rendering of this place, viz. *Thy way O God is holy*, I find it very difficult to assign any meaning to these words, and still more difficult to connect such a sentiment with the context.

In addition to the places referred to above, and as an example of the *collective* meaning of קדש, I would call attention to Lev. xxi. 6, והיו קדש *And they* (sc. the priests) *shall be holy*.

v. 17. *The waters saw Thee, &c.* Comp. the expressions of this verse and the next with Hab. iii. 10, 11. This passage in Habakkuk has been supposed to be the original upon these grounds, viz. (*a*) that the expression יחילו הרים is more natural than the מים יחילו of this Psalm; and (*b*) that the verbal form זרמו of the Psalm is found no-where else, whereas the זרם of Hab. iii. 10 is a word of ordinary use.

Upon the same grounds it may perhaps be argued that the expressions in v. 3 are borrowed in a clumsy fashion from Lam. iii. 49.

Psalm LXXVIII.

That this Psalm, in which the history of the chosen people is given in such minute detail, ends with the mention of David's reign, might seem to warrant the assertion of the title, viz. that it was written by Asaph. But the disruption of the kingdom is so clearly the main subject of the composition that such an ending must be otherwise accounted for. And on the supposition that the Psalm was written on the occasion of that disruption, or soon afterwards, it will easily appear why the narrative should end with that which might seem to be the consummation of God's purposes towards His people, viz. the establishment of David in the kingdom. Up to this point, all goes well: beyond it, all goes wrong. These considerations determine the point at which the narrative should end, although the occasion of the Psalm arises from subsequent events.

Let it be borne in mind, that Ephraim, in this Psalm, as in the prophecy of Hosea, and elsewhere, is the representative of the revolted tribes. "From the time of the revolt in two senses the history of Ephraim is the history of the kingdom of Israel, since not only did the tribe become a kingdom, but the kingdom embraced little besides the tribe."*

vv. 1, 2. For the similarity and the difference between this place and Ps. xlix. 4, 5, see the note there.

v. 2 *Shall I open my mouth in a parable, and utter old-fashioned riddles?*

v. 3. *(No), the things which we have heard and known, and which our fathers have told us, (will I utter).*

This meaning is given here, because it is beyond all doubt that it expresses the character of the Psalm, which is an historical narrative, removed as far as possible from the משל or חידה.

For the marking of the difference between the חידה and plain speech, see Numb. xii. 8.

v. 5. *For He made it an ordinance in Jacob, and instituted it a law in Israel, when He commanded our fathers to tell them (sc. His wondrous works) to their children.*

The meaning here given to אשר, as equivalent to כאשר, is that adopted by the Syriac

---

*Smith's Dict. of the Bible, sub v. *Ephraim.*

translator. The allusion seems to be to the oft-repeated injunction that the Israelites should tell to their children the wondrous works that God had wrought for them. The usual interpretation of this verse is to the effect that the injunctions themselves were to be taught to the children. The meaning I have adopted, and given above, seems much more suitable to the occasion, which is concerned with a reminder not of God's *laws* so much as of His dealings with His people.

v. 9. This mention of Ephraim seems here so utterly out of place that one feels inclined to regard the whole verse as an interpolation. Taking it, however, as it stands, how are we to interpret the words נושקי רומי קשת? The expression רמה קשת, *a shooter* (with) *a bow*, occurs in Jer. iv. 29, but it is doubtful whether the construct form of the text can bear this meaning.

It is somewhat surprising to find that commentators and critics, for the most part, either neglect or decline to institute a comparison of the text (*a*) with v. 57 of this Psalm (*b*), and Hosea vii. 16 (*c*).

(a) נושקי רומי קשת הפכו.
(b) נהפכו כקשת רמיה.
(c) ישובו היו כקשת רמיה.

Let it be observed that the words of Hosea (c) are, like those of the text (a), spoken expressly of Ephraim. The result of the comparison to my mind is, that the רומי קשת of (a), is equivalent to, and represents, the קשת רמיה of (b) and (c). The meaning will thus be that the children of Ephraim drew back in time of need just as bows with relaxed strings recoil. For the הפך, in these two places, refers primarily to the recoil of the bow, and is then figuratively applied to those who similarly delude one's expectation in time of need.

The primary idea of רמה,—I mean of that root from which מרמה and רמיה are derived— was certainly that of *relaxation, remissness*. It is closely akin to רפה, which has both in Hebrew and in Syriac this same meaning. Both the disappointment in the day of battle, and the cause of the disappointment, which are mentioned in the text, will be appreciated by the English reader who remembers that the result of the battle of Crecy was determined at the outset by a shower of rain that relaxed the strings of our enemy's bows.

I do not think it is intended in the text that Ephraim did on any special occasion of battle turn his back, as if in cowardice. The mention of *the day of battle* is appropriate to the illustration (sc. the bow), not to the thing illustrated (sc. Ephraim). The meaning seems to be that Ephraim was wanting to the occasion, just as bows with relaxed strings fail in the day of battle. What the occasion was, I do not pretend to know.

Having thus attempted to indicate the outlines of the meaning of the text, it remains to offer a detailed explanation of the text itself. The word נשק means to *lay hold of*, sc. weapons in general, but especially to draw the string of a bow. The words רומי קשת may therefore be taken as the object. The word רמיה in v 57, and in Hos. vii. 16, is the fem. form of the same Kal active participle, and ought to be pointed as such; just as פריה, in Ps. cxxviii. 3, is the fem. form of the participle פרה. But the Kal form of רמה has a meaning that we express by a passive form, viz. *to be relaxed*. Consequently,

רומי קשת means *the relaxed strings of the bow*. In the other two places, the bow itself is spoken of as being relaxed.

The construction is therefore not so unusual as is that which is commonly assumed, viz. that which regards קשת as the object of both the preceding participles. Taking נושקי as the governing verb, and רומי קשת as the object, the construction presents no difficulty; saving the remark that I have made upon lxxvi. 6, viz. that such an accumulation of nouns in the construct state was often avoided by the adoption of some other syntactical contrivance.

v. 12. *The field of Zoan.*

"A sandy plain, as vast as it is dreary, called at this day San in remembrance of the ancient name of Zoan, and covered with gigantic ruins of columns, pillars, sphinxes, stêlæ, and stones of buildings,—all these fragments being cut in the hardest material from the granite of Syene,—shows you the position of that city of Tanis, to which the Egyptian texts and the classic authors are agreed in giving the epithet of 'a great and splendid city of Egypt.' According to the geographical inscriptions, the

Egyptians gave to this plain the name of Sokhot Zoan, 'the plain of Zoan,' the origin of which name is traced back as far as the age of Ramses II. The author of the 78th Psalm makes use in two verses (12 and 43) of precisely the same phrase in reminding the Hebrews of his time of the miracles which God wrought before their ancestors the children of Israel, in Egypt, *in the plain of Zoan*. This remarkable agreement is not accidental, for the knowledge of the Hebrews concerning all that related to Tanis is proved by the note of an annalist, likewise reported in Holy Scripture (Num. xiii. 22), that the city of Hebron was built seven years before the foundation of Zoan." . . . . . "This (Zoan-Ramses) is the very city where the children of Israel experienced the rigours of a long and oppressive slavery, where Moses wrought his miracles in the presence of the Pharaoh of his age; and it was from this same city that the Hebrews set out, to quit the fertile land of Egypt." *The Exodus and the Egyptian Monuments*, by Brugsch Bey.

v. 24. *He rained down upon them manna for food, and of the corn of heaven He gave to them.*

The expressions here are all appropriate to the gift of manna.

v. 25. *Lordly food did man eat:* **He** *sent them meat,* (lit. *game,* or *venison*) *to satiety.*

The expressions here are all appropriate to the gift of quails.

v. 26. See also the consecutive use of יסע וינהג in v. 52.

v. 29. *And He fulfilled their desire,* והאותם יבא להם. For this use of the verb, see cv. 19, and note on lxxiv. 4, 5.

v. 30. *They had not yet got so far as the loathing of their lust, for the meat was yet in their mouths.*

v. 31. *When the wrath of God arose against them.*

It can hardly admit of doubt that זרו in v. 30 is identical in meaning with the זרא of Numb. xi. 20, to which this passage is to be referred: —*Ye shall eat* (sc. the quails) *for a whole month; until it come out at your nostrils, and it be loathsome* (לזרא) *unto you.*

v. 41. *The Holy One of Israel.* See Ps. lxxxix. 19.

id. הרוו, *They put a mark upon the Holy One of Israel.* This is clearly the meaning, if the reading is correct. For תו does not mean *a sign*, as some suppose, but a mark to know a person or thing by. See Ezek. ix. 4. But the word *mark*, as denoting a criterion, a critical test, gives the proper meaning of the word, and a very significant one in this connection. How, said the Israelites, are we to know that Jehovah is our God? We will try Him (נסה) and put this test to Him, whereby we shall mark Him and recognise Him. This test is proposed in verses 18-20 :—It is true that He has done such and such things for us,—But can He provide flesh in the wilderness? If He can do this, then we shall acknowledge Him :— this is the mark whereby we shall know Him.*

It was in this way, as it seems to me, that Israel demanded a continually repeated token of that love which needed no such miraculous tokens of its continuance. Except they saw continually repeated signs and wonders they

---

*So Caliban, in *The Tempest* :—
" That's a brave god, and bears celestial liquor:
I will kneel to him."

would not believe. The very opposite of this, viz. what they ought to have done, is indicated in the following verses, 42-55. They ought to have *remembered* all those manifestations of God's regard for them which in these verses are recounted.

v. 43. אתותיו שם. *He wrought His signs.* See note on Ps. lxxiv. 4. See also cv. 27.

v. 47. בחנמל. The root of this word is certainly to be sought in נמל i.q. מול, *to cut off, to devastate by cutting off.* It is therefore probably a mere synonym of ברד,—χάλαζα. For the same thing that destroyed the vines destroyed also the sycamores. With this obvious meaning agree pretty nearly the LXX., ἐν τῇ πάχνῃ; the two phenomena being also associated in Plato, Symp. 188. B, πάχναι καὶ χάλαζαι. So also the Lat. Vulg. *pruina*, and the Syriac.

v. 48. In this verse ברד seems to have been mistaken from the preceding verse. It ought probably to be דבר, *pestilence*, which is associated with רשף (as it is here) in Hab. iii. 5. See note on Ps. lxxvi. 4. We thus take v. 47 to refer to the plague of hail, and this 48th verse to the murrain of beasts, thus:—He gave up their cattle to the plague, and their flocks to burning pestilences. Two MSS. give the reading דבר. It must be acknowledged, certainly, that their authority is infinitely outweighted by that of the LXX., who read ברד, as did also the Syr. On the whole, however, the reading דבר, *pestilence*, seems preferable, and more probable.

v. 51. ראשית אונים, *The first-fruits of genital power*, i.e. the first-born. See Gen. xlix. 3, and Ps. cv. 36.

v. 57. קשת רמיה. See note on v. 9 of this Psalm.

v. 60. *He forsook the dwelling in Shiloh*, &c. That a distinct reference is made to the disastrous defeat of Israel by the Philistines (1 Sam. iv.), wherein the Ark of God was taken, seems clear from the consideration that there is here no mention of the transference of the Ark from Ephraim to Judah, but of God's utter withdrawal from His earthly dwelling, the tent that He had pitched amongst *men*. The same reference is indicated also by the next verse:—

v. 61. *He gave his strength into captivity and His ornament into the enemy's hand.* For these two words, *strength* and *ornament*, are elsewhere appropriated to the Ark of God. See note on Ps. lxviii. 29, and cv. 4.

v. 63. *Their virgins were not celebrated with nuptial song.* The LXX. read הילֵלוּ, ἐπένθησαν, and this reading is adopted by Gesenius in order to make these words accord with those of the next verse,—*their widows wept not.* See note on next verse.

v. 64. *Their widows wept not.* See the same words in Job. xxvii. 15.

If we seek to maintain a correspondence between the הוללו of the preceding verse, and the הבכינה of this, we ought to be sure that the parallelism is complete throughout. But it is not. There is no such correspondence between the *young men* of v. 63, and the *priests* of v. 64. The two verses must therefore be interpreted, not as continuing one sequence of ideas, but as two distinct and independent propositions.

The 63rd verse is more complete in its obvious meaning than the 64th. There the virgins are not married because the young men are slain. In this 64th verse, it is not so clear why the priests' widows should not weep, when their husbands fell by the sword. The only explanation that occurs to me is that which is suggested by the history referred to. When Hophni and Phinehas fell in battle, the wife of the latter died in premature labour. In this view, the Prayer Book Version seems to give the intended meaning :—*There were no widows to make lamentation,* sc. because they too were dead. This seems also the meaning of the same words in Job xxvii. 15.

v. 65. *As a giant exulting* (lit. *shouting*) *from wine.* Gesenius is certainly wrong in rendering this place, *like a mighty man overcome with wine.* The mighty man, far from lying down in drunken sloth, arises for exulting victory.

v. 66. *He smote their enemies behind,* referring probably to the particular disease wherewith the Philistines were smitten for their detention of the Ark. See 1 Sam. v. 9.

v. 67. *And He passed over the tabernacle of Joseph,* i.e. He declined to choose it. See note on Ps. xiv. 6, p. 120.

Psalm LXXIX.

There is no event that will answer to the representations of this Psalm earlier than the taking of Jerusalem by Nebuchadnezzar. This gives the *maximum* of age.

How is the *minimum* to be determined? Since there are many passages common to this Psalm and to the writings of Jeremiah,—then either (1) Jeremiah copied the Psalm, or (2) the Psalmist copied Jeremiah. Upon the latter supposition, some later devastation than that by Nebuchadnezzar may be the occasion and subject of the Psalm. If the former seem more probable, then the maximum and minimum data will coincide, sc. in the destruction of Jerusalem by Nebuchadnezzar.

For the determination of this problem, the principal test passages are the 6th and 7th verses of the Psalm, and Jer. x. 25. The variations are these

Psalm LXXIX.		Jer. X.	
v. 6.	אל הגוים	v. 25.	על הגוים (a)
	ועל ממלכות		ועל משפחות (b)
v. 7.	כי אכל את יעקוב		כי אכלו את יעקוב (c)
			ואכלהו ויכלהו (d)
	ואת נוהו השמו		ואת נוהו השמי (e)

With regard to the variation in clause (*a*) it may be admitted that the אל of the Psalm is less appropriate than the על of Jeremiah. But this goes for nothing as a test of priority, unless it can be shown that the two compositions are separated in time by a considerable interval, and that the use of אל for על prevails at one more than at the other limit of this interval. But neither of these suppositions is available.

On the other hand, if one composition is copied from another, where may we reasonably look for an abnormal form or construction? Certainly not in the copy, where the copyist would not be likely to introduce an irregularity, but would be rather prone to correct such irregularity and bring it into pedantic conformity. The abnormal is more likely to be the original than the normal.

The same remarks will apply to the slight variation under (*c*).

Under (*b*) the variation is not so important to the inquiry as might at first sight appear. The word משפחות, which invariably means some lower subdivision of the *gens*, cannot appropriately be co-ordinated with the גוים, as in Jeremiah. The proper co-ordinate is the ממלכות of the Psalm. But משפחות is a very favourite word with Jeremiah. Upon the supposition that he quoted the Psalm, it is easy to see how he would introduce his own peculiar phraseology. But on the supposition that the Psalmist quoted Jeremiah, it is equally easy to discern the inducement (as in the case of *a*) to correct an obvious solecism.

With regard to the variation under (*c*), viz. the addition that appears in Jeremiah as (*d*), it will be observed that Jeremiah gives an amplification of the Psalmist's words. This means that the Psalmist gives the text, and Jeremiah the application. Further, that the amplification of the text consists in a play upon the words אכלהו and יכלהו.

Which of the two is more likely to be the original,—the text without the play upon it, or the text and the play upon it?

We may put the matter thus:—

The Psalm: *They have eaten Jacob, and devastated His dwelling.*

Jeremiah :—*They have eaten Jacob :—*
    They have indeed eaten him, and eaten him up too,—
    And devastated his dwelling.

It is hardly necessary to ask the question, Which of these two is the original: The sober statement of the Psalm, or the passage wherein a punning amplification thrusts itself into the middle of that sober statement?

This last test seems to me decisive, and upon the strength of it, chiefly but not solely, I conclude that Jeremiah made an adaptation of the Psalm. And since the disaster lamented in the Psalm can hardly be of earlier date than the destruction of Jerusalem by Nebuchadnezzar, and since the adapting of the Psalm by Jeremiah precludes the supposition of a later date, I conclude further that the date and occasion of the Psalm are to be identified with Nebuchadnezzar's invasion.

Would Jeremiah quote, and vary to his purpose, the writing of a contemporary? There seems no reason why he should not. He would perhaps have less scruple in varying and amplifying such a writing than one of venerable antiquity.

Did Jeremiah himself write the Psalm? It is not impossible; but even so, it seems certain that Jer. x. 25 is not the original composition. And he would not scruple to amplify and apply his own writings.

v. 10. *Why should the heathen say, Where is their God? Let it be known* (sc. where He is) *amongst the heathen, in our sight,* (by) *the avenging of Thy servants' blood that is shed.*

v. 11. *By the greatness of Thy power, keep alive a remnant of them that are appointed unto death.*

v. 12. The mention of insulting *neighbours*, here and in v. 4, must not be overlooked. They were not the persecutors, but they exulted in the persecution of God's people.

v. 13. The last word of the Psalm is *Tehillah*; the one crowning privilege of God's people: the exulting and triumphant confidence in God which only His chosen can entertain and express. It is here placed in splendid contrast with the reproach of the heathen, and of the malicious neighbours, mentioned in the preceding verse. *Let them curse, so long as Thou dost bless.*

Psalm LXXX.

v. 3. *Before Ephraim, and Benjamin, and Manasseh.* The explanation long ago proposed, viz. that these three tribes took the lead in the march through the wilderness, seems quite satisfactory. See Numb. ii. 17-24. It should be added that the word הופיע here, meaning *Shine forth,* is the very word that Moses uses in Deuteronomy xxxiii. 2, to express the divine splendour whereby that march was conducted:— *The Lord came from Sinai, and rose up from Seir unto them: He shined forth from Mount Paran, and He came with ten thousands of His saints.*

Therefore the prayer of the text, *Shine forth before Ephraim, Benjamin, and Manasses,* &c., means only, *Be Thou our leader now as Thou wast of old.*

v. 4. השיבנו. *Restore us.* I have remarked upon Ps. lxviii. 22, 23, that "the word does not always mean restoration from captivity, but is often used, generally, of restoration from evil to good."

v. 5. On account of the preterite tense of the verb, it has been proposed to render the words עדמתי עשנת, *How long hast Thou been angry!* But it is certain that עדמתי means *quousque*, without any retrospective reference : *until when,*—not *since when*. On the other hand, the preterite force of the verb must be acknowledged. The difficulty is not peculiar to this place. We find precisely the same expression,—*How long hast thou refused?*—in Exod. x. 3. The construction must be taken as a compound of two incomplete constructions, concerning which I refer to my quotation from M. Renan in note on Ps. xiii. 2.

The full meaning of such expressions is to be found and represented by separating and separately expressing their mingled ideas, or rather intentions. Thus :—

Exod. x. 3. *Thou hast refused so long!*
  How much longer wilt Thou refuse?
Ps. lxxx. 5. *Thou hast been angry so long!*
  How much longer wilt Thou be angry?

For עמך at the end of this verse the LXX. read עבדך or עבדיך.

v. 6. *Thou hast fed them with tears as if it were bread.* See Ps xiv. 4, and note on lvi. 2.

שָׁלִישׁ. This word speaks for itself, as a measure that is *one-third* of a larger measure, just as our *quart* is one-fourth of a gallon. The larger measure is possibly the *ephah,* since the LXX render איפה (*an ephah*) by τρία μέτρα in Exod. xvi. 36, and Isaiah v. 10; and שׁליש by ἐν μέτρῳ here. An expression quite analogous to that of the text would be, *by the quart,* an exaggerated expression to denote a great quantity.

v. 16. The על in the latter clause of this verse must be taken in connection with some verb in the former. This verb is כנה, imperat. of כנן i.q. גנן, which is regularly followed by על. In this place, the Psalmist, neglecting the rule in the former clause, observes it in the latter. The meaning is:—*Protect that which Thy right hand hath planted, and the branch that Thou hast nurtured for Thyself.*

I give *nurtured* instead of *strengthened,* as being more appropriate in this connection. The same word is used in the same sense in Isaiah xliv. 14,—*the cypress and the oak which he hath nurtured.*

It has been supposed, not unreasonably, that the mention of בן and ימין, here and in v. 18, points to *Benjamin.*

For בן or בנה, in the sense of *branch*, see the blessing pronounced upon Joseph in Gen. xlix. 22. A reference to that blessing may here be intended.

v. 18. *Let Thy hand be over* (sc. as a protection) *the man of Thy right hand.*

We could not have given this as the meaning but for the use of על in connection with כנה in v. 16. Without this clue we might as well translate *Let Thy hand be against the man* &c.

id. *Over that branch of the human family* (בן אדם) *which Thou hast nurtured for Thyself:* i.e. Israel,—the allusion to the vine brought out of Egypt being still maintained.

Psalm LXXXI.

v. 4. It seems nearly certain that the *new moon* and the כסה of this verse are to be referred to the *seventh month,* and that therefore the reference of the whole passage is to the feast of tabernacles. The word חג is, as I have remarked upon xlii. 5, specially appropriated to this festival.

Why the *new* moon, as well as the *full* moon, of this month should be celebrated, does not immediately appear. I quote, however, the following remarks from Ewald's *Antiquities of Israel.* After having spoken of the seventh month as the "sabbath-month," he adds—

Hence this month was to be distinguished from all the rest, and receive a sacred consecration, by its *new-moon* being saluted more solemnly than that of any other, and even being exalted to the dignity of a special annual festival. With the remaining new-moons the law concerned itself but little . . . . The law never insisted on their celebration by the whole people, or placed them on a level with the sabbaths. On the seventh new-moon, however, there was to be a public celebration of a great festival by all the people, during which work was suspended; and the importance of the occasion was to be loudly proclaimed by the priests from the Sanctuary.

It would thus appear that where, as in this Psalm, especial mention is made both of the new moon and of another festival in the same month, the moon intended must be that of the seventh month, and that therefore the occasion of this Psalm is the celebration of the feast of booths. The following remarks are introduced here, not only as being of general interest in connection with this great festival, but as being necessary for the elucidation of the text.

The purpose of this feast is briefly stated in Lev. xxiii. 42, 43 thus :—*Ye shall dwell in booths seven days* .... *That your generations may know that I made the children of Israel to dwell in booths (Succoth) when I brought them out of the land of Egypt.* It occurs to remark that *Succoth* is hardly the word that would have been used if *tents* had been intended. It is quite certain that the Israelites, during their march through the wilderness, could not have lived in *booths*, such as are denoted by *Succoth*. The event to be commemorated is therefore to be dissociated from the mere dwelling in tents. Yet it is expressly connected with the departure from Egypt; and in this connection we cannot but

F

call to mind that the first encampment of Israel was at a place called *Succoth*. It matters little to our inquiry whether the name was given to the place on this occasion by the Hebrews, or whether it is a Hebrew form of an Egyptian name, since we know how prone the Hebrews were to adapt to their own circumstances proper names that had their origin in totally different circumstances.

This first encampment of the Israelites was, however, marked by an extraordinary phenomenon. Then, for the first time, their camp was overshadowed by a cloud that plainly marked God's protection of His people, and as plainly indicated His will with regard to their movements. So long as the cloud rested over them, they must rest. When it moved, they must move.

Amongst the many wonderful manifestations of divine protection and guidance which signalized the Exodus, this phenomenon does not seem to meet with its share of commemoration, unless, as I suppose, it is commemorated in the feast of Succoth. It is, however, often referred to indirectly by the Old Testament writers, and the allusions to it in this 81st Psalm are, as I shall show, numerous and unequivocal. But the most direct reference to it is that made by St. Paul in 1 Cor. x. 1, 2, where he reminds his brethren that *all their fathers were under the cloud, and all passed through the sea ; and were all baptized unto Moses in the cloud and in the sea.* Observe the order, repeatedly observed,— first the cloud, then the sea ; from which it would appear that the protecting cloud was a subject of commemoration preceding, in respect of time, the passage of the sea.

By such considerations we are induced to this conclusion, viz. that, whatever may be the origin and proper meaning of the name Succoth, it was connected in the minds of the Israelites with their first experience of God's shielding and guiding cloud, and then, etymologically, with the verb סכך, which is appropriate to such connection.*

The dwelling in tents was a necessary and insignificant incident of the Exodus. It was totally unconnected with any manifestation of

---

*Comp. Ps. cv. 39. *He spread out a cloud for a covering,* לםסך.

God's power and love. There seems, therefore, no reason why it should be the occasion of a commemorative feast on a level with that of the Passover. On the other hand, the shielding and guiding cloud, first appearing at Succoth, and accompanying Israel throughout the long journey, was a worthy occasion of such a festive commemoration.

If this conclusion be established, we may discover what has hitherto been vainly sought, viz. the origin of the word כסה, as it appears here, or כסא as it appears in Prov. vii. 20,—the word being found no-where else. By the early Hebrew commentators it was supposed to be a poetical synonym of חדש, and to denote the *new moon*. The etymology suited this notion, since the word might be taken to mean *the hidden moon*. But when it appeared certain that the *full moon*, or rather something coincident with the full moon, was denoted, the etymological account of the word was strangely forced. "The etymology," says Gesenius, "is not clear to me, for it is not satisfactory to say that it is so called from the whole moon being then *covered* with light." Now the word seems certainly to denote *the feast,* κατ' ἐξοχήν, in Prov. vii. 20, and it can hardly be doubted that it denotes the *feast of booths* in this Psalm. The same feast is probably intended in both places. And since כסה and ככך are equivalent in meaning, as they are allied in form, the conclusion seems at least probable that כסה denotes, not the full moon, but the feast of booths. That this feast was coincident with the full moon of the seventh month is no reason for assuming that the word כסה denotes the full moon of any other month. That it denotes the feast of booths, as a commemoration of the shielding and guiding cloud, seems probable from the further consideration that it is the word regularly used, in the Mosaic history, in connection with this cloud.*

---

* The argument, so far as it concerns the origin of the *Feast of Booths*, may be thus summarized :—

The word כסה denotes something coincident with the full moon of the seventh month. This is the feast of booths. It has been customary to seek the origin of this feast exclusively in the word *Succoth*. But if we find the feast itself denoted by the word כסה, we are warranted in looking for this origin in something more general than the idea of *booths,* sc. in the general idea of covering, sheltering. And since this word כסה is frequently used to denote the operation of the sheltering cloud that first

In this view the הרנינו of v. 2 may be connected with the בסכה of v. 4, in accordance with the ירננו ותסך עלימו of Ps. v. 12. In both places the Israelites *shout for joy because God is their shelter.* See also Ps. xlii. 5, where this joyful shouting (רנה) is specially associated with the feast of booths; and Ps. cv. 43, where this same רנה is mentioned in close connection with the appearance of the sheltering cloud in v. 39.

v. 6. *When He went forth over the land of Egypt.*

The use of the preposition על in this place both confirms the foregoing conjecture and is explained by it. The feast of booths was instituted when God went forth *over* the land of Egypt. The *overshadowing* cloud suggests the preposition על, just as, in Ps. lxxx. the על of v. 18 is to be understood only in connection with the כסה of v. 4.

id. *Where* (sc. in Egypt) *I heard a language that I knew not.* See Ps. cxiv. 1.

v. 7. *I removed his shoulder from the burden: his hands forsook the clay.*

---

appeared at Succoth, we are further warranted in regarding the festival as a commemoration of that sheltering cloud.

I adopt this interpretation of דוד with some misgivings. It is conjectured as a synonym of חמר in Exod. i. 14. That the word does not mean a *basket*, as the LXX. and some modern writers suppose, appears from the consideration that the *basket* in which the burden was to be carried would be borne on the shoulder. Now the shoulder and its burden are mentioned in the former clause. It is hardly likely that the same burden would be mentioned, in connection with the *hands*, in the second clause. An instructive Egyptian picture given by Wilkinson, and reproduced in Smith's Bible Dictionary *sub v. brick*, is a perfect commentary on the text. We here see foreign captives busily engaged with their *hands* in the various processes of brickmaking, whilst a load is being placed by one of these captives on the *shoulder* of another.

v. 8. *In trouble didst thou cry, and I delivered thee: I sheltered thee with my thundercloud.*

I take אענך to mean *I sheltered thee*, from ענן.* So the Syriac, using here the verb כסא.

With regard to the word סתר, let it be

---

* Comp. Ps. cv. 39, *He spread out a cloud for a covering* ענן למסך.

observed that it is used as equivalent to כסה in Ps. xviii. 12, xxvii. 5, and xxxi. 21:—as equivalent to אהל in Ps. lxi. 5, and to צל in Ps. xci. 1. It is therefore not unwarrantable to take כרה here as referring to the *Succoth* which I suppose to be the occasion and the subject of the Psalm.

The change of person in v. 7 would seem abrupt and unaccountable but for the supposition that the Psalm is intended for use on the great feast of booths. It is certain that one feature in the celebration of this feast was the solemn recital of God's dealings with His people in the past. See Deut. xxxi. 10, 13, and Neh. viii. 18. I suppose, therefore, that to the end of the 6th verse the Psalmist states the occasion of the recital of God's manifested power and love, and devotes the rest of the Psalm to the recital itself. *This is the occasion whereon ye ought to remember God's gracious dealings with you: Ye are therefore and hereby reminded of them.*

The remainder of the Psalm is little more than a formula of reminiscence. We are therefore not surprised by its abrupt ending. Much the same account is to be given of the abrupt ending of Ps. lxxvii.

Psalm LXXXII.

v. 1. *God sitteth in the congregation of the mighty. In the midst of the judges He judgeth.*

It is not here meant that God sits in judgment upon the judges; but rather that their tribunal is His. This consideration accounts for the use of the words אל and אלהים. For although elsewhere these words serve to denote *human* judges, their use in this place is somewhat perplexing. We should not ordinarily expect the word to be used in one sense in the former clause, and in another sense in the latter clause, of the same verse. Here, however, the intention is to represent the human judges as God's vicegerents: perhaps as assessors with Him in His tribunal. They are therefore mentioned by the name that identifies their office with that of God.

v. 6. *I myself have spoken of you as gods,*—as indeed, for that matter, ye are all of you (high and low) *children of the most high,*—See Deut. xiv. 1.

v. 7. *Nevertheless, ye die like common men, and together* (sc. with common men) *do ye princes fall.*

This meaning of אכן, *nevertheless*, is warranted by many examples. See Ps. xxxi. 23, lxvi. 29, and Isaiah liii. 4.

This meaning of כאחד, *together*, is found in many other places. It is proposed here by Ewald and others. We may compare the sentiment of this passage with Ps. xlix. 3 and 11, and the use of כאחד here with יחד there.

The *princes* of v. 7 are the *judges* to whom the expostulation of the Psalm is addressed. This we know from the history. See also Zephaniah iii. 3, where שׂרים and שׁפטים seem to be identified.

v. 8. *For all the nations are Thy possession.*

These words might be taken to show that the Psalm has a reference to unjust rulers in general,—not to those of Israel in particular. In the second Psalm the nations are given to the Son of God for a possession; and, in immediate connection with this fact, the judges of the earth are exhorted to the wise and just discharge of their duty. In this 82nd Psalm the same grand and general fact is declared, as in Psalm ii., but probably with more limited reference, viz. to the judges of Israel.

Psalm LXXXIII.

The Psalmist, praying for help in a present emergency, calls to mind, as a ground of encouragement, the deliverance from the Midianites under Gideon, and that from Jabin king of Canaan under Deborah. Now it seems to me almost certain that if, at the time this Psalm was written, these old deliverances had been outshone by something more recent, the more recent would have been mentioned. If the Psalm had been written after the destruction of Sennacherib's army, this defeat would have been specially referred to:—the more especially since the possibility of Assyria's joining the confederacy against Israel is expressly mentioned in the Psalm. If after the overthrow of Sennacherib's army Assyria again contemplates hostilities against Israel, then the prayer will surely be, *Do to them as Thou didst to them before*, rather than *Do to them as Thou didst to Midian, &c.* Admitting that Assyria is only indirectly an occasion of fear, yet, even so, the very mention of her name would recall the appalling circumstances of her overthrow, if this had been an event of the past when the Psalm was written.

Upon these grounds there seems little room for doubting that the occasion of the Psalm is to be sought in circumstances antecedent to the reign of Hezekiah. There is now no difficulty in assigning it to the time of Jehoshaphat. In his reign we read that *Moab and Ammon and some of the kindred nations** (2 Chron. xx. 1), *and Edom* (xx. 10), *menaced Israel.*

Gebal, Amalek, Ishmael, Philistia, Tyre, Assyria:—these names occur in the Psalm, and not in the history.

Of these, I do not take Gebal to be a proper name, but a verb. See note on v. 8. Those who take it as the name of a place or of a people connect it with Phœnicia; but its place in the list discredits this assumption. Neither is the existence of such a city in the slightest degree to be inferred from Ezek. xxvii. 9.

---

*In thus translating 2 Chron. xx. 1, I have borne in mind that the word עמון by itself denotes simply *kindred*. The full name of the Ammonites is בני עמון, *sons of kin*, i.e. children born of incest. Because *Ammon*, by itself, is used frequently, as an abbreviation, for the people who had such an origin, the proper meaning of the word is not to be overlooked.

We find *Amalek* allied with Moab and Ammon against Israel in Judges iii. 12, 13. They are therefore presumable allies of the enemy on this occasion.

The Ishmaelites are included in the *kindred* mentioned in the Chronicles.

Philistia and Tyre may possibly stand for *Philistia and Syria*, united in enmity to Judah as in Isaiah ix. 12. Of the Philistines it may be said that they were almost always on the alert to unite with other foes against the chosen people, whether Judah or Israel. They are here mentioned as *possible* enemies, viz. as allies of Moab and Ammon. The same may be said of *Assyria*.

I suppose therefore that whilst war was declared, or hostilities actually commenced, only by the peoples mentioned in the Chronicles, the known hostility of other tribes or peoples warranted the apprehension expressed in the Psalm: —that thus the circumstances under which the Psalm was written may be identified with the troubles of the reign of Jehoshaphat.

v. 5. *That the Name of Israel be remembered no more.* It must be considered that

God had put His Name upon Israel. The impious purpose expressed in these words is probably directed against the God of Israel. This consideration throws light upon the last verse of this Psalm. See also notes upon Ps. lix. 12.

v. 8. גבלו עמון ועמלק. So I divide the first two words: and translate the whole verse thus:—

Ammon and Amalek are joined together: Philistia (is joined together) with the inhabitants of Tsor.

The verb גבל denotes union by conjunction. It is used for the most part of conterminous regions, and thence comes the notion of *demarcation* expressed by the Hiphil form of the verb in Exod. xix. 12, 23. But that the proper idea of the word was that of *joining together* appears from all the other usages of the verb and of its derivatives. It is easy to see how the idea of demarcation, apparently so opposite, would grow up and invest the word, if we consider that the line which separates any two territories is precisely the line wherein they adjoin to one another. So strangely do extremes meet.

The verb occurs in Kal in Deut. xix. 14,

of the marking out of a territory; but there it is plainly denominative from the גבול, the territory so marked out. The meaning is, *Thou shalt not remove the allotment of thy neighbour, which they of old time allotted.* It occurs also in Josh. xviii. 20, where the river Jordan is mentioned as a boundary. But a boundary is not necessarily a demarcation. It is a summation. See also Zech. ix. 2, where the verb means plainly *to be adjacent to.*

The noun substantive גבול denotes constantly the territory itself. This could hardly be if the primary idea was that of separation. It means really *my bit of land that comes up to my neighbour's bit;* and this idea of coming up to, joining on to, fitting in to, is precisely the idea of the verb.

We call a man who fits and joins timbers together *a joiner.* The same expression was applied to the stone-fitters, or stone-squarers, who were employed to dress the stone for Solomon's temple. They are called גבלים, 1 Kings v. 18. When we remember that these stones had to be dressed, so as to fit exactly, before they were brought to the site of the temple, we see how appropriate the word is, denoting not simply *hewers* of stone, but *fitters*, or *joiners*. These *gobelim*, however, are usually supposed to be the inhabitants of the imaginary city of Gebal, in Phœnicia!

The idea of joining together appears also in the word גבלות, applied to linked or woven chains of gold in Exod. xxviii. 14 and 22. Whether they were linked or woven, or both, the idea is that of uniting into a continuous chain. Compare our English word *knit*, *to unite*, concerning which see note on Ps. lxxxvi. 11.

v. 14. *My God, make them like chaff, or chaffy husks before the wind.* בלגל is nothing more than a synonym of קש. It is identical with Syr. גלא, chaff or husk,—the word used, *e.g.*, in Matt. vii. 3, to represent the Greek κάρφος. See Isaiah xvii. 13.

v. 15. The context shows that some rapid and superficial devastation by fire is intended: —something analogous to the superficial action of the wind when it sweeps away chaff and dry husks. We may therefore understand the rapid burning of bushy thickets (יער) and of herbage

(הרים) in dry seasons. With regard to the latter, the hills are usually spoken of as pastures; (See Ps. l. 10,—*On the hills of the oxen*, and cxlvii. 8, *He causeth the hills to bring forth grass*). And for the intentional, as well as accidental, burning of these upland pastures, see note on Ps. xxxvii. 20.

v. 17. *That they may seek Thy Name (which is) Jehovah.* This last word, Jehovah, is not an unmeaning expletive. It is the name by which God was known especially as the God of Israel. To seek this is to seek after the one living and true God. In the last verse of this Psalm this identification of the knowledge of God with the knowledge of His sacred Name is remarkably expressed.

v. 19. *And they shall know that Thou, Thy Name Jehovah,* &c. This construction has been the subject of much comment. It has not yet been noted that it **is a construction** peculiar to the occasion,—an occasion which in at least two other places is marked by the same construction. The peculiarity is this, that the Name of Jehovah is identified with Jehovah Himself. Now Jehovah may speak in the first person, may be addressed in the second, or may be spoken of in the third. But the word *Name* remains always in the third person. Yet in all three cases the two words *(Jehovah* and *Name)* are found in apposition. Thus:—

First person, Exod. vi. 3, *My Name Jehovah I was not known unto them.*

Second person, Ps. lxxxiii. 19. *They shall know that Thou Thy Name Jehovah art* (or *is*) *most high over all the earth.*

Third person, Ps. lxviii. 5. ביה שמו, *Unto Jehovah His Name.*

Psalm LXXXIV.

v. 1. מה ידידות, LXX. ὡς ἀγαπητά; Lat. Vulg. *quam dilecti;* and both our English Versions, *How amiable!* In view of all these correct translations it is surprising that some modern commentators should give the word *lovely*, which conveys a totally different idea, and one that is unsuitable to the context. If *amiable* is objected to as un-English, then the word *loveable* presents itself. But the idea is better expressed in English by *beloved:—O how beloved are Thy dwellings.*

v. 3. נכספה, *longeth.* The word seems to denote primarily *paleness, whiteness;* hence כסף, *silver.* The idea of *longing* is similarly expressed by the Latin *pallere.* Not to mention the *palleat omnis amans* of Ovid, (*Ars Am.* 1. 729), the word is thus used more generally in Hor. Sat. II. 3, 78,—*Ambitione mala aut argenti pallet amore.*

The word occurs with the same meaning in this same Niphal form in Gen. xxxi. 30, and in Kal in Ps. xvii. 12.

v. 4. דרור seems to mean *a swallow.* Whether this word is derived from a root that denotes flying in a circle, because these birds fly in circles, which is the opinion of Gesenius; —or from a root that denotes flying in a straight line, because these birds fly in straight lines, which is the opinion of Delitzsch,—I do not pretend to decide. A probable conjecture is that those learned writers knew as much about swallows as these happy birds knew about them.

The word, as denoting some kind of bird, is found only here and in Prov. xxvi. 2.*

---

* Prov. xxvi. 2. *Like the sparrow for fleeing: like the swallow for flying; so the groundless curse shall not be*

v. 5. *O happy they who dwell in Thy house: they are still exulting in Thee:*

v. 6. *O happy (also is) the man who has a strong refuge in Thee: in their heart are the highways,* sc. that lead to that refuge.

This, which is the usual rendering of the latter part of v. 6, seems at first sight far-fetched. But I think it is warranted by the following considerations.

The preceding words, אשרי אדם עוז לו בך, are usually taken to mean, *Blessed is the man whose strength is in Thee*,—as if the reading were עוזו instead of עוז־לו. The strictly accurate translation is, *Blessed is the man who has a strong refuge in Thee*. The sentiment is to be taken in connection with that which immediately precedes,—*Blessed are they that dwell in Thy house*. Then comes the sequel:—*Blessed also are they that have that house of Thine to flee unto*. With which compare Ps. xlvi. 2,—*God is our hope* (מחסה) *and refuge* (עוז): *a help to be found especially in adversities*. As עוז in

---

fulfilled; i.e., it shall vanish at the slightest challenge, as birds do at the slightest scare. צפור is here connected with the verb נוד, as in Ps. xi. 1,

this forty-sixth Psalm is found in connection, and almost as synonymous, with מחסה,* so מגדל עז and מחסה are connected in Ps. lxi. 4. It would thus appear that עוז in the text before us stands for the fuller form, " tower of strength." That is, the word denotes the sanctuary of God as a place of refuge.

All this can hardly be better expressed than it has been by Hammond. He gives: *" Blessed is the man that hath in Thee strength, help, or protection; being allowed liberty (as the former part of the Psalm determines the sense) to resort to God's sanctuary, which is sometimes called עוז, and from whence that protection and aid in all exigencies may be had."*

Having ascertained this as the meaning of עוז, we shall have less difficulty than we should otherwise find in referring the מסלות of this verse to the *highways* that led to Zion. For the mention of those who habitually dwell in God's Sanctuary is thus associated with the mention of those who, though they cannot so habitually

---

* The two coalesce for the expression of one and the same idea in Ps. lxxi. 7,—מחסי עז.

dwell, are yet blessed in being able to resort thither in time of need.

Since this passage, like many others, can be adequately rendered only by a paraphrase, we may frame one upon the words of the Collect for Ascension Day :—

Blessed are they who " *continually dwell* " *in Thy house: Blessed are they who* " *in heart and mind thither ascend.*"

For מסלות the Chald. read בכלות, *confidence.*

v. 7. עברי בעמק. A noun in the construct state is sometimes, in poetry, followed by a preposition, as here.

If the *Valley of Weeping* were, what many have supposed it to be, a valley with streams trickling, like tears, from its rocky sides, then the force of the verb ישיתוהו would be completely annulled. The pilgrims would find a spring of water, and they would make it, or regard it, as a spring of water; which is absurd. The meaning is plainly to this effect, viz. that something disadvantageous to the pilgrim is turned to advantage by him, or for him. Now the one thing that a traveller in Palestine would recognise as a disadvantage would be the want of water. The supply of water is a blessing. Therefore, whatever other account we may give of this word בכא, the one above mentioned is certainly to be excluded.

We must suppose that a certain place was called *Baca* from some lamentable occasion. By a play upon the word, the Psalmist says that this Valley of Weeping weeps blessings for the pilgrim;—a figure of speech which he expounds in the same breath by saying that the rain covers it (sc. the place), or him (sc. the pilgrim) with blessings.

This is, without doubt, a poetical representation of the truth that God makes all things work together for the good of His people. A representation of the same truth, under the same figure, is found in Isaiah xxxv. 6, 7, 8,—a passage in connection with which the words of the text may be explained. In this passage of Isaiah, a *highway* (מסלול) is prepared, wherein waters break out in the wilderness, and streams in the desert. In the Psalm, highways (מסלות) are contemplated, wherein the most doleful stage is turned into a refreshing fountain of water.

v. 8. *Appeareth before God in Zion.* Comp. xlii. 3. The promiscuous use of Sing. and Plural in this verse and in v. 6 may be noted. It is, however, of such common occurrence as to create no difficulty.

v. 9. *O God, behold our shield, and look upon the face of* Thine *anointed.*

The order of the words compels us so to render them, though the ancient and modern translators take ראה as used absolutely. They did so because they could not understand what was denoted by *the shield* upon which God was required to look : misled also by the fact that in this same Psalm (v. 12), as often elsewhere, God Himself is spoken of as *a shield* ;—but forgetting the decisive passage in Ps. lxxxix. 19,— *Our shield is of Jehovah, and of the Holy One of Israel is our king,**

The prayer of this verse is therefore a prayer *for the king.* It is by no means necessary to suppose that the Psalm was composed *by* the king. The prayer is appropriate, because,

---

Comp. Ps. xlvii. 10, where *the shields of the earth* are synonymous with the *princes of the peoples.* See also Hos. iv. 18.

as Delitzsch remarks, " when his king prevails, the poet will at the same time be restored to the sanctuary," the hope of which is the one subject of the Psalm. He adds that it is beyond all doubt that " we have before us a Psalm belonging to the time of David's persecution by Absalom."

Psalm LXXXV.

v. 2. This Psalm commences, as it closes, with God's returning favour to the *land*, manifested by a fruitful season. See v. 13.

In this connection it can hardly be doubted that the expression שבות שבת is used figuratively :—*Thou hast restored the prosperity of Jacob*. See the instance specially cited by Gesenius for the exemplification of this meaning, viz. Job xlii. 10, *And the Lord turned the captivity* (שב את־שבות) *of Job*, as it is rendered in our Authorised Version: *Jehovah le rétablit dans son ancien état*, as M. Renan gives it.

We may therefore suppose that God's anger had been manifested by unfruitful seasons; and, from verses 5-8, we may assume that these indications of divine wrath had not been wholly removed: that the land was not yet fully blessed with its wonted fertility.

v. 3. For the equivalence of עון and חטאת. see Prolegomena §§ 24, 25.

v. 5. The first word of this verse, שובנו, seems to indicate the meaning of שבת שבות in v. 2. If that means, *Thou hast returned our captivity*, then the prayer of this verse, *Restore us*, sc. from captivity, is meaningless. But if that refers, as I suppose, to some incomplete blessing, then this is a prayer for its completion.

Although the word שבות is derived from a root distinct from שוב, yet it is not improbable that in an uncritical age the difference in origin of these two words might be obliterated by their similarity in form and sound. Thus the expression which originally denoted *the return of exiles* might come to mean a *reversion to prosperity;* and to assume this more general meaning not only conventionally but upon supposed etymological grounds. That is to say, the expression שוב שבות might erroneously be taken to mean directly and expressly the bringing about of a return in one's fortunes; as if שבות were derived from שוב.

With regard to the terms which denote the prolonged displeasure of God, here and in the next verse, it is easily observable that they are of milder import than those which appear in the preceding verse. There it is fierce wrath; here it is lingering displeasure :—this lingering, long drawn out, displeasure being equally indicated by the verb תמשך in v. 6.

v. 9. *O let me hearken! What is it that God the Lord is speaking? Yea, He speaketh peace to His people!*

If we accept the usual rendering, viz. *I will hear what the Lord saith, &c.*, we shall overlook the interrogative power of מה. This word never corresponds to our equivocal English word *what;* which may be either an interrogative or a compounded relative and antecedent, with the meaning of *that which.* See my note on Ps. lxxiv. 9.

For the meaning here assigned to כי, "*Yea,*" see Isaiah xxxii. 13, where it so rendered in our English Version, and Gesenius *sub v.* See also Ps. xci. 3, and cxvi. 2.

v. 10. That God's salvation was nigh unto His people in order that His glory might dwell in their land, is the usual interpretation of this verse. But the inversion of this sentiment surely must be intended; viz. that God's nearness to His people was assured to them by the fact that even His glory tabernacled amongst them. We must therefore take the ל of לשכן to mean *adeo, to this extent*, for which see Gesenius sub v. ל. *His salvation is so nigh, that even His glory tabernacles in our land.* Comp. John i. 14.

The same meaning is probably to be assigned to the same expression in Ps. lxviii. 19; a meaning, however, which I overlooked in my note upon that place:—*Such gifts didst Thou bestow upon Edom, yea upon those rebels, that even the Jehovah God tabernacled amongst them.*

That כבוד here refers to the Sanctuary of God will appear from a comparison of many other places. As a parallel to the לשכן כבוד of the text, it may suffice to cite Ps. xxvi. 8, where משכן כבודך is synonymous with מעון ביתך.

v. 11. If we render this verse, as it is usually rendered, *Mercy and truth are met together*, we seem to warrant the usual interpretation, viz. that God's eternal justice is somehow reconciled with His mercy. No such meaning is intended. See Prolegomena § 20. God's *loving-kindness* is denoted by חסד, and this attribute is co-operative with His *faithfulness* for the good of His people. Righteousness and Peace, are the *gifts* of God. The expressions " meet together," and " kiss each other," refer to the two spheres wherein these attributes are manifested, and the two sources from which these gifts are bestowed, viz. heaven and earth. The *goodness*, or *loving-kindness*, חסד, that is poured down from heaven, meets the faithfulness, אמת, that springs forth from the earth,— i.e. the fruits of the earth that are produced in accordance with God's faithful covenant with the earth. So, further, the *peace*, or *prosperity*, which is enjoyed on earth, kisses, or embraces, the *righteousness* which, in the next verse, is said to appear from heaven. The same idea is expressed in v. 13, where God (from heaven) gives that which is good; and the earth (i.e., of course, God from the earth) gives its increase.

v. 12. *Faithfulness flourisheth from the*

earth, and righteousness looketh down from heaven.

In the somewhat fanciful arrangement of the ideas of the text, we find, in v. 11, two pairs of expressions, viz. *loving-kindness* (A) and *faithfulness (a)*; then *righteousness* (B) and *prosperity (b)*. In this 12th verse, one term is taken from the first pair, and another from the second; so that a third pair of terms, viz. B and *a*, expresses the truth which is intended to be taught, viz. that God is the one source of all the blessings of nature and of grace: of those that spring out of the earth, and of those that are shed down from heaven.

Moreover it is to my mind by no means a fanciful supposition that the Psalmist, who is so remarkably stirred up to listen to the Word of Peace that God is speaking, hears by anticipation, and expresses, somewhat of that angelic song that heralded the advent of the Prince of Peace:—*Glory to God in the highest: Peace* (שלום) *on earth: Goodwill* (חסד) *towards men!* It is doubtless for this reason that the Psalm finds a place in the Church's Services for Christmas Day.

v. 14. *Righteousness shall go before Him and shall make a way for His footsteps.*

We may either suppose that לדרך פעמיו stands by transposition for דרך לפעמיו,—such unaccountable transpositions being not very unusual,—or, (which is more satisfactory), we may understand, as the object of the verb וישם, something vaguely connected with לפניו. As we speak vaguely of one's *antecedents,* and of one's *surroundings,* so we may here understand τὰ לפניו, *His precedings,* as the object of the verb. A more literal rendering of לפניו than is ordinarily needful may serve our purpose here:—Righteousness goes in the van; in the *forelyings.* These forelying places are crooked and rough. Righteousness goes before to make them straight and plain, for the way of His footsteps.*

The interpretation is warranted by two very important considerations. First, that the expression שום ל is that which is constantly used to denote the using of anything for a purpose, or the converting of anything to a purpose.

---

* Comp. Isaiah xlv. 2, *I will go before thee and make the crooked places straight.*

Secondly, that שׂום דרך is the proper expression for *making a road.* See especially Isaiah xliii. 19; and also xlix. 11; li. 10; and Ezek. xxi. 20.

Delitzsch suggests that שׂים is to be taken in the sense of שׂים לב, to give heed to anything, as in Job iv. 20. I do not object to this, since I have proposed the same elliptical use of שׁית, for שׁית לב, in Ps. xlix. 15. But the meaning thus arrived at is unsatisfactory. "Righteousness," says Delitzsch, "goes before Jahveh, who dwells and walks abroad in Israel, and gives heed to the way of His steps; that is to say, follows carefully in His footsteps." But how can this be? That which *goes before* God can hardly be said to *follow* in His footsteps.

Psalm LXXXVI.

With regard to the authorship of this Psalm, of one thing only can we be certain, viz. that it was not written, as the title says it was, by David.

The frequent use of the word *Adonai,* for the divine name, has been often pointed out; but the import of this usage will hardly appear, unless we take it in its proper sense as correlative to עבד. Throughout the Psalm the writer represents himself as a *servant*, and God as his *Master*. This is one of the features of the Psalm which lead me to suspect that its author may have been an alien by birth, either wholly or on the mother's side.

v. 2. *Preserve Thou my soul, for I am a partaker of Thy covenant goodness*. For this, which is the proper meaning of the word *chasid*, see Prolegomena, § 20. With perfect accuracy Dr. Perowne remarks that the writer " here pleads his own covenant relationship to God ; for this is implied in the adj. here used, *chasid*."

But why this emphatic assertion of covenant relationship? Such relationship would be assumed, and the assertion of it would not be thought of, by one who originally and fully belonged to the covenant nation. But it is just what would occur to a man who had been engrafted upon the covenant stock, and whose complete privilege might perhaps be called in question by his enemies. Just as St. Paul's question, *Am I not an apostle?*, would be unmeaning from the mouth of Peter, or James, or

John, but is accounted for by the fact that his call to the Apostleship was irregular, and was by some denied; so the assertion, *For I am chasid,* is most probably to be accounted for by the supposition that the writer's covenant relationship was not regular, (i.e. did not come by birth,) and had perhaps been challenged.

To the same effect is the parenthetic *Thou, my God,* in this same verse. The full import of the prayer seems to be this:—*O save Thy servant,—Thou who art my God as well as theirs,—Thy servant who trusteth in Thee.*

v. 8. *Among the gods there is none like unto Thee.*

In reference to a national trouble, for the relief of which the one living and true God was appealed to, as in Psalm lxxxix. 7, this remark is obviously appropriate. But in reference to the writer's personal emergency, it is appropriate only on the supposition of his having had, in the past, relations towards the heathen gods;—that is, that he had wholly, or in part, sprung from a gentile stock.

v. 9. *All nations . . . shall come . . . . and shall glorify* (יכבדו) *Thy Name.* With this compare v. 12, *I will glorify* (אכבדה) *Thy Name*. Though this point is not too closely to be pressed, it yet seems as if the writer regarded himself as one coming from amongst the heathen to glorify God's Name.

v. 11. *Unite my heart &c.* That is, *Make it wholly Thine*, so that, as in the next verse, I may praise Thee *with all my heart :—*

That all my powers with all their might
In Thy sole glory may unite.

v. 14. This verse is taken literally from Ps. liv. 5, with the substitution of *zedim* for *zarim*, *superbi* instead of *alieni*. We can see a reason for this on the supposition that the writer was himself an *alien;* though we are not of necessity driven to this supposition.

v. 16. The expression, *Thy servant . . . . the son of Thine handmaid*, is so remarkable that we can hardly regard it as a tautological amplification. For a man to describe himself as God's *servant* is only what might be expected, and what we often find. But that the man should thus particularize his relation to God, *Thy servant and the son of Thine handmaid*, is a circumstance that surely calls for some remark, and which may perhaps require some explanation. What, then, would these words mean as between man and man? They would express a more devoted fidelity on the part of the servant than would be expressed by the term *servant* (עבד) alone.* A slave captured in war, or bought with money, is not likely to attach himself to his master's interests as the home-born slave does. The expression would also imply a participation in the privileges of that family of which the home-born slave had become an associated member. Therefore, as between man and God, we are permitted to regard these words as uttered by *an affiliated member* of God's household. And this is the relationship which I have already assumed as existing between the writer of this Psalm and God. The same expression occurs in Ps. cxvi. 16.

v. 17. *Show towards me some token of Thy covenant goodness.* This seems also to indicate that the covenant *status* of the writer had been questioned.

The expression ויבשו may be regarded as

---

* See Ewald, *Antiquities of Israel.*

parenthetical, and in an English translation may be put off to the end of the sentence, thus: — *Show some sign of Thy covenant-goodness towards me; so that they who hate me may see that it is Thou Jehovah who hast holpen me and comforted me,—and may be ashamed.* It is herein implied that the enemies had presumed that the Psalmist had no interest in the covenant-God Jehovah. The Psalmist's prayer is that this presumption of theirs might be confuted, and that they themselves might thus be confounded.

Psalm LXXXVII.

This Psalm is thought to correspond in sentiment, and to some extent in form, with the latter portion of the writings that stand in Isaiah's name. For this reason some modern critics assign to it a comparatively late date.

I am unable to find in it the missionary spirit that some have detected. Like the passages in Isaiah xlix. 21, 22; lx.; lxvi. 7-12; this Psalm speaks of triumph, (it may be of spiritual triumph,) over the Gentiles, rather than of incorporation with them, or of conceding to them the privileges of divine sonship. The only place that can be utilised for such a purpose is v. 6, which may be interpreted to mean that when God takes account of the nations He will record that "this (nation) was born in Zion." But this meaning is altogether dependent upon the question whether the word זה *(this)* refers to a Gentile.

Traditionally, however, the Psalm has been supposed to refer to the adoption of the Gentiles to sonship together with Israel. *Sion mater gentium* is assumed as its subject. The LXX. were so impressed with the thought that they either interpolated or read the word יולדת, before the word ציון in v. 5; where now we find only two letters of such reading, viz. ול. They give, μήτηρ Σιών ἐρεῖ ἄνθρωπος, καὶ ἄνθρωπος ἐγενήθη ἐν αὐτῇ. If, however, their Hebrew text contained anything to warrant their rendering, we may conjecture that the correct form of their reading was מולדת rather than יולדת, the initial מ being dropped through its being confounded with the final מ of the preceding word. The meaning of such a reading would be very straightforward, and very consistent with the context, viz. *A man shall be spoken of as of Zion's kindred.*

The Septuagint rendering of this verse seems to have been in St. Paul's mind when he spoke of Jerusalem as *" the mother of us all,"* Gal. iv. 25, 26.

We have, however, to deal with the text as it comes before us; and of this I give the following paraphrase, as more adequately representing the original than a literal translation could do.

v. 1. *His (city) that is founded upon the holy hills.*

v. 2. *Of all the dwellings of Jacob, Jehovah loveth the gates of Zion.*

v. 3. *Honourable mention shall be made of thee thou city of God.*

v. 4. *In conversation with my acquaintances I make mention of Egypt and Babylon,— pointing also to Philistia and Tyre,—as the birth-place of such a one.*

v. 5. *So also of Zion shall it be said, Such and such a man was born in her; and (with the more reason for this boasting, because) He, the Most High, hath founded her!*

v. 6. *Jehovah shall record it when He*

writes the records of the peoples,—This was born there!

v. 7. (An orchestral direction for) *both singers and trumpeters:—*

All my springs are in thee.

v. 1. With regard to the verbs יסד, here, and כונן, in v. 5, it may be observed that they are used as synonyms in Ps. xxiv. 2.

v. 2. It is stretching the licence of Hebrew poetry too far to regard מדבר as intended to be in accordance with the fem. plural נכבדות. It is better to regard it as an impersonal form, and the following plural as used adverbially:— *Gloriose de te locutum erit.*

v. 4. *This was born there.* Zion has not yet been mentioned as an honourable birth-place. It is formally introduced, as competing for such honourable mention, in the next verse. The word "*there*" in this place must surely refer to the nations mentioned in this place. It is inconceivable that it should refer to Zion.

v. 5. It is certain that the introductory ולציון is intended to present Zion in antithesis to, and in favourable comparison with, the nations mentioned in the preceding verse. It is this consideration that warrants the rendering of this preceding verse which I have given above. If "*of Zion also can such boast be made,*" it seems to be implied that the boast has been made before with reference to the heathen nations.

It is with reluctance that I give up the evangelical interpretation of this verse. But I can find no foundation for such an assertion as Delitzsch, followed by many others, makes, when he says that, in v. 4, "Jehovah Himself takes up the discourse, and declares the gracious, glorious, world-wide mission of His chosen and beloved city, which shall become the birth-place of all nations," sc. of Egypt, Babylon, Philistia, Tyre, and Ethiopia ;—adding that " שם *(there)* refers to Zion."

v. 7. The preceding verse ends with the musical direction *Selah.* It seems likely that the opening words of this 7th verse, which have never yet been satisfactorily explained, are merely an amplification of this musical direction. The vocal and instrumental elements are to combine in the grand chorus, which bears all the burden of the Psalm,—*All my springs are in thee.*

The special reference to this chorus is to *the well-spring of life,* in allusion to the *birth in Zion* which is the subject of the Psalm,—We may compare Ps. xxxvi. 10, *With Thee is the well of life,* though the word here is מקור.

Psalm LXXXVIII.

In its general tone, and even in some remarkable points of detail, this Psalm bears some resemblance to the Book of Job. There are, however, considerations that greatly avail to dissuade us from the supposition that the two compositions proceed from one hand and one mind. It is sufficient to mention that Job no-where appears as a member of the covenant-nation. Whether really or artistically, he stands aloof from the sphere of Israel.* But the writer of this Psalm appeals to the covenant, and ex-

---

* " Job est le prêtre de sa famille : il a des rites à lui, qui ne se rattachent à aucun des usages particuliers de la religion d' Israel :—pas une allusion n'est faite aux usages mosaïques ni aux croyances particulières des Juifs." *Renan ; Livre de Job.*

presses himself in terms of the covenant. In the opening verse, Jehovah is the *God of his Salvation.* In v. 12 mention is made of God's covenant *goodness and faithfulness:* in v. 13 of His *righteousness,* and of the *wonders* that He works specially for His people. For the import of these allusions I refer to my Prolegomena.

But although the Psalmist thus makes mention of covenant privileges, he speaks of himself as debarred from them, or at least from the exercise and enjoyment of them. And the bar is a peculiar one. It is not a transgression of the covenant to be expiated in the ordinary manner by penitence and formal penance. The Psalmist is, actually or prospectively, removed from the *power* of God's grace (מידך נגזרו), as completely as if he were dead. Even to the Jewish mind the saying that "God is not the God of the dead but of the living," might have suggested the truth that in connection with Him there is no death. Yet we find here the expression of the hopeless thought that neither His love nor His faithfulness extend beyond the grave. It is this "death in life" that haunts and troubles the writer of this Psalm.

One condition, on the part of the writer, may account for these peculiarities. He may have been a *leper*. But even to this supposition a weighty objection occurs. In such a case the grievance would be more definitely expressed, and the prayer for restoration more determined to its object.

Another supposition, more satisfactory to my mind, is that the Psalm was composed, like the prayer of Hezekiah, by one in fear and peril of death : under sentence of death, so to speak. The main sentiment of the Psalm is identical with that attributed to Hezekiah in Isaiah xxxviii. 11, 17, 18, 19.

This view seems to be confirmed by v. 4,— *My life draweth nigh to Sheol.* So also in the next verse,—Though not yet dead, *I am counted with them that go down to the pit.* Upon this supposition, the extremity of the evil is anticipated, and described as if it had actually come about, in verses 7, 9, 11, 12, 13, and 19.

The subject of the Psalm being thus a matter of common experience, it is not worth while to attempt to ascribe it to any particular writer. The circumstances are such as are common to man, and the sentiment such as all must share in and sympathise with;—excepting only the Christian, who through the grave and gate of death expects to pass, not out of the sphere of God's care, but into "the everlasting arms" of His love.

v. 6. The rendering proposed by Gesenius,—*My couch is amongst the dead,*—is far-fetched. The word חפשי may retain its usual meaning of "*free*," and yet with no emphasis upon the *privilege* of freedom. The state to be expressed is, as I have observed above, the state of "life in death." The expression במתים חפשי must therefore be taken to denote a characteristic of life, (viz. freedom of will) combined with the surroundings of death. This presents the horror of the situation:—a Mezentian torment, which

"Complexu in misero longa sic morte necabat."

id. שכבי קבר. For the construction comp. Ps. lvii. 5.

v. 8. *Thy wrath hath weighed heavily upon me.* The double use of the word סמך, namely (1), as here, *to bear down upon,* and (2) *to bear up, support,* is a philological illustration of the mechanical truth, that action and re-action are equivalent.

id. וכל משבריך עניח. *And Thou hast afflicted me with all Thy billows.* A supposed difficulty in the construction has induced some strange interpretations. The same construction, (and, as it happens, with the same verb), is found in Ps. cii. 24, *By His power He afflicted me in the way,*—ענה בדרך כחו.

v. 11. Putting aside all that has been conjectured concerning the *rephaim*, it is sufficient for our present purpose to collect the obvious notices of Holy Scripture. These have been well indicated by Gesenius. He speaks of the *rephaim* as " *Manes,* shades living in Hades, void of blood and animal life, therefore weak and languid like a sick person; but not devoid of powers of mind, such as memory." This is precisely the state in which the writer of the Psalm imagines and pictures himself:—a state in which thought survives actuality, and the will survives the power. See above under v. 6.

id. פלא . . . . . יודוך. For the connection in idea of these two, comp. v. 6 of the next Psalm.

v. 16. *Death* and *youth* are here connected by the same horrible tie that connects death and consciousness in v. 6. It is the same morbid imagining of "life in death" that characterises the whole Psalm.

id. *I have borne Thy terrors in an ever-recurring series.* Ever dying, yet never dead. This terrible description in the latter part of the verse is a worthy balance to that of the former. The figure is taken (as in other languages) from the revolutions of a wheel: not the wheel of fortune that turns up now joy and now sorrow; but the wheel of Ixion: an endless revolution of evil. The word אפונה is an adverbial form of the substantive אופן, *a wheel.*

It is very difficult to account otherwise for the word אפונה. If it is a verb in the first person singular, there is no root פון to fall back upon. There is no account to be given of the final ה. Supposing these objections to be set aside; even so, the resulting interpretation is inane. After the appalling description of God's wrath inflicted upon a being capable of suffering yet incapable of resistance, it is intolerable that such a being should be represented as saying that "*he was troubled.*"

v. 17. The form צמתתוני is very irregular. This is a case wherein it is difficult to suppose a corruption of the text. We can only conclude that in Hebrew, as in all other languages, some verbs make a law for themselves; and that this is one of the lawless verbs.

Psalm LXXXIX.

The features of the Psalm are these:—

(1) Mention of God's covenanted goodness to Israel in general, and especially to David and his seed, as representative of Israel.

(2) Apparent failure of the promise to the royal representative.

(3) Deprecation of such failure.

It is easy to see that these conditions are applicable to almost any king of the house of David, excepting perhaps Solomon.

I refer the reader to a preliminary note upon Ps. xlv. for some important points of correspondence between this Psalm and that.

v. 2. *I would fain sing* (אשירה) *of the*

kindnesses of Jehovah. The song soon sinks into a dirge. However the Psalmist would desire to celebrate God's promised kindness, this is not his subject. It is the apparent failure of the promise, the cessation of the kindness, that forms the theme of this Psalm.

The second clause, according to the law of Hebrew poetry, is under the influence of the former. What is expressed in the former is to be understood in the latter. The verb in the second clause of this verse may therefore be taken in an optative sense, in accordance with the preceding אשירה.

v. 3. כי אמרתי. The LXX. read אמרת, *Thou saidst,* and this must surely be the right reading. It prevents the awkward and unaccountable change of construction that appears, as the text stands, in the next verse. The meaning, according to the Septuagint reading is this:—

v. 3. *Thou saidst that Thy covenant goodness should for ever be built up unto the heavens: that upon them Thou didst found Thy faithfulness.*

(v. 4.) *I have made a covenant, &c.*—

a speech still put into the mouth of God, with only the very usual change from the indirect to the direct narration.

It will be observed that, in v. 3, I have connected שמים with יבנה. My chief reason is, that to connect this word with the latter clause, as is usual, puts too much emphasis upon it. Such a construction seems to me almost ridiculous. There is no antithesis between the heavens and anything else, that can claim such a position of emphasis for the word *heavens.* The emphatic word of the second clause is *faithfulness.* It would be reasonable to say, *As for Thy faithfulness, Thou foundest it upon the heavens;* but it seems little less than absurd to say, *As for the heavens, Thou foundest Thy faithfulness upon them.*

The word שמים, then, is used adverbially, (as in 1 Sam v. 12, and Ps. cxxxix. 8) for השמימה.

For the assertion, compare Ps. xxxvi. 6, " *Thy goodness* (חסד) *is in the heavens, and Thy faithfulness (reacheth) unto the skies.*

v. 6. *And the heavens shall acknowledge Thy wondrous works, O Jehovah; and Thy faithfulness (shall be acknowledged) in the congregation of the saints.*

All the terms here used are such as are appropriate (and have been appropriated) to the relations between God and His chosen people. It may seem that the mention of *the heavens* is an exception ;—as if it were meant that some of God's attributes were acknowledged by angels in heaven, and others by saints upon earth. But we need not thus split up the sentiment, if we consider that it has just now been stated that God's faithfulness (towards His people) was founded in or upon the heavens. Whatever this may mean, it is certain that only men upon earth are concerned in the meaning. I therefore understand the Psalmist to say that God's covenant goodness and faithfulness were acknowledged wherever their foundations had been laid : *in the heavens* (whatever this may mean) and *upon earth,* in the congregation of the saints.

We may compare the solemn summons of the fiftieth Psalm, v. 4,—*He shall call upon the heavens above, and upon the earth, for the judgment of His people*, and the assertion in v. 6 of the same Psalm,—*The heavens shall declare His righteousness.* See note upon Ps. l. 4; and compare Ps. xcvii. 6.

v. 9. חסין, occurring only here, is a word of more frequent use in Aramaic. LXX. δυνατός.

Considering that the word is here associated with אמונה *faithfulness,* and that in this Psalm אמונה and חסיד are associated no less than *seven* times; there is a great temptation to read חסיד, instead of חסין, in this place also.

v. 10. The mention of God's stilling the waves of the sea seems here to have special reference to the passage of the Red Sea by the Israelites :—the next verse being concerned with the discomfiture of Egypt on that occasion.

v. 11. *It is Thou who hast smitten Egypt mortally,* כחלל. So in the preceding Psalm; v. 6, כמו חללים *as those who are utterly slain.* Comp. Isaiah li. 9. המחצבת רהב מחללת תנין.

v. 12. *Of Thine ordinance are the heavens: of Thine ordinance also is the earth.* The same construction as in v. 19.

The retrospection, lighting first upon the

deliverance at the Red Sea, as being nearest in time, passes on to the work of creation. We find the same subjects, in the same order, in Ps. lxxiv. 13-17.

v. 14. זרוע עם גבורה, does not mean "a mighty arm." Such a construction, for such a meaning, is unknown in Hebrew; whilst, for this meaning, the ordinary construction of a noun substantive with an adjective would suffice. In this place, if one of the words had a concrete, and the other an abstract, meaning, we could hardly help placing the one to the other, in the relation of substantive to adjective. But both words may be taken with an abstract signification here, just as they are both undoubtedly used in Ps. lxxi. 18.

That זרוע is properly a concrete term is certain; but it is so often used in the abstract sense of *help*, that there is no special pleading required for its use in this sense in this place.

גבורה is very frequently used of Divine power specially—see note on Ps. lxxi. 16,—and is here to be interpreted in connection with גבור in v. 20. This word denotes a divine champion. The title is often appropriated to the house of

David, and is one of the exquisite appellations of the Messiah in Isaiah ix. 6. See also Ps. xlv. 4. In such close connection with the גבור of v. 20, it may be assumed that the גבורה of this 14th verse denotes the divine power wherewith God's champion was endued.

We may now take the opening words of this verse to mean, *Of Thee comes help allied with divine power.* To the same effect is v. 20,— *I have laid help upon my champion* (גבור). The construction of לך will correspond with that of לך in v. 12, and of ליהוה in v. 19, and in Ps. xxii. 29.

v. 16. "*Blessed are the people to whom the Teruah is a familiar sound.*" The Teruah (תרועה) was a solemn sounding of trumpets upon triumphal or festive occasions. It was associated with all those events in Jewish history that were celebrated with joy and exultation. Its meaning, therefore, comes very near to that of *Tehillah*, (Prolegom. § 23); and although it does not always convey an idea of covenant privilege, as *Tehillah* does, it certainly seems to intend such an idea in this place. It is also found with this appropriated (or, as we may say, *consecrated)* meaning in Ps. xxvii. 6, where זבחי תרועה, *sacrifices of exultation*, are spoken of, just as *sacrifices of righteousness* are elsewhere mentioned.

It is to be admitted that all such interpretations of the text have an appearance of being made up for the occasion. It is therefore not surprising that some should adopt the alternative method, viz. of making the occasion, (that is, the *reading*) suit the meaning. It has been plausibly suggested that for תרועה we should read זרועך, *Thine arm;* viz. the divine arm that has just before been mentioned. For the pronominal suffix:—this we already find in the Syriac. For the interchange of ז and ת, the Aramaic supplies, phonetically, an intermediate link. דרוע might easily be confounded with תרוע. It is added, that in Ps. xliv. 4, *Thine arm and the light of Thy countenance* are conjoined, as they would be here upon the hypothesis, according to which the meaning would be, *Blessed are the people, O Lord, that recognize Thine arm: They walk in the light of Thy countenance.*

v. 19. *For by the appointment of Jehovah*

is our shield: by the appointment of the Holy One of Israel is our king. The same construction as in v. 12. The account of the appointment of the king (David) by Jehovah follows immediately.

It might be thought that the expression in Ps. xxii. 29, ליהוה המלוכה, was entirely parallel. But the meaning there seems to be simply that the whole world is Jehovah's realm.

v. 20. *Then Thou spakest &c.,* When? The only answer to this question implies the correctness of the rendering of the preceding verse given above. If that verse mentions God's appointment of David, the word "*then*" refers us back to that event. If it means only that the shield and the king are Jehovah's, there is no event to which this word "*Then*" can refer.

Hupfeld's objection to עזר shows that he does not properly recognize the functions of the גבור.

Thou spakest in a vision to Thy saint, sc. to Nathan. See 2 Sam. vii.

v. 23. *The son of wickedness shall not hurt him,* is word for word taken from 2 Sam. vii. 10.

v. 28. *And there is a faithful witness* (sc. of all the foregoing promises) *in heaven*. Some have supposed the faithful witness in heaven to be the moon; which is improbable, since this has just been mentioned:—others suggest the *rainbow*, which is inconceivable, since this transitory phenomenon, notwithstanding its association with God's promise, would hardly be chosen to illustrate the stability of David's throne. Moreover it seems to me certain that if it had been intended to continue the illustration in these words, we should find וכעד instead of ועד.

v. 40. *Thou hast profaned his crown to the ground.* See note on Ps. lxxiv. 7.

v. 44. *Thou hast turned the edge* (צור) *of his sword.* There seems to me no room for doubting that the word is to be traced to the ancient use of stone weapons. See Joshua v. 2, 3. That stone knives were used for circumcising children, long after the use of metal had become general, is of a piece with that which is found almost universally, viz. that the circumstances of religious ceremonies maintain their primitive and archaic character. Illustrations of the truth present themselves abundantly in modern ecclesiastical vestments, buildings, usages, &c. This ceremonial usage of stone knives, therefore, points to the same origin as is indicated by the etymological usage of the text; viz. to the time when the only cutting tool was a flint-stone. As I have observed upon Ps. liv. 9, the relics of barbarism, however they may have disappeared from the life of the Hebrews, are yet wonderfully preserved in their language.

v. 45. *Thou hast caused him to cease from his brightness, and hast cast his throne down to the ground.*

The sentiment is to be understood in connection with v. 37, where the promise is recalled that *David's throne should be as the sun before God.* From this splendour it has waned: from this height it is degraded.

v. 48. אני מה חלד. No satisfactory account of these words, as they stand, has ever yet been given. I therefore approve of the suggestion to substitute חדל for חלד, so as to bring this place into conformity with Ps. xxxix. 5, מה חדל אני. The same two words are confused in Isaiah xxxviii. 11; where, conversely, חדל seems to stand for חלד.

v. 51. *Remember, O Lord, the reproach of Thy servants, how I bear in my own bosom the contumely of the people.*

"The reproach of Thy servants" means, of course, the reproach that Thy servants bear. So also we may suppose "the contumely of the people" to mean that which Thy people suffer. This supposition is confirmed by the next verse, wherein God's enemies are mentioned as the reproachful ones. But for this mention, it would have been allowable to take "the people" of v. 51, as the antecedent to the relative, אשר, of v. 52. As it is, we must connect the two verses thus :—" *the reproach of Thy people, wherewith Thine enemies have reproached Thee, &c.*

We can hardly avoid taking the infinitive שׂאתי in connection with some word (expressed or understood) that denotes *reproach*, or *contumely*, since נשׂא חרפה is the regular expression for *bearing reproach &c.*

Further,—with regard to the expression, " *I bear in my bosom,*"—the clue to the meaning of these words is most unfortunately lost by those who see in them only an image of tender care. To maintain their connection with the reproach (חרפה) which is the subject of the whole passage, we need refer only to Ps. lxxix. 12, where we find the same sentiment in the same words,—*Render . . . . into their bosom their reproach* (הרפה) *wherewith they have reproached Thee.*

With these considerations in view, it seems certain that we must understand some word denoting *reproach* after the words *in my bosom.* This has been always admitted. Now in the existing Hebrew text, after these words, *in my bosom,* we find כל רבים עמים, words that are syntactically inexplicable. But the LXX. did not read כל, and Jerome read something that he renders *iniquitates.*

It is here to be carefully observed, that the Hebrew text is doubtful just at the point where, from perfectly independent considerations, it is necessary to supply some word denoting *reproach.* The insertion of the requisite word after בחיקי will supply the want, but will not remove the difficulty of the following words. To repeat הרפה will not account for the reading כל רבים. But if, with Böttcher, we read כלמת this will answer all the requirements of the passage, and will leave untouched the two letters, כל, of the existing text. For the rest, it seems certain that the Syriac translator read the letters כלרנ . . . ., where we now read , . . . כלרב. This is note-worthy, since the Syriac reading thus approximates somewhat more nearly to the proposed reading כלמה, which I have little doubt is the true one, and according to which I have rendered the passage as above.

Psalm XC.

This Psalm is attributed to Moses the Man of God. There may not be much evidence in support of this assumption; but it is certain that the arguments of Ewald in the opposite direction are not very convincing. He says that "so general and profound a feeling of human frailty is only gradually formed, and that the certain tokens of the times of Moses and David do not admit the possibility of such a song at so early a period." He adds that the Psalm probably belongs to the kingdom of the Ten Tribes, because "in that kingdom the transitoriness of all human things, and the necessity of deepest penitence, might be recognized far earlier than in Judah." This, I suppose, is "higher criticism." I do not presume to criticize it, since I do not understand it.

In trying to form an opinion as to the age of this composition, we must carefully compare it with that which appears in Deut. xxxii. as the *Song of Moses.* If these two had borne any general resemblance, the one to the other, we could easily understand how both might be attributed to the same author. But it is very observable that the general drift and tenor of the one are totally different from the drift and tenor of the other. We observe further, however, that in point of style, and in some matters of detail, the two are closely connected. Now it is certain that the collectors of the Psalms did not pretend to be critics of style, and would not be likely to observe the minute points of resemblance between this Psalm and Deut. xxxii. It follows that there are two distinct and independent lines of testimony converging to the supposition that Moses wrote this Psalm. The resultant may not be sufficient to sway our opinion, or to enable us to form an opinion. It is yet worthy of observation, that the tradition, as indicated by the title of the Psalm, is supported by evidence which could not have suggested the title, and which is therefore independent.

v. 2. *Before the mountains were born, or the earth and the world brought forth.* The figure, derived from child-bearing, is certainly to be maintained in both clauses. So in Job xv. 7, *Art thou the first man that was born, or wast thou brought forth before the hills?*, we find the same two verbs in the same order.* So also in Deut. xxxii. 18,—*Of the Rock that begat thee thou art unmindful, and hast forgotten God that brought thee forth.*

v. 3. *Thou turnest man back to the dust* (sc. of which he was made); *and sayest, Turn again* (sc. from the dust) *ye sons of men.* See Ps. civ. 29, 30.

---

* For the second verb in this place, which I have rendered *brought forth*, our English Version gives *made*; as, in Ps. xc. 2, and in Deut. xxxii. 18, they give *formed*. But I think there can be little doubt as to the correctness of my rendering of both places. Of Job xv. 7, Renan gives—*Es-tu donc né le premier des hommes ? As-tu-été enfanté avant des collines ?* He adds in a foot-note,—*Allusion à la Sagesse divine, née, selon les idées des Hébreux, avant toutes les créatures. Les mêmes expressions se retrouvent dans les Proverbes, viii. 24, 25.*

"These are Thy wonders, Lord of power,
Killing and quickening."

So was the meaning of this place accurately comprehended, and beautifully reproduced, by George Herbert. The idea is continued through the next verse, (4) into the fifth.

v. 4. *For a thousand years in Thy sight are only like the vicissitudes of day and night to us mortals.*

v. 5. *Thou didst sweep them away with the flood* (sc. the great Deluge in the days of Noah): *again they are:—like grass that springs up again in the morning* (sc. however it may be withered by the heat of the preceding day).

So would I render the words שנה יהיו. The word שנה undoubtedly expresses *iteration*, even when it is used for the more special denotation of *a year*. But the idea of *iteration* is so plainly intended by the context, that we can hardly get away from it here.

For חלף does not mean simply to sprout, or grow, but *to sprout again** Comp. Hab. iii. 2,

---

* The proper idea of חלף is that of replacing one thing by another. The word denotes the growth of plants; but in this sense always implies a previous life, growth, wither-

—O Lord, in the midst of vicissitudes revive Thy work.

We may here observe another trace of the hand of Moses. The historian of the deluge is not likely to lose sight of that catastrophe in reviewing the vicissitudes of human existence. The same observation is appropriate to v. 3, wherein Moses (if he be the author of the Psalm) is only repeating the words of the primal doom, *Dust thou art, and to dust shalt thou return.*

v. 6. *In the morning it flourishes and revives: in the evening it is cut down and withered.* In this one verse three stages of vicissitude are implied. The grass *revives.* This implies a former withering. The revival is the second phase: the withering again is the third.

---

ing, sc. of the thing replaced. So that it means really *to revive.* It is used of the *changing* of raiment, i.e., not of merely wearing a garment, but of replacing an old or soiled garment, with a new or clean one. It is used also, sc. in Ps. cii. 27, of those cosmical changes which, in our own time, are denoted by the word *evolution.*

It is remarkable that so many ages ago men were familiar with the truth which we of this age claim to have discovered, that *destruction* means only *change of form.*

v. 7. Up to this point the Psalmist adduces general considerations. When all but eight persons had been swept away by the flood, from that small remnant humanity flourished again. So, all along, the decayed residuum of the old is the natal soil of the new. These considerations are now applied to the case of God's people. They have been in a state of depression. Their turn is surely due. As the withered grass revives, so surely it is time for the well-nigh dead hope of Israel to revive also.

The same idea, viz. of life resuscitated when extinct, or near extinction, occurs in Ps. xcii. 15,—*In extreme old age they shall sprout again.*

v. 9. *For our days are all declining in Thy displeasure: we spend our years as it were sighing* (lit. *as a sigh*).

This meaning of הגה (quite a warrantable meaning) is necessary here, in order to make the second clause balance the first. If, in the first, days decline in God's anger, it is a lowering of the sentiment to say, in the second, that years pass away like a breath, or a sound, or a whisper. Something of the sorrow that clouds the former clause must appear in the latter.

The strange rendering of the LXX., τὰ ἔτη ἡμῶν ὡς ἀράχνη ἐμελέτων, is very commonly misunderstood, as if they rendered כבו הגה by ὡς ἀράχνη. This is not so. The word *spider* represents some word that the LXX. read before הגה, which is reproduced in the word ἐμελέτων.

For my rendering of ימינו פנו, see Jer. vi. 4, פנה היום, "*the day is declining.*"

v. 10. *As for the days of our years, in them are seventy years, or if by reason of strength they be eighty years, yet this extension of them is only labour and sorrow, for a scare comes upon us, and away we fly.*

For רהב I would read רחב. This is appropriate to the *extension* of time as contrasted with *limited* time. See Ps. cxix. 96, *I have seen an end of all that is (apparently) complete, but Thy commandment is extended exceedingly,* sc. beyond that worldly perfection.

I render חיש *a scare*, since the word occurs no-where but in this place, and the primary meaning of the root, is that of *haste with alarm, or trepidation.* For the meaning of גז I follow the LXX. who give ἐπῆλθε. Like some other Hebrew verbs, it seems to have for the same form an intransitive and a transitive meaning. For the latter see Numb. xi. 31.

So much by way of positive justification of my rendering. As against the usual renderings, it may be observed that the last words of the verse certainly profess to account for the fact that the years of man's life, prolonged beyond the usual term, are only labour and vanity. Now it is no account to say that human life is quickly brought to a close. This is true of youth, as well as of old age. Any account to be given of the irksomeness of extreme old age must express something of positive and specific evil, rather than reiterate common-place sentiments about the shortness and uncertainty of life in general. Therefore, it is a very poor and unsatisfactory meaning to put upon the words, to make them say of extremely prolonged life, what might be said of any life whatever, that it is quickly brought to a close. The word *quickly* is, in truth, as inappropriate a word for the occasion as can well be imagined.

Ewald supposes אם בגבורת to mean *scarcely, hardly*, and gives " *seventy years, or scarcely eighty.*" He compares Lat. *vix*, and Greek μόλις. He might have added our English word *hardly*. But it is certain that the Hebrew words will not bear this meaning, since גבורה always denotes *power*, which is a very different idea from that of *toil, labour*. The Syriac *may* be understood in this sense, but we are quite at liberty to take it as a literal translation of the Hebrew.

Who regardeth the power of Thine anger, or Thy displeasure according to the reverence due unto Thee? So Delitzsch and Perowne. I have before remarked (under Ps. xxxvi. 1), that פחד is the word appropriate to the denotation of *terror;* whereas יראה rather denotes *reverential regard*.

v. 12. הודע means *make me to know (a thing)*. We are not thence warranted in making it mean *Teach me how to do a thing*, which is the meaning usually assumed in this place.* Since in the preceding verse the question is asked *Who knoweth the power of thy wrath?* &c., it seems

---

* There is indeed one place in which this meaning cannot be avoided, viz. 2 Chron. xxii. 9; but this solitary example from a later writer can hardly be adduced for the present occasion.

inevitable that we should understand the same object to the same verb in this verse: *Make us to know it* (sc. *the power of Thy wrath &c.*)

What then will become of the first two words of this verse למנות ימינו? Since in v. 9, it is said that *our days are declining* (ימינו פנו) *in Thy displeasure:* since in v. 11, the question occurs, *Who knoweth as he ought to do Thy displeasure?*; and since in this 12th verse the prayer is found, *Make us to know (Thy displeasure),* it is certainly implied that this knowledge may be looked for *even in our declining days.* This is not only implied, but expressed, if for למנות ימינו we may be allowed to read לפנות ימינו. This slight emendation I propose, and with less diffidence because it is certain that no warrantable meaning has, as yet, been assigned to the text as it stands.

I give the following outline of the meaning of these verses.

v. 9. *Our days are declining in Thy displeasure.*

v. 11. *Yet who sufficiently regards Thy displeasure, in accordance with the reverence due unto Thee?*

v. 12. *Yet even in the declining of our days make us so to regard it, that we may bring a wise heart* (sc. to Thee or to the reception of this instruction).

v. 14. This verse is connected with v. 12, thus:—There, even in the declining of our days, it is not too late to seek the knowledge of the wrath of God that leads men to repentance; but here something better is prayed for, viz. God's covenant-goodness throughout the *whole* of life, from youth to old age:—*O satisfy us in the morning (of our days) with Thy goodness, that we may rejoice and be glad all our days.*

v. 15. This verse, again, is a continuation of the sentiment of vv. 3-6. As the race of man was swept away and re-appeared: as grass cut down and withered yet revives; so the Psalmist prays for the revival of Israel as the due alternation of past depression. *Make us glad according to the days wherein Thou hast afflicted us, and the years wherein we have seen adversity.*

The forms ימות and שנות are among the unusual expressions common to this Psalm and xxxii. 7.

v. 17. *Let the pleasantness* (נעם) *of the*

Lord our God be upon us. It seems a pity to lose sight of the peculiar meaning of this word by giving for it any more common word, such as *grace,* or *favour.* There are other words to express these ideas, and it is plain that the Psalmist intended to express something distinct from them.

Psalm XCI.

The difficulties in this Psalm, arising from the frequent change of person, are certainly not to be removed by such textual alterations as will produce a prosaic uniformity. If a simpler text, so produced, can be assumed as the original,— how is it possible to account for the existing text? To this case the maxim is certainly applicable, that a difficult reading is to be preferred to one that is at the same time easy and obvious.

In the study, not only of the Hebrew Scriptures, but of any ancient writings, there is no attempt less fruitful than that which is often made, viz. to apply to them, prosaically and pedantically, common rules of grammatical or logical construction. It is forgotten that the rules were made from the compositions, and not the compositions according to the rules. "Il est également superficiel," says M. Renan, "et de chercher des *règles* rigoureuses dans des anomalies où il n'y avait que choix instinctif, et d'envisager ces anomalies comme des *fautes*."

The confusion of persons, in the same discourse, may thus be regarded as a trait of primitive simplicity. But even so, it will be most likely to occur in such compositions as the Hebrew Psalms, where man's thought of God is assumed to be that which God first suggests to man. Under these circumstances, the inspired person uttering the sentiments of the Inspirer speaks sometimes in His person: sometimes in his own; sometimes in the part of a third person. See note on Ps. xxvii. 8. This view has, in effect, been adopted by Ewald in this 91st Psalm.

It is quite impossible for a translation of this Psalm to be at the same time literal and adequate. The first two verses, for example, are an address to the devout and trustful soul. According to our western and modern usage, this address ought to be expressed in the second person. But there is no such necessity in the old Semitic languages. The person addressed

may be mentioned, as here, in the third person.*
I shall, however. give a literal translation of the
first three verses, with this notice, viz. that the
expression, *Dwelling in the hiding-place of the
Highest ; abiding under the shadow of the Almighty*, means in adequate English, *Thou that
dwellest . . . . Thou that abidest, &c.*

v. 1. *Sitting in the hiding-place of the
Most High, he lodgeth himself under the shadow
of the Almighty,*

v. 2. *Saying of Jehovah, He is my trust
and my fortress, my God in whom I confide :—*

v. 3. *Yes! It is He that delivereth thee*

---

* Other examples will occur to the student. But in confirmation of what is here asserted, it is sufficient to remark that in Hebrew the definite article is used in the vocative case. Of course this is only an illustration of the general truth, that, in all languages, expressions for the denotation of the first and second persons are only modifications of those that denote the third. As I have elsewhere remarked, (*Relations of Language to Thought, p.* 38), " the analysis of the personal pronouns discloses no fundamental differences between them. *I* and *thou* and *he* are only conventional distinctions between *this* and *this* and *this*."

from the snare of the hunter: from the noisome pestilence.

For this rendering of כי by " *Yes*," see the precisely parallel place in Ps. lxxxv. 9, and my note there.

v. 4. The word סחרה is found only here as a noun substantive. It is found here in connection with צנה. From Ps. v. 13, where צנה is associated with the verb עטר, we may conclude that it was a piece of defensive armour that to some extent *surrounded* the body. And since the verb סחר also denotes *surrounding*, we may assume that the expression צנה וסחרה stands, by *hendiadys*, for צנה סחרה, *an encompassing shield.*

This meaning, of *surrounding*, is assigned to the word סחרה by the LXX.; though they take it as a verb.

v. 7. *Though there fall at thy side a thousand, and a myriad at thy right hand, it shall not touch thee.* This verse affords an illustration of the law of sequence in Hebrew poetry, as laid down in my note on Ps. lxviii. 21. Another illustration occurs in v. 13.

v. 9. If we could read מחסך for מחסי, it might seem that all difficulty would be eliminated. The rendering would then be, *Because thou hast made Jehovah thy trust, the Most High thy dwelling place, Therefore &c.* But even with this change of reading, the translation would be inadequate. It is quite certain that the emphatic אתה of the former clause refers to Jehovah. It is quite certain that this former clause means only, *For Thou Jehovah art my trust.* Any emendation that can be suggested for the removal of the difficulty must be deferred to the second clause.

Of this second clause it is equally certain that the meaning is, *Thou hast made the Highest thy refuge.* No textual change will avail to change this meaning.

We must therefore fall back upon those general principles which we have indicated as ruling the construction of the whole Psalm. The Psalmist begins this verse in the first person *(Thou Lord art my hope)* and ends it in the second; that is, with a reflective glance at himself. This transition from the subjective to the objective would not appear so abrupt to those early writers in whose minds, and in whose language, the conventional distinction between the two had not been distinctly formed.

The Hebrew stands thus :—*For Thou Jehovah art my refuge: thou hast made the Most High thy dwelling-place.* The corresponding English is :—*For Thou Jehovah art my refuge: I have made the Most High my dwelling-place.*

Psalm XCII.

Some coincidences between this Psalm and the 90th may be noted ; as, in v. 3, *goodness in the morning*, compared with xc. 14 ;—in v. 5, *makest me glad with Thy work*, compared with xc. 15, 16 :—in v. 15, *resuscitation of life that is supposed to be extinct*, compared with xc. 5, 6, 7.

v. 2. It is remarkable that here, as in v. 9, of the preceding Psalm, *Jehovah* is spoken of (in the third person), and the *Most High* is addressed (in the second).

v. 4. עלי הגיון. Since the same preposition, עלי, has already occurred twice in this verse in reference to musical instruments, it is most certain that, when it occurs for the third time, it is with the same reference. We are thus compelled to take the expression עלי הגיון בכנור as a poetical expansion of עלי כנור. Now the form of this word הגיון, leads us to הגה as its root; and this Gesenius gives. But its *meaning* strongly inclines us to connect it with the verb נגן. For it is remarkable that, wherever this verb occurs, it is always used, either expressly or by implication, in connection with כנור, the harp, or lyre. And, as against the supposition that הגיון is connected with הגה, it is certain that this root cannot be tortured into any meaning that will be appropriate to this case. It never means to sing, or to play upon a musical instrument, or indeed anything beyond meditation, or suppressed utterance. In this last sense it is used in Ps. xxxv. 23. There the oppressed and humbled writer closes his mournful representations with the two-fold prayer,—firstly, that upon the return of God's favour to him, his friends might shout for joy; and then that his own tongue might find utterance, not in shouting exultation, but in subdued thankfulness. It is impossible to take this as an example of the word being used to denote demonstrative praise. It is just the opposite of this that the word is chosen to denote.

So in Psalm lxxi. 24; where the daily and hourly gratitude that rises from the heart, and is but just murmured from the tongue, brings the Psalm to a soft close, as with an inward echo of those outward and grand utterances of praise that have been mentioned in the preceding verses.

The word הִגָּיוֹן is found also in a musical direction appended to Ps. ix. 17. In such a situation, viz. as referring to an interlude between the parts of a vocal composition, the reference is undoubtedly to some instrumental music. It is indeed generally understood in this sense in this ninth Psalm; and so, I have no doubt, we ought to understand the word in the text, notwithstanding the difficulty of its form:— *With the ten stringed lute, and with the lyre: with twanging upon the harp.*

v. 5. *Thou, O Lord, hast made me glad through Thy work.* Comp. Ps. xc. 15, 16:— *Make us glad . . . . Let Thy work appear, &c.*

v. 7. *The brutish and foolish do not know*

or consider this,—v. 3, *viz. that when the ungodly sprout forth, they are like hay-grass, (i.e. for cutting); and that the workers of iniquity bloom for their eternal destruction.*

This rendering differs very little from that which is usually given; but the difference will be appreciated by those who are competent to see the difficulty of reconciling the received rendering with the received construction of this verse. It is impossible to admit that the last words, להשמדם עדי עד, are dependent upon a verb that is not expressed. Again,—making every allowance for the Hebrew licence in changing constructions in the same sentence,—the change from the infinitive בפרח to the finite ויציצו upon the supposition of one continuous proposition, is unexampled and unaccountable. My own rendering supposes two propositions. Lastly,—it is certain that the words בפרח - - - כמו עשב cannot mean *to sprout like grass*. The word עשב is precisely the word that would *not* be chosen for such a meaning. It means, invariably, dry grass, hay, withered, or prepared by drying for being stored up. For the express distinction of this meaning, see Prov. XXVII. 25:

To assimilate the construction of the former clause of this verse to that of the latter,—that is, to show that the verse contains two propositions,—we may understand the verb היו in the former; thus,—בפרח רשעים (היו) כמו עשב.

The supposition that the word עשב may denote young, sprouting, or blooming, grass, might seem to have some warrant from the expressions in Ps. lxxii. 16. But the emendation of the text which I have there proposed removes such warrant. In truth, my argument there is enforced by this consideration, viz. that the expression יציצו כעשב is incongruous;— since עשב denotes, not the grass in its tender germ, or in blossom, but the dry hay,—cut, or fit for cutting.

v. 11. *My anointing,*—i.e. my being anointed,—*is with fresh oil.* The English idiom seems to correspond exactly with that of the Hebrew.

v. 13. ישׂגה *shall be multiplied,* like a number of trees: not, *shall spread abroad,* as one tree. See note on Ps. lxxii. 16. The verb שׂגה denotes numerical increase, rather than growth in stature or bulk.

v. 15. *They shall sprout again in extreme old age,*

v. 16. *that they may declare &c.*

This is not only the result, but the purpose, of this renewed vigour, viz. to manifest God's faithfulness. Compare Ps. lxxi. 17, 18. We may compare also St. Paul's more perfect realisation of the same truth :—*Though the outward man perish, yet the inward man is renewed day by day.*

With צורי ולא עלתה בו compare Deut. XXXII. 4, הצור - - - - - ואין עול.

Psalm XCIII.

We find here a comparison, tending to an identification, of the power of God with the power of Nature. The Psalm expresses only a theoretical assumption of Jehovah's supremacy. See note on Ps. lxxv. 4.

v. 1. *Jehovah reigneth. He hath clothed, He hath clothed Himself with majesty. Jehovah hath girded Himself with strength.*

What though the world be immovably fixed !
v. 2. *Fixed is Thy throne of yore : Thou art from eternity.*

It is plain that the last clause of v. 1 belongs to v. 2, as I have here placed it.

The same comparison of the powers of Nature with those of Jehovah occupy the next two verses.

v. 3. *The floods lift up, O Jehovah, the floods lift up their voice, the floods lift up their clamour.*

v. 4. *Jehovah on high is mightier than the voices of many mighty waters, the breakers of the sea.*

Upon v. 1, it is to be noted that אִם stands, as often elsewhere, for אִם אִם. It is well represented by the English *What if?*, or *What though?* So in Ps. xliv. 10, the word אִם introduces the *protasis:—what though thou hast cast us off* &c. The *apodosis* occurs in v. 18, —*All this has come upon us, yet have we not forgotten Thee.* See also Ps. xcvi. 10.

The same sort of rivalry, if I may so speak, appears in the third and fourth, as in the first and second verses. *However stable the world's foundations may be, the foundations of Jehovah's throne are as stable. However grand and mighty the waves of the sea may appear, Jehovah on high is grander and mightier.*

v. 5. *The attestations of Thy power and love towards Thy people have been confirmed. For a good long time Thy house has been regarded as sacred.*

The writer's faith in Jehovah has an historical foundation only. It seems to come into collision with his enforced belief in the powers of Nature. He seems rather to suppose that God and Nature are antagonistic, or rival, forces, than that they are One. That for some little time God's sanctuary at Jerusalem had been unviolated seems a thing worth balancing against the permanence of natural phenomena.

In thus rendering this 5th verse, I have taken נאוה as an adjectival form,* from נאה *to dwell.* In the expression לביתך נאוה we may regard the construction with ל as the very usual alternative of that which is known as the *status constructus.* It is thus the exact equivalent of נות בית in Ps. lxviii. 13. But even if it be regarded as a verb, there is no more difficulty attending the construction with ל when it means *dwelling* than there is when it means

---

* This view is preferred by Delitzsch, in accordance with a punctuation adopted by Heidenheim and Baer.

becoming. Since the former is undoubtedly the primary meaning, the construction is that which is appropriate to it. In any aspect, therefore, the expression לביתך נאוה קדש may with good warrant be taken to mean, *Sanctity hath been an inhabitant of Thy house.**

With regard to the expression ארך ימים, it is certain that it never elsewhere means more than *length of days*, sc., for the most part, the days of a man's life. It would never have occurred to any one to give it a more extended meaning here, but for the necessity imposed by the erroneous rendering of the preceding words. If they mean, *Holiness becometh Thy house*, they express a truth that is true for ever. Consequently, it was thought, the words ארך ימים must mean *for ever.*

I do not expect to find this assertion confronted by Ps. xxi. 5. Because there God promises to extend the days (sc. of the Messiah) for ever and ever, it by no means follows that

---

* The meaning here assigned to קדש is adopted also by Delitzsch:—" *Holiness becometh Thy temple* . . *that is to say, it is inviolable, sacrosanct.*"

eternity is denoted by words that express only extension of days.

PSALM XCIV.

v. 4. *All the workers of iniquity lord themselves* (יתאמרו), sc. over Thy people. The word occurs only here. It seems to be equivalent, and akin, to התעמר in Deut. xxi. 14; xxiv. 7, and to התימר in Isaiah lxi. 6.

v. 8. בינו בערים בעם, *Observe the people, ye fools.* That is, Take notice what the attitude of God's people is under these circumstances. You say that God does not see their affliction (v. 7). But this can hardly be. He that made the eye can surely Himself see, &c. &c., (vv. 9, 10). The attitude of His people, which you mistake, but which you might observe, is this,—that God has taught them submission: He has made them to cower down, so to speak, השקיט (v. 13), until this tyranny be overpast: until the pit be digged for the ungodly. For the Lord will not forsake His people (v. 14).

It is this attitude of submission on the part of the chosen people that the tyrant fools are called to observe, in the words ביגו בעם. They think such submission is the result of their own tyranny, and a mark of abasement. Let them learn that it is rather a manifestation of divinely-taught patience.

To this interpretation one is led by the consideration that the whole Psalm is directed against the enemies of God's people, and that, therefore, the expostulation of the 8th verse cannot be addressed to any amongst His people. עם is the appropriate word to denote them, as distinguished from the heathen (גוים), and it is used consistently in this sense throughout the Psalm.

The construction of בין with ב is not unusual, especially, as Gesenius observes, in the later Hebrew. For an example completely corresponding with the text see Ezra viii. 15,— ואבינה בעם, *And I viewed the people*. See also Nehem. xiii. 7, ואבינה ברע, *And I discerned the evil*. The more usual construction is with ל.

v. 9. *He that erected the ear.* See note on Ps. xvii. 1.

vv. 10, 11. *He that chasteneth the heathen,*

will He not convince them,—even He that teacheth man knowledge, Jehovah, who knoweth man's thoughts,—(will He not convince them) that they are but vanity? i.e. the men, not the thoughts.

The same two words, יסר and הוכיח, are used of God's benevolent correction, in Job v. 17. The conviction of sin and error is the purpose of chastisement.

v. 15. *For judgment will return to righteousness,* the actual to the true, *and all the true-hearted shall follow in its train.*

Although משפט is sometimes used in an abstract sense, as almost equivalent to צדק with which it is found coupled, yet here it is to be understood as denoting *a judicial process,* which may be just or unjust. See, for this meaning, Lev. xix. 15, 35, *Do no wrong in judgment,* במשפט. It is here promised that, in the future, such judgment shall be brought back to the standard of absolute righteousness. To the same effect Isaiah says (xlii. 3), *He shall bring forth judgment unto truth,* לאמת יוציא משפט. In the meantime the Psalmist complains, as in

v. 20, that iniquity is dispensed under the form of equity.

v. 20. *Shall the judgment seat of iniquity, that mouldeth mischief by decree, be associated with Thee?* See note on Ps. lvii. 3.

If it were permitted to assign a Maccabean origin to this Psalm, this verse and the next would be fully explained by the attempt of Antiochus Epiphanes to assimilate the laws and the worship of the Jews to those of the Greeks, and by his persecution of those that resisted the attempt. See 1 Macc. I. 41, 49, 60, &c. For this attempt did not at first appear as an assault upon all law and order, but as inviting to a compromise such as is indicated in this 20th verse, and much the same as was offered to the early Christians when a place in the Pantheon might have been allowed to Christ.

PSALM XCV.

v. 4. תוֹעֲפוֹת. According to the analogy of יְגִיעַ and of עָמָל as used in Ps. cv. 44, this word may here denote the result of labour, that is *wealth*. Against this, it has been urged that the meaning of *heights* is required as antithetical to that of *depths* (מֶחְקְרֵי) in the former clause. Yet I am unable to discover why this meaning of *depth* has been assigned to this word. It occurs only here, but it is plainly derived from חָקַר to *seek, search for*. It is improbable that such a word should be chosen to denote that which is unsearchable and inaccessible. On the other hand, it is quite an appropriate word to express that which is the object of search, viz. *treasure*. I therefore render this 4th verse thus:—*In whose hand are the treasures of the earth, and the riches of the hills are His also.* We have thus not an antithesis of opposite ideas, but two expressions of ideas that differ from each other but slightly. Some difference, indeed, there is; since the metals that are found in the hills are in other places of Holy Scripture distinguished from those that may be elsewhere found.

v. 7. We might perhaps expect *the people of His hand and the sheep of His pasture*. The existing order is to be accounted for by the Hebrew love of collocating in a sentence the words that express congruous ideas, even to the detriment of the general sense. To have the words *sheep* and *pasture* standing side by side it was thought worth while to sacrifice the congruity of the whole sentence.

v. 9. *When your fathers tested me, tried me, yea and obtained the result of such testing and trying, for they saw my works.* See my note on Ps. lxxviii. 18, 41, where we see the manner and the result of such testing. The Israelites professed dissatisfaction with the evidence already before them, and asked to see further *works*. These God *did* shew them, but in anger. It is all this that is referred to in this 9th verse.

PSALM XCVI.

This Psalm is a perfect example of a *Tehillah*. As such it is spoken of in the first verse as *a New Song ;* for the full meaning of which see my notes on Ps. xxxiii. 1 and 3.*

v. 4. *For Jehovah is great, and to be boasted in* (מהלל) *exceedingly: He is to be feared* (נורא) *above all gods.*

I call attention to these two expressions as corresponding with the נורא תהלות of the Song of Moses (Ex. xv. 11).

I have remarked upon Ps. xxxiii. 3, that the *New Song,* wherever it is found in the Psalter, seems to be framed upon the theme of the Song of Moses at the passage of the Red Sea; and that in the Book of the Revelation

---

* In the notes referred to I have remarked that *The New Song* is identified with the *Tehillah* in Ps. xl. 4. I ought to have added that the same identification is found in Ps. cxlix. 1, and Is. xlii. 10, and I ought also to have added this 96th Psalm to the three Psalms there compared for the purpose of illustrating the meaning of the *New Song.* For the present, I would refer the reader to Ps. xxxiii. 3, Ps. xl. 4, Ps. xcvi. 1, Ps. xcviii. 1, Ps. cxlix. 1, and Isaiah xlii. 10.

(xiv. xv.) the New Song is identified with the Song of Moses.

v. 6. In the adaptation of this Psalm found in 1 Chron. xvi., we find חדוה במקמו instead of the תפארת במקדשו of the text.

vv. 8, 9. See Ps. xxix. 1, 2.

v. 10. *Tell it out among the heathen that Jehovah is King,—however immovable the foundation of the world may be.*

For this meaning of אף see note on Ps. xciii. 1. There is here to be detected some trace of that which I have there noted, viz. a boastfulness that betrays diffidence. The truth was not always, nor ever fully, grasped by the Israelites, that their special God, Jehovah, was the one universal God. In the language of those who most completely realized it, it is asserted almost tentatively. For so long a time the world of Nature was regarded, as it seems to be even now by some Christians, as lying beyond the scope of God's world, that even when the grand truth was acknowledged it could hardly find adequate expression. And the argument from the continuity of natural phenomena seems to have been long ago urged against the supposition of

Divine interference in the world's course. See 2 Pet. III. 4. Thus the assertion of the world's eternal stability seems to have been understood as made in opposition to Jehovah's claims.

Now in this place we find first (viz. in v. 9) the heralding of Jehovah's kingly presence, in the words *Tremble before Him, all the earth;* and then in v. 10 the assertion that *He is King however fast the world may stand.* The connection of the two clauses was observed by the writer of 1 Chron. xvi. 30, and was emphasized by putting them in immediate juxtaposition, thus :—*Tremble before Him, O earth, however immoveable the world's foundations may be.*

In both places (viz. of the Psalm and of the Chronicles) it will be admitted that there is an inconsistency,—not to say an absurdity,—in the rendering which first makes the earth tremble at God's presence, and then immediately adduces the world's stability in attestation of His kingly rule.

v. 13. *He shall judge the world in righteousness, and the peoples in His faithfulness.*

These words point to an extension to the whole world of privileges hitherto supposed to be restricted to the covenant people. And this is, in truth, the drift of the whole Psalm. The powers of Nature are manifestations of Jehovah's power. The kingdoms of the world are to become the kingdom of our God and of His Christ.

Psalm XCVII.

v. 6. *The heavens declared His righteousness.* See note on Ps. lxxxix. 6.

v. 10. *They who love the Lord hate that which is evil: He preserveth the souls of His saints &c.*

By pointing שֹׂנְאוּ as for indicative Kal, instead of imperative, we avoid the intolerable abruptness of the change from imperative to indicative which is found in the text as at present pointed.

v. 11. *Light is shed abroad* (זֹרֻעַ) *for the righteous.*

It is absurd to introduce here the utterly inappropriate idea of *sowing*. Almost identical is the expression in Ps. cxii. 4, *In the midst of darkness, light is shed abroad* (זָרַח) *for the upright.*

It is quite unnecessary to point זרע in the text as Paul. It is indicative Kal, just as the corresponding זרח is. Both verbs have an active power, though I have rendered them as passives. The literal meaning in each case is that light *spreads itself* abroad.

Psalm XCVIII.

v. 1. All the characteristics of the New Song, the Tehillah, as noted in Ps. xxxiii. 1, 3, are observable in this Psalm.

v. 3. The LXX. give, *He hath remembered His goodness to Jacob, and His faithfulness to the house of Israel.*

v. 6. The LXX. read ליהוה at the end of the verse:—ἐνώπιον τοῦ βασιλέως κυρίῳ.

Psalm XCIX.

v. 1. *Jehovah reigneth; let the nations tremble:* (*He reigneth*) *seated* (sc. as a rider) *upon the cherubim; let the earth be moved.*

For the idea of *riding* upon the cherubim see Ps. xviii. 11. For the same expression as in the text see Ps. lxxx. 2. The intention is plainly to express God's going forth to overcome the obstinacy of the world. The earth's stability has seemed to symbolize this obstinacy. See notes upon Ps. xciii. 1, and Ps. xcvi. 10.

v. 4. *And the King's power loveth judgment.* The King is certainly Jehovah, whose reign of majesty and justice is the subject of the Psalm. To say that His power or majesty loves judgment is much the same as to say that which is often elsewhere asserted, viz. that Jehovah loves judgment. The expression is amplified in the text as if to indicate that His kingly power is exercised, not like that of earthly kings, in tyranny, but in equity. And this is the reason why the peoples are represented, in v. 3, as praising God's great and terrible name; because His greatness and His terror are manifested in behalf of righteousness. The manifestation, indeed, was made primarily in and for Israel; but its intention to the whole world is here proclaimed. God who is great in Zion is also exalted over all peoples, in v. 2. In this 4th verse, the foundations of that kingdom of righteousness which is to prevail throughout the world have been laid *in Jacob.*

v. 6. Of those men through whom God's

manifestations of Himself were made to Israel, the Psalmist names Moses and Aaron, as priests, and Samuel as prevailing in prayer. There is perhaps some allusion to the meaning of the name *Samuel*, viz. *heard of God.*

v. 7. *He spake unto them in a pillar of cloud.* That this is true of Moses and Aaron, but not of Samuel, is a very inconsiderable matter. The statement concerns all Israel at the time of giving the law; and so does the statement of the next verse.

Psalm C.

Excepting the expression, *all the earth,* in the first verse, there is nothing in this Psalm that extends its application beyond the limits of the chosen people. On the contrary, there is everything to restrict it within those limits. God is specially designated as Jehovah: the people addressed are *His* people; the sheep of *His* pasture. It is inconceivable that, at the time the Psalm was written, such expressions could be used as applicable to the heathen. In v. 4. the entering into the gates of Jehovah's temple &c. is a thing impracticable to all except Israel. In the same verse, the mention of the *Tehillah* indicates the same exclusive reference. Lastly, in v. 5, the *goodness* (חסד) and the *faithfulness* (אמונה) are the constant characteristics of Jehovah in His covenant relationship towards Israel. These the Israelites could always plead; whilst, on the other hand, and even in Christian times, the utmost that the Gentiles could plead was the commiseration, the pity, the unconvenanted mercy, of God. See Rom. xv. 8, 9, 10. Yet even here, viz. in the last of the verses here quoted, the Gentiles are called to *rejoice with God's people.* Perhaps hardly as much as this,—certainly no more,— is intended in the first verse of this Psalm:—*Shout unto Jehovah all the earth!*

Notwithstanding this restriction of its meaning, or rather, perhaps, in consequence of such restriction, this hundredth Psalm is a grand example of a *Tehillah*, for the characteristics of which see *Prolegomena*, §. 23.

v. 3. If this address had been made to the Gentiles, it would surely have taken this form: —"Know ye that Jehovah is *your* God: It is He that made *you*, and *you* are His." As it is, we find the complacent self-gratulation, *It is He that made us, and we are His.*

I adopt the reading לו for לא since the latter, the existing text, cannot plead much in its favour.

Psalm CI.

The drift of this Psalm is obvious. The writer desires to live a godly life himself, and he resolves to insist upon godly living in his household. These desires and resolutions are entertained with a view to a state of preparedness for God's presence in the household. The idea of this household may be extended, and, in view of v. 8, must be extended, so as to denote a kingdom. The Psalmist, therefore, is a king of Israel, and probably David. "In the repeated mention of *the house*," says Ewald, "we readily observe that only as great a king as David could thus speak, ... who could call all Jerusalem *his*, and look upon it as *his home*, without overlooking the fact that it was at the same time the city of a still Higher One."

The purpose of this preparation is throughout implied; but it finds expression in the aspiration of v. 2,—*O when wilt Thou come unto me?*

The occasion of the Psalm is thus determined, with a great degree of probability, to the bringing of the Ark of the Covenant to Jerusalem, from the house of Obed-Edom. This was surely an occasion of seeking, and worthily claiming, the divine blessing. In 2 Sam. vi. we read how David, upon the fearful punishment of Uzza, was afraid to bring the Ark to his own house. *How*, he said, *shall the Ark of the Lord come to me?* Which question of his corresponds with that of the text, *When will Thou come unto me?* And, as there we find David afterwards encouraged to bring home the Ark, because God had therewith blessed Obed-Edom and his house-hold, v. 11, and upon joyful reception of the same returning to bless his own household, v. 20,—so here we find him seeking, claiming, and preparing for, the special blessing of God's specially manifested presence in his household.

v. 2. The question, *When will Thou come unto me?*, seems abruptly intruded, if the preceding verbs are understood as simple futures. But they are clearly *optatives*, and the rhetorical question is therefore only a slightly varied expression of the same optative meaning,—

Fain would I sing of goodness and judgment: to Thee, O Jehovah, fain would I play upon the harp. I would walk wisely in a perfect way; O when wilt Thou come unto me?

To avoid the supposed abruptness, it has been proposed to deprive מתי of its interrogative power. But no-where,—not even in Prov. xxiii. 35,—is the word used otherwise than as an interrogative. The promiscuous use of relative and interrogative forms in English may mislead us in such cases. See my note on Ps. lxxxv. 9.

In this same verse, it is worth while to observe the change from the optative אשכילה to the simple future אתהלך. In the former, the Psalmist prays, or desires, that he may *walk in a perfect way.* In the latter, he resolves that he will *walk with a sincere heart.* The former is an aspiration: the latter is a resolution. *A perfect way* is something to aspire to and to strive after. *A sincere heart* is something to offer. *The perfect way* is the realization of the desires of *the sincere heart.* Therefore, while he prays for the former, as a result of God's grace co-operating with his sincere will, he guarantees the latter, viz. the sincere will, on his own part.

With the expression of the text, *I would walk wisely*, אשכילה, *in a perfect way, O when wilt Thou come unto me*, Compare 1 Sam. xviii. 14, *And David was prudent*, משכיל, *in all his ways, and the Lord was with him.*

v. 3. From this point, to the end of the Psalm, evil is regarded objectively. How shall I purge it from my household? How shall I regulate the conduct of my dependents?—This is now the problem. For this reason, as well as for others, it is impossible to take the words עשׂה כטים שׂנאתי to mean *I hate to commit transgressions*. The meaning undoubtedly is, *I hate him that committeth &c.;* the word עשׂה being taken as the participle *Poel* as in v. 7. So the LXX., except that they read the word in the plural. The remainder of the verse confirms this rendering:—*He shall have no connection with me.* To say, *I hate to commit transgressions: it* (sc. the commission) *shall not cleave to me*, is sufficiently clumsy and senseless. I therefore take the latter part of this verse to mean, *I hate the doer of transgressions: he shall have no connection with me.*

For דבק is a usual expression of loving or friendly connections. But סטים is undoubtedly the same as שטים in Hosea v. 2.* Whilst, however, it seems there to mean *transgressors*, we can hardly, in the text, avoid the meaning of *transgressions*.

I have already observed that this verse begins with a very express mention of evil objectively considered:—*I will set before mine eyes no thing of Belial:* i.e. no vain idol. For this meaning of the expression, *thing of Belial*, see note on Ps. xli. 9.

---

* In Hosea v. 2, we read ושחטה שטים העמיקו, and in Hosea ix. 9, העמיקו שחתו. In both places the context requires that we should understand the expressions as concerned with the laying of snares, digging of pit-falls, &c. It is therefore highly probable that שחטה in the former passage is equivalent to שחת in the latter. I find that this is admitted by Ewald, though I am not indebted to him for the suggestion. But the result is, that, in Hos. v. 2, שטים means, not *transgressions* but *transgressors*. This is a difficulty to which one feels bound in honesty to call attention. Yet let it be observed that it is no more opposed to my rendering than to any others that have been suggested. Whether we say *I hate to do* &c., or *I hate the doers of* &c.,—the word in question must equally denote, not *transgressors* but *transgressions*.

v. 5. *Him that privily slandereth his neighbour will I put to silence,* אצמית. Although this verb is elsewhere used more generally, sc. of *destroying,* it is worth while to mark its proper meaning where it is so appropriate as in this place. Another place where the proper meaning of this verb is not usually brought out, is in Lam. iii. 53, where the English Version gives, *They have cut off my life in the dungeon.** But Jeremiah's life was *silenced,* not *cut off.* Unless we observe this meaning the great beauty of the following verses will be lost. In the dungeon the voice of his life was silenced, (v. 53), so far as his fellow-men were concerned. But from that silent dungeon he could call upon the Lord (v. 55), with the assurance that He could hear his voice, yea even his *breathing* (v. 56).

---

* In this place Ewald gives *They have bound my life,* taking צמת as i q. צמד, which is quite unnecessary. For רוחתי in v. 56, he proposes to read צוחתי.

Psalm CII.

The circumstances under which this Psalm was composed are sufficiently indicated by the Psalm itself:—the inscription, as usual, adding nothing to our information. The opening verses (2 and 3) consist of familiar phrases gathered from older Psalms.

v. 4. *For my days are consumed in smoke, and my bones are scorched like a fire-brand.*

The meaning of the verse is so plain as to require no comment. If however it should be urged that *days* and *bones* are incongruously mentioned, let it be considered that by the former is denoted *the time of life:* by the latter, *the living body.* The one vanishes like smoke: the other is the burning material which produces that smoke.

See Ps. xxxvii. 20, and my notes thereupon.

v. 5. הוכה כעשב, *Smitten like dry herbage.* The same verb is used to express the effects of excessive heat in Ps. cxxi. 6, and Hosea ix. 16. And, as I have elsewhere remarked, עשב is quite the proper word to denote dried herbage, hay, &c. See also v. 12 of this Psalm.

id. כי שכחתי מאכל לחמי. *For I have been delirious in the matter of my food.* This delirious or depraved appetite is more particularly described in v. 10, *I have eaten ashes as it were bread.* A medical writer, describing this depraved appetite, speaks of the patient as craving " things unfit for food, or incapable of nourishing, as coals, ashes," &c.

I feel warranted in thus rendering this passage, partly because it is, so far as I know, the only place in which the verb שכח is followed by the preposition מן. It seems therefore allowable to take it in its primary meaning of *wandering*. So the Syriac translator, who here uses the verb טעא.* To this verb the Hebrew תעה corresponds; and this, through the form שגה, still meaning *to wander*, is linked on to שכח.

---

* This Syriac word does indeed, in a very few places, denote *forgetfulness*. Castellius having adduced Gen. xxvii. 44, in support of this meaning, Michælis adds :— " No unico loco credatur *obliviscendi* notio, addo et alterum, Hos. ii. 13. Cæterum verbum Syris peculiariter de hæresi ponitur, ut Hebræis Chaldæisque de idolatria." The proper meaning is that of *wandering*, or *erring*.

A further warrant is derived from a comparison of this place with Isaiah xliv. 20,—*He feedeth on ashes: a deceived heart* (לב הותל) *hath turned him astray.* These Hebrew words certainly express a delirious or depraved inclination, manifesting itself in using ashes as food. It is observable that here also the Syriac uses the verb טעא.

Not that, in this particular case, ashes were actually eaten; but that the eating of ashes was usually regarded as the mark of a depraved appetite consequent upon insanity, and is here mentioned as an ordinary expression and denotation of the idea of insanity.

v. 9. *All the day long do mine enemies reproach me: they that have driven me mad make me a by-word,*

v. 10. *Because I have eaten ashes as it were bread, &c.*

For this, as a token of madness, see note on v. 5.

The word מהוללי is the participle of the Poël conjugation. This form of the verb is found, with the meaning *to make mad*, in Job

xii. 17; Ecc. vii. 7; and Isaiah xliv. 25. The participle, as here, is found in Ecc. ii. 2.*

The words בי נשבעו, which I have rendered *make me a by-word*, mean literally *have sworn by me*, as if it were an imprecation, *Let him be like so and so*. At least, this is the meaning put upon the words by nearly all modern commentators. They compare Isaiah lxv. 15. This does not seem quite satisfactory. It is only because I am unwilling to diverge too widely from the current opinion that I do not render this place thus:—*They that have driven me mad swear against me* (or *concerning me*) *that I have eaten ashes &c.*

v. 12. *My days are like a stretched out*

---

* This Poël conjugation is most frequently found, as Gesenius observes, in verbs *double Ayin*. He gives as examples, הולל, סובב, and חונן. He adds, "Its signification, like that of Piël, is often causative of Kal"; and of this causative meaning he cites הולל, *to make mad*, as an example.

It has been customary to compare מהוללי in the text with קמי in Ps. xviii. 40, and קמיו in Deut. xxxiii. 11. But, as I understand the word, its construction is perfectly regular, whereas those forms are almost unaccountably irregular.

shadow, viz. such a shadow as indicates the close of day. So in Ps. cix. 23. Compare the verse towards the end of Milton's Lycidas :—

"And now the sun had stretched out all the hills."

id. *And I am dried up like hay*, as in v. 5.

v. 13. *And Thou Jehovah endurest for ever.* For this use of the verb see note on Ps. xxii. 4.

v. 17. The past tenses in this and the next verse must be understood prospectively; and conditionally also, in connection with v. 16; thus :—*The nations shall fear Thy name &c. &c. Because Jehovah has built up &c. &c.* The meaning to us is this :—*If Thou wilt build up, then the nations shall fear &c.*

This imagining of future glory for Zion continues to the end of v. 23.

v. 24. Here the writer falls back from the dream of prospective blessedness upon his present actual misery. *By His power He afflicted me in the way.*

For a precisely identical construction, with (as it happens) the same verb, see Ps. lxxxviii. 5, and my note there.

There is something dramatic in this sudden transition from familiar pleading with God to the situation from which He is regarded as without, as afar, as wielding the scourge.

v. 27. חלף, in Kal, means *to be changed:* in Hiphil, *to cause to be changed*, i.e. *to change.* See foot-note on xc. 5. The sentiment of the text is equivalent to that of Ps. civ. 30, *Thou renewest the face of the earth.**

v. 29. *The children of Thy servants shall continue*, (ישכונו): this verb being used absolutely, as in Isaiah lvii. 15; and as ישב is used in v. 13 of this Psalm and elsewhere. It is very unnecessary to suppose an ellipsis of a supposed object, as is usual, sc. of *the promised land* in the text, and of *heaven* in Isaiah lvii. 15. For it ought to be considered that words denoting such an abstract idea as that of *continuance*

---

* "There is nothing here," says Dean Perowne, "which contradicts the promise made elsewhere of *new heavens and a new earth.*" We may go further, and say that in the text this renovation of heaven and earth is clearly implied. The former heavens and earth are to be replaced by others, as a worn out garment is replaced by a new one.

must necessarily be adapted from words of more material and actual signification: that *to continue*, meaning *to hold together*, as opposed to dissolution; *to abide*, meaning *to dwell*, sc. in a certain place; and *to endure*, meaning *to overcome hardship by hardihood*, have all advanced to denote an idea abstracted from the particular ideas of which each is made up. We ought not to ignore in Hebrew the natural and necessary evolution of the meanings of words which we recognize in modern and more familiar languages.

I suppose שכן, which means *to dwell in a place*, has come to denote the abstract idea of *continuance*.

Psalm CIII.

The occasion of this Psalm is the recovery of its author from sickness and peril of death. See verses 3 and 4. The occasion being thus common to man, and there being no mention of special circumstances, it seems useless to enter upon any speculation as to the Psalmist's personality.

v. 3. *Who forgiveth all thy sin: who*

healeth all thy sickness. So Christ said to the cripple who was brought to Him, first, *Thy sins be forgiven thee,* and then, *Arise and walk.*

v. 5. המשביע בטוב עדיך. *Who satisfieth thy times* (i.e. vicissitudes of life, occasions of need &c.) *with good.* I take עדיך to be the plural noun עדים (*i.q.* עדות in Ps. xxxi. 16) with suffix. The passage is beset with difficulties, from the midst of which only one thing seems clear to my mind, viz. that עדיך here is not the same word as עדיו in Ps. xxxii. 9. That the reading either here or there may be corrupt seems probable from these considerations.

(a) That none of the old versions give the same rendering to the word here as is given there.

(b) That this is the more surprising, since either the Septuagint or Syriac rendering of the word there would give a very suitable meaning here.

(c) That according to the constant usage of this Psalm, both before and after this word, it ought to appear as עדיכי.

Taking the word as it stands, the rendering

given above seems the best, though I am by no means satisfied with it.* It may, however, be connected with the remainder of the verse by the consideration that God fills with good the successive periods of His servants' lives, so that they seem continually to renew their youth.

id. *Thou renewest thy youth as the eagle renews her pinions.*

Whether the eagle does this or not, is a question of no importance whatever, either to criticism or to religion. Compare Isaiah xl. 31,—*They who wait for Jehovah shall renew their strength: they shall put forth fresh pinions as eagles do,*—πτεροφυήσουσιν ὡς ἀετοί.

---

* Ewald takes the word to mean *jaws* (as the LXX.) in Ps. xxxii. 9, but *spirit* (*Muth*) in the text: here also professedly in accordance with the ἐπιθυμία of the LXX.

Psalm CIV.

v. 3. *Who buildeth His chambers in the waters,* sc. in the waters that are above the firmament, to use the expression of the Book of Genesis. From these exalted chambers He pours down rain upon the earth, as is said in v. 13.

v. 4. *He maketh the winds His messengers, and the flaming fire His ministers.*

The translation of the LXX. admits the meaning adopted by the writer of the Ep. to the Hebrews. No such meaning can be forced upon the Hebrew text. In this connection, however, it is possible that the word רוחות, *winds*, may be used with reference to the Spirit (רוח) of God that "moved on the face of the waters."

v. 6. *With the deep as with a garment Thou coveredst it,* sc. the earth. Since ארץ, the earth, is fem., and since the gender has been strictly observed in the preceding verse, the masculine suffix of this word כסיתו might lead us to look for some other object than the earth. But this we can hardly do, in view of the expression לכסית הארץ in v. 9.

id. *The waters stand above the hills.*

v. 8. *Up rear the mountains : down go the valleys.*

v. 10. *He sendeth forth springs into rivers,* i.e. until they become rivers. Or it may mean simply that the springs flow *into the rivers,* as tributaries.

v. 14. *He causeth green stuff to sprout forth for cattle, and ripened stuff for the service of man ;* sc. to make *bread.*

This is the distinction which is everywhere observed, and which I have elsewhere indicated, between חציר, דשא, &c. on the one hand, and עשב on the other. The one is *green stuff* for cattle : the other is something *ripened,* whether hay or corn, for man or for the service of man. As ripening implies drying up and withering, the word עשב is sometimes used of that which is dried up and withered to no purpose.

v. 15. *And wine that maketh glad the heart of man, and oil to make him a cheerful countenance, and bread to strengthen man's heart.*

This is our Prayer Book Version, which here and very often elsewhere cannot be equalled for accuracy or for beauty. Ewald shuts out *oil* from the constituents of bodily welfare. He says instead that *wine rejoices man's heart so that his face shines more than with fat!* Does he really think that in this short list of *corn* and *wine* and *oil*, the oil is only mentioned to be put in the background?

The construction is incomplete, and somewhat vague. But it is impossible to miss the meaning. The infinitive להצהיל of v. 15, is co-ordinate with the inf. להוציא of v. 14.

v. 16. *Well nourished* (ישׂבעו) *are Jehovah's trees: the cedars of Lebanon which He hath planted.*

These trees seem to be mentioned as of God's planting in distinction from trees, shrubs, crops, &c. of ordinary agriculture. The distinction is observed by our Saviour, in His Sermon on the Mount, between things that man cares for, domestic animals, crops, &c., and things that, as we might say, care for themselves. For the latter God cares, and God provides. The cedars of Lebanon are the Lord's trees, because man has not appropriated them. The ravens, the sparrows, the lilies of the field, man does not concern himself to maintain. But they too are the Lord's. He careth for them, and not in vain:—they are full, satisfied, well-nourished.

v. 25. זה is here, as often elsewhere, an interjectional demonstrative. Turning from the contemplation of the earth, the Psalmist says,— *Behold the great and broad sea !*

v. 29. *Thou hidest Thy face, they are troubled: Thou takest away their breath, they die, and return to their dust.*

v. 30. *Thou sendest forth Thy breath, they are created, and Thou renewest the face of the earth.*

See notes upon Ps. xc. 3, &c. Such expressions as these are remarkable. They indicate a very hopeful view of death and dissolution. These are only the preludes of new life and re-construction. Not that this in the slightest degree approaches the Christian view of immortality. The Psalmist's παλιγγενεσία is of the race, not of the individual.

v. 33. *As long as I live would I sing unto the Lord: I would play upon the harp to my God whilst I have my being.*

v. 34. *My meditation shall be pleasant to Him.* The Authorised English Version is, *My* *meditation of Him shall be sweet.* This is plainly wrong. The order of the words themselves is against it. Then the ensuing clause אנכי אשמח ביהוה, puts the Psalmist in such strongly marked antithesis to the subject of the former clause, that we are for this reason compelled to assume that God is the subject of whom the pleasure of this former clause is predicated.*

The connection of this verse with the preceding is note-worthy. There the singing and playing upon the harp to Jehovah constitute active praise. This shall go on so long as life shall last. But death comes to choke the voice and to chain the hand. Yet even so, neither shall God lack praise nor His servant joy. *When I can no longer sing His praises, or play upon the harp, my thought of Him shall be acceptable to Him, and shall bring joy to myself.* When my lips shall be dumb, and they who stand by shall look in vain for a token of consciousness, the joy in which my heart shall still

---

* The antithesis may be thus represented :—*Pleasing to Him shall be my meditation : I too shall be glad : I shall be glad in Jehovah.*

exult in Him will be an acknowledgment, a silent tribute of praise, which He will listen to, *" For all the anthems of the boundless sky."*

v. 35. *Sinners shall be exterminated from the earth, and the wicked shall be no more.*

These have no part or lot in that hopeful future to which righteousness tends. In accordance with that view which regards immortality as only the continuance of the race, it is here assumed that the hope of posterity is denied to the ungodly. See to the same effect Ps. xxxvii. 37, 38.

Psalm CV.

The subject of this Psalm is the fulfilment of God's promise to Abraham, that he and his seed should possess the land of Canaan. The promise itself is recited in v. 11, and the remainder of the Psalm recounts the various dispensations of God's providence whereby its fulfilment was brought about. Apart from this consideration, it would not be easy to see why the Psalmist dwells at such length upon the circumstances that led to the sojourning of Israel in Egypt, or why he so completely omits to mention the passage of the Red Sea upon Israel's return.

The scope of the Psalm being thus determined, its purpose may be conjectured; and there is much probability in Hengstenberg's supposition, that this purpose was to hold up the hope of restoration to the Babylonian exiles.

The variations between the text as found here and that in 1 Chron. xvi., are unimportant.

The difference between a *Hodu* Psalm and a *Hallelujah* Psalm, which is usually noted, is one that I cannot discriminate.

v. 2. שירו - - - זמרו - - - שיחו. The same words, in the same order, as in Ps. civ. 33, 34.

v. 4. *Seek the Lord and His strength,* עזו. The LXX. took this last word as a verb, "*be strong.*" But there is no difficulty in the word as it stands; since עז is used of the majestic manifestation of God's presence, and since this divine presence is plainly the object that His people are here exhorted to seek, as may be gathered from the word פניו in this same verse. See notes on Ps. lxviii. 29, and lxxviii. 61.

v. 6. *O ye seed of Abraham, His servant: ye children of Jacob, His chosen.*

This address seems to confirm the supposition that the purpose of the Psalm was to encourage captive Israel with the hope of restoration. To such an occasion the address is appropriate, and the appeal effective. Under ordinary circumstances, both would seem superfluous.

v. 10. *And He confirmed it to Jacob as an ordinance* (חק) : *to Israel as an everlasting covenant* (ברית).

It is important to observe that the two words seem here to be used as equivalents.

v. 18. *They bound his feet with fetters: iron entered into his soul.*

The full form, *fetter of iron*, כבל ברזל, is found in Ps. cxlix. 8. This full form is distributed in the text; half of it being found in the first clause, and the other half in the second. In like manner, the ענו of the first clause, and the ברזל of the second, are found in closer connection in Ps. cvii. 10, אסירי עני וברזל.

I am quite unable to agree with those who render the latter clause, ברזל באה נפשו, *his soul came into iron*, that is, shared the fate of his legs. Because, although the verb בוא is sometimes found with an accusative, without a preposition, yet this happens only, I think, when the accusative *follows*, and follows immediately. As the words stand in the text, we should certainly find בברזל, if this meaning were intended; just as in Gen. xlix. 6,—*My soul, come not thou into their secret*, which is a perfectly parallel place, and in poetic form also, we find בסדם אל תבא נפשי,*

v. 19. *Until the time that his* (sc. Joseph's) *word was fulfilled:* (when) *Jehovah's oracle attested him,* (sc. as innocent of the charge brought against him).

For בוא, meaning to come to pass, to be fulfilled, as a dream, or a prophecy, see 1 Sam. ix. 6; Jer. xvii. 15, and note on Ps. lxxiv. 4, 5.

For the meaning here assigned to the verb צרף, see note on Ps. xvii. 3, 4, where it is said that " this word, wherever it is found, denotes

---

* If, in the first word, we substitute ב for ז, and read ברגל באה נפשו, a meaning appears which satisfies all the grammatical and all the historical requirements of the passage :—*His soul came into calumny*. This, however, I do not propose. I have adduced considerations sufficient to warrant the text as it stands.

actual purgation." The word is most appropriately used here. The dreams of Pharaoh and his servants were *tests* of Joseph's honesty, and specially of his favour with Jehovah. The interpretation and fulfilment of these dreams constituted the purgation of his character from the calumny wherewith it had been assailed, and the attestation of his innocence.

For דברה, I have followed the rendering of the LXX., who give τὸ λογίον. It is certain that the word is used, almost exclusively, of divine utterances. I am not aware that the peculiar connection of this word with the verb צרף, as in the text, has been hitherto observed. In Ps. xviii. 31, 2 Sam. xxii. 31, and Prov. xxx. 5,—which places I put together, because there is really only one instance to be gathered from them of the usage which I am now considering, but also in Ps. xii. 7, in Ps. cxix. 140, and in the text before us, the two terms are found in close connection.

v. 25. *He* (i.e. God) *turned their heart*, as in v. 29, *He turned their water*.

id. נכל to deal fraudulently, Mal. i. 14. *Hithpa.*, in same sense, here and in Gen. xxxvii. 18.

v. 27. אהותיו - - - שמו. See lxxviii. 43, and note on lxxiv. 4, 5. The use of דברי here, and elsewhere, is not pleonastic, as Gesenius assumes, but seems to denote the details, the particulars, of that wherewith it is conjoined. Thus it may be used almost in contempt, as we speak of petty details. So in 1 Sam. x. 2,— *Thy father has left off thinking about this little matter of the asses.* In Ps. lxv. 4, the meaning seems to be that the Psalmist's iniquities rise up in detail against him; and in Ps. cxlv. 5, דברי נפלאתיך means much the same as דברי אהותיו in the text, viz. particular manifestations of God's power as exercised in behalf of Israel.

v. 28. In consideration of the insuperable difficulty of this verse, as it stands, I propose to read ראו instead of מרו. The rendering of this and of the preceding verse will thus be :—

v. 27. *He showed His tokens* (דברי אהותיו) *amongst them, &c.*

v. 28. *He sent darkness and darkened (them), that they did not discern His tokens* (דבריו).

For the justification of this reading and of this rendering, I postulate first, what I think will readily be conceded, viz. that the דבריו of v. 28 stands for the fuller דברי אתותיו of v. 27;—whatever may be the precise meaning that we put upon דברי*. The usage, common enough under any circumstances, happens to be in keeping with that which we have noted in v. 18 of this Psalm, where we find first כבל and then ברזל put for the full form כבל ברזל.

Again,—Some such meaning as I have given above must be assumed in order to account for the mention of *darkness* at this stage, since this was the *ninth* in the order of the ten plagues. Hengstenberg has rightly assigned this as the reason for mentioning the darkening of Egypt in the first place, viz. that the Psalmist has regard to the moral, as well as to the physical, aspect of this visitation. It is regarded not so much as a plague, in itself, as a symbol of that blindness and hardness that persisted throughout the whole series of plagues.

With regard to the slight textual alteration that I propose, let it be considered that the necessity of some such alteration was felt by the

---

* That this word, even by itself, may denote *deeds*, will appear from 1 Kings xi. 41, and from other places.

LXX. and by the Syriac translator, who solved the difficulty by omitting the negative, לא. Yet nothing can be more certain than that this negative properly belongs to the text. Such a word could not have slipped in by accident, and could not have been interpolated for the sole purpose of making nonsense. And what can be more nonsensical than, in the face of the history, to begin the recapitulation of that history by saying that God wrought His wonders amongst the Egyptians, and they were *not* disobedient? The supposition that the statement is made of the obedience of Moses and Aaron is offensively absurd.

I do not wonder that the old Greek and Syriac translators made a textual alteration; but I think they made it in the wrong place.

In proposing now the reading ויחשיך ולא ראו I adduce, by way of illustration of the meaning so arrived at, תחשכנה עיניהם מראות from Ps. lxix. 24.

The gain effected by this emendation, and therefore the warrant of the emendation itself, is two-fold. First, it accounts for what has hitherto seemed unaccountable, the mention of *dark-*

ness as if it were first in order of the plagues, whereas it was really ninth. Then, and thereby, it puts a clear and worthy meaning upon a passage which has hitherto expressed only an inanity, and has expressed this only with the help of a far more material alteration than that which is here suggested.

It is quite unnecessary to remind the reader that the idea of *moral darkness and blindness* is one that finds frequent expression in the writings both of the Old and New Testaments; and that this blindness, this infatuation, is spoken of consistently, in both the Old and New Testaments, as sent by God. This 28th verse, therefore (wherein, as I suppose, it is asserted that God sent darkness upon the Egyptians and so darkened them that they did not discern His tokens), is of a piece with the assertion of the 25th verse, viz. that God turned the hearts of the Egyptians to hate His people. This is not perhaps the language that *we* should choose; but it is the unmistakeable and oft-repeated language of Holy Scripture.

vv. 34, 35. ארבה and ילק may denote two distinct species of locusts, as Bochart asserts; or the two words may be poetical synonyms. The latter supposition seems probable, since the former only of these words is used in the narrative in Exodus, and of this one subject the same thing is predicated as of the two in the text, viz. that it devoured all fodder (עשׂב) and fruit (פרי); Exod. x. 15.

v. 36. See Ps. lxxviii. 51.

v. 39. *He spread out a cloud for a shelter*, למסך. This word is derived from the verb סכך, and so is also the name of the place where this sheltering and guiding cloud first appeared, viz. *Succoth*, סכות. It seems likely that the place took its name from this event, and also that the Feast of Succoth was instituted in commemoration of the same event. See the investigation of this subject in my notes on Ps. lxxxi. 4.

v. 40. For שאל read שאלו. Of two *vau's* coming together the scribe omitted one, *de more*.

Psalm CVI.

This Psalm is a *Tehillah,* to which the first five verses constitute the author's personal prologue. The second and third verses may thus be paraphrased :—

v. 2. *Who shall be privileged to speak the Tehillah of God?*

v. 3. *This is the privilege of them that keep, &c.*

v. 4. *Remember me,* &c. Compare Nehemiah v. 19 ; xiii. 14, 22, 31.

v. 7. As the text is usually read, the latter part of this verse is interpreted to mean,— *They were disobedient at the sea, at the Red Sea,—* על ים בים סוף. Such repetition is supposed to be used for the sake of poetical effect, and is indeed often so used with very good effect. But in this case it is impossible to see what is gained in impressiveness, or in effect of any kind, by the repetition. Moreover, if anything of this sort had been intended, it seems certain that the same preposition would have been used in both members of such an expression. Whatever may be gained in poetical effect by amplifying the Sea of the first member into the Red Sea of the second, there is no conceivable purpose served by varying the preposition. If that which is accepted as the meaning of the words had been intended, we should certainly find על ים על ים סוף.

To one who feels these *a priori* difficulties it is a relief to find that the LXX. read עלים, the Kal participle plural of עלה, instead of the two words על ים. The meaning which they thus saw is one that can hardly be rejected :—*They were rebellious going up* (sc. from Egypt), *at the Red Sea*. The verb עלה is used constantly in this connection, viz. of the departure of Israel from Egypt. This meaning might perhaps be better reproduced thus :—*Even in the exodus itself, at the very outset, they were rebellious*. The reference is, probably, to the narrative in Ex. xiv. 11, 12.

v. 15. *And He granted their request, and sent gratification to their lust.*

Israel's lusting after flesh-meat is mentioned in Ps. lxxviii. 18, in these words :—לשאל אכל לנפשם, *by asking meat for their lust*. The same two words, viz. שאל and נפש, occur here ; and, it can hardly be doubted, with the same meaning. The account given here of the gratification of this lust, ישלח רצון בנפשם, is equivalent to that in Ps. lxxviii. 25, שלח להם לשׂבע.

It is certainly unnecessary to cite examples of the use of נפש to denote the seat of appetite, or the appetite itself; since the word is used in this sense perhaps more frequently than in any other.

I suppose the word רזון to stand for רצון; the meaning of which is invariably *the gratification of desire.* The rendering of the LXX., πλησμονή, *satiety,* is adequate and appropriate.

For the appropriate connection of רצון with נפש, compare Isaiah xlii. 1,—רצתה נפשי, *my desire is gratified.*

From general considerations, it seems certain that the second clause of this verse is the usual poetical tautology of the first clause. If the subject of the second clause had been antithetical to that of the first,—as is usually assumed,—the antithesis would surely have been marked by the varied and emphasized position of the second subject. The uniformity of the construction throughout is alone sufficient to shew that no such antithesis was intended.

v. 20. *They changed their glory &c.* I suppose it is called *their* glory, as being displayed in their behalf. It is of course God's glory that is spoken of. See Rom. i. 23.

v. 23. *Had not Moses His chosen stood before Him in the breaking forth* (בפרץ) sc. of His anger.

The occasion referred to is the sin of the people in the matter of the golden calf, when Moses had gone up into the Mount. Before he went up, orders were given that the people should not press in and pry too closely, *lest*, it is said, *the Lord break forth* (פרץ) *upon them.* Exod. xix. 21, 22. This, then, fixes the meaning of פרץ in the text. It appears as θραῦσις in the Septuagint Version. But by this same word they render מגפה in v. 30. They seem therefore to have associated and identified the breaking out of God's anger with plague or pestilence.

To *stand before* does not elsewhere mean to *stand in opposition*, which is the meaning usually and very naturally assumed here; but rather *to attend in subservience.* See the places cited by Gesenius, viz. Gen. xli. 46; Deut. i.

38 ; 1 Kings i. 28, and x. 8. The idea of *standing in the breach*, as of a stormed fortress, is quite foreign to the author's purpose.

v. 27. ולהפיל זרעם בגוים ולזרותם בארצות.
With which compare Ezek. xx. 23,—

להפיץ אתם בגוים ולזרות אותם בארצות.
It will be seen that the verb הפיל is appropriate in v. 26 of the text, but inappropriate in v. 27. In this 27th verse, therefore, we may feel at liberty to make the reading conform to Ezek. xx. 23, by reading להפיץ, a very suitable word, instead of the very unsuitable להפיל of the text. I have no doubt that Hitzig is right in regarding the repetition of להפיל as an error of the copyist. It is, however, a very old one, since it is adopted by the LXX. But the Syriac read according to our proposed emendation; using the same word (בדר) here that is used to represent the להפיץ of Ezekiel.

v. 28. *And they were joined to Baal-Peor.* See note on Ps. l. 19. *Initiati sunt*, sc. by prostitution.

id. *They did eat the sacrifices of corpses.*

These words, which have given rise to many speculations, admit of a very simple explanation. The פעור of the compound Baal-Peor, in the form of בגור, (the φεγώρ of the LXX.), is identified with פגר, *a corpse*, for the sake of the play upon the words. As in the first clause of the verse we find פעור (which is taken as i.q. פגר) and in the second clause מתים,—so in Isaiah xxxvii. 36, we find the two combined,—פגרים מתים. This combination is found no-where else; since פגר alone denotes a *dead body.**

---

* In Arabic two powers of the consonant ע are distinguished:—the one of a softer and more evanescent character; the other harder, and more permanent. The latter must have been very much alike and akin to ג (*g*). Now the ע of פעור is marked in Arabic as of this latter power. Independently, to a great extent, of this distinction, the LXX. almost always represent the Hebrew ע by the Greek γ.

We may therefore very certainly assume such a close similarity in sound between פַּעֲר and פָּגֶר as to warrant the play upon the words which I suppose to be here intended: —remembering that such *jeux d'esprit* were often suggested to the Hebrew mind by even a smaller degree of similarity in the words. For examples,—see שִׁיר and שׁוּר in Ps. lxix. 31, 32; אַחֲרִית לְהַכְרִית in Ps. cix. 13; and מִשְׁפָּט and מִשְׂפָּח, together with צְדָקָה and צְעָקָה, in Isaiah v. 7; and וַאֲכָלֻהוּ וַיְכַלֻּהוּ in Jer. x. 25; for which see note on Ps. lxxix. 7.

It is obvious that the play upon the words was suggested by the fatal consequences of this following of Baal-Peor. *They that died* (המתים) *in the plague . . . in the matter of Peor . . . were twenty-four thousand.* Numb. xxv. 9 and 18. This was sufficient occasion for the association of the name of *Peor* with *death:* of פגר with מת.

v. 30. *Then stood up Phinehas and executed judgment,* ויפלל. This seems on the whole the most justifiable rendering; since it suits the usual meaning of the verb in this Piel form, and is in accordance with the history. On the other hand, it is to be considered that all the ancient versions take the word to denote *praying, interceding,* or *propitiating,* and that these meanings do belong to it in one of its forms, viz. the *Hithpael.* The LXX. give ἐξιλάσατο : the Latin

---

In the case before us, the similarity between פער and פגר approaches very nearly to identity.

We must make some allowance for the *juventus mundi* if we think such *plays* too frivolous for serious writers, and must remember that serious writers of other nationalities used to indulge in them. When Cicero, in his essay *De Amicitiâ,* asks—*Quis tam esset ferreus, qui eam vitam ferre posset?*—this is by no means his worst pun.

Vulgate *placavit:* the Syriac צלי, *oravit,* and so also the Targum.

v. 33. *Because they provoked his spirit, and he spake unadvisedly with his lips.*

The obvious meaning is that they provoked the spirit of Moses. But it is not quite certain that we ought not rather to understand the Spirit of God. The ordinary usage of the Hiphil form of the verb favours this latter supposition. Moreover, on the occasion referred to, Moses addresses the people as *rebels,* הממרים, – the Kal participle of the same verb. Now it seems certain that they were regarded as rebels against God, and not as against Moses. From which it might be inferred that God is the object of the rebellion or provocation mentioned in the text. This supposition seems, lastly, to be confirmed by Isaiah lxiii. 10.

For בטא, *to talk rashly,* in Kal, see Prov. xii. 18; in Pi. Lev. v. 4, where, as here, the meaning of the verb is more fully indicated by the added words, *with his lips.* This remark is due to Gesenius.

Psalm CVII.

The subject of this Psalm is Jehovah's providential and beneficial control of the affairs of men :—of men in general; although the first illustration is derived, as is natural, from the history of *them whom Jehovah had redeemed.* The redemption is, not that old one from Egypt, but from subsequent exile. The 2nd, 3rd, 4th, and in part the 5th, illustrations are concerned with those adversities that are common to all men. Yet with regard to these, all men are exhorted to render their acknowledgments to *Jehovah :*—not to any vague notion of deity, but to the one God of Revelation, who is the only living and true God.

The detailed subjects of the Psalm are these :—

(1) Return from exile, 2-9.

(2) Deliverance from prison, 10-16.

(3) Restoration to health, 17-22.

(4) Preservation from the perils of the sea, 23-32.

(5) Divers illustrations of God's overruling providence, 33-41.

(6) General conclusion, 42, 43.

v. 3. *From the East and from the South: from the North and from the West.*

The order in which these points are named is quite Hebraic.

I take מערבה here to stand for ערבה, *the Arabah,* the southern limit of Palestine, a low-lying tract of country extending from the Dead Sea to the Red Sea. It will not be objected that this could be only a local designation of the *South;* since the same objection lies against the recognized designation of the *West* as *The Sea.* The designation of the South seems to have been more varied than that of the other points of the compass. See note on Ps. lxxv. 7.

v. 10. *Affliction and iron,* עני וברזל. See note on Ps. cv. 18.

v. 14. מוסרותיהם ינתק. See the same expression in Ps. ii. 3.

v. 29. יקם here is equivalent to ישם in v. 33, and is used with the same construction. It is not elsewhere found in this sense. The other place referred to by Gesenius, viz. Deut. xxviii. 36, is not parallel. As there used the word means to *set up*, (sc. a king); which is its ordinary and proper meaning.

v. 38. עֹצֶר, *oppression*. This meaning hardly appears in the Hebrew root, but is found in the corresponding Syriac עצר, *to press;* whence מעצרתא, a *wine-press*.

v. 43. *Who is wise?* . . *Then* (sc. as being wise) *he will observe these things.* See Hos. xiv. 10. The proper interrogative power of מי in such a sentence (with which compare Ps. xxv. 12), is not to be overlooked. It is, in effect, the *protasis*, whereof the *apodosis* appears in the following verb.

Psalm CVIII.

This is made up of the latter part of Ps. lvii. and the latter part of Ps. lx.

Psalm CIX.

In the 69th Psalm, I have put the cursings (vv. 28, 29,) into the mouth of the Psalmist's adversaries. At first sight it might seem possible to transfer the odium of the maledictions of this Psalm in the same manner. Thus the 6th verse, in which these maledictions commence, looks very much like the expression of the malice of which the Psalmist complains. But this supposition is forbidden by v. 16, and still more decisively by v. 20.

In the title of the Psalm David is assumed as its author. This goes for little, but is quite equivalent to any warrant that has hitherto been adduced against the assumption.

v. 1. *O God of my praise* (Tehillah) *be not silent.* That is,—O God, in whom I have boasted with exulting confidence, let not this boasting seem in vain, or this confidence misplaced. See Prolegomena, § 23.

v. 2. *For a wicked mouth, and a deceitful mouth, have they opened against me: with a false tongue have they talked with me,*—דברו אתי. For the usual rendering, viz. *They have spoken against me,* there is no warrant. After verbs of striving, contending, fighting, the preposition את is indeed used, just as we speak of *fighting with* an enemy. But we cannot therefore put the meaning of *against* upon this preposition even in connection with these verbs:—much less in any other connection. Moreover, it is in conversation *with* a person, that the false friend speaks deceitfully. Compare the expression שוא ידברו איש את רעהו in Ps. xii. 3, and see my note there. See also 1 Kings viii. 15.

v. 4. ואני תפלה. LXX. ἐγὼ δὲ προσηυχόμην. The LXX. read here, or understood, a finite verb. And this seems necessary.

The context before and behind requires that the תפלה should denote *supplication for others, intercession*. This meaning must be maintained. I suppose that the writer's intention would be conveyed by the reading אתפלל, *I make intercession*, sc. for those who return only their malediction. The text, as it stands, will bear this meaning, and no other. But the construction, for this or for any other meaning, is strange, and full of difficulty. I do not, however, propose any alteration; but assume only that the expression of the text, אני תפלה, is equivalent to אני אתפלל. *I, for my part, make intercession for them.*

v. 13. יהי אחריתו להכרית. An alliterative play upon words.

v. 23. *Like a shadow when it is lengthened out.* See cii. 12.

v. 24. *My flesh faileth of fatness,* i.e. lacketh fatness.

v. 31. *He standeth at the right hand of the poor, to save (him) from them that judge his soul.* That is,—God is the poor man's advocate.

Psalm CX.

This Psalm, which was certainly written by David, is described by him as *An oracle of Jehovah to his* (sc. David's) *Lord.* Its subject is, therefore, the future Messiah. No difficulty whatever arises from the consideration that David's future Lord was to be his son, *quoad humanitatem;* nor does Christ by any means try to put this His human sonship into the background, much less to deny it, when He asks— *If David call Him Lord, how is He his son?* See the question in its two forms, viz. πῶς υἱὸς αὐτοῦ ἐστι in Matt. xxii. 45, and Luke xx. 44;

and πόθεν υἱὸς αὐτοῦ ἐστι, in Mark xii. 37. The point of it, in each form, is—*In what sense do you regard the Messiah as David's Son?*, and the effect of it is to induce the belief that He had a higher sonship than this, yet consistent with this.

As the composition is short, and very important, I give a translation of it in full; premising that the Psalm is probably incomplete. Making every allowance for poetical brevity, and for allusions that have long ago and for ever lost their meaning, it is difficult to trace any continuous line of thought. What Ewald says of v. 4, that it is " manifestly the mere echo of a more ancient Divine oracle," may perhaps be asserted of the whole Psalm.

The mention of sacred armies, with a Priest-King at their head, may induce the belief that *moral* conquests are indicated by the somewhat blood-thirsty language of the sixth verse. The sentiments of the writer must not be reduced to the level of the language that he is compelled to use.* Thoughts grow and are refined.

---

* See notes upon Ps. xx. 4, and liv. 9.

Language is fixed. So true is the old saying, that "*Word is thrall, but Thought is free.*"

(1) An oracle of Jehovah to my Lord:—Sit Thou at my right hand, until I make Thy foes Thy footstool.

(2) Jehovah sendeth the staff of Thy strength out of Sion: Rule Thou in the midst of Thine enemies.

(3) Thy people are free-will offerings in the day of Thy might, in sacred attire. Fresh from the womb of the morning, Thou hast still the dew of Thy youth upon Thee.

(4) Jehovah hath sworn, and will not repent, Thou art a priest for ever, after the order of Melchizedek.

(5) The Lord at Thy right hand (O Jehovah) hath smitten kings in the day of His wrath.

(6) He hath fully executed judgment among the heathen:—fullness of corpses. He hath smitten him who is the head over a vast land.

(7) He drinketh of the river in His course: therefore doth He lift up His head.

v. 2. *Rule Thou* (רדה) *in the midst* (בקרב) *of Thine enemies*. One would expect rather *Rule over &c.* But the reference seems to be primarily to that which is recorded of Solomon (1 Kings v. 4, in the Hebrew: iv. 24, in E.V.),—that he ruled over (רדה ב) all the kings on this side of the river. This was a friendly sovereignty; and in reference to this the expression of the text is quite appropriate.

v. 3. The two expressions, *free-will-offerings* and *sacred attire*, in this verse, taken in connection with the mention of a *priest-king* in the next, point to a sacred mission. All the expressions imply *consecration*.

There is much to be said in favour of the Septuagint reading of the first word of this verse, which takes עם as the preposition:—*with Thee*, instead of the noun substantive *Thy people*.

But no interpretation of the former part of this verse must be allowed to disturb the obvious meaning and simple beauty of the latter part:— *Fresh from the womb of the morning, Thou hast still the dew of Thy youth upon Thee.* Those who take ילדותך to mean *Thy youth*, in the sense of *Thy young men*, do not consider that the word never has this meaning; and forget that the same association of the words משחר and ילדות that is found here, appears, with a slight modification, as הילדות והשחרות in Eccl. xi, 10, where undoubtedly both words denote the *season of infancy and youth*.

v. 4. *After the order* (על דברתי) *of Melchizedek.* It has been remarked under Ps. xviii. 48, that the primary meaning of דבר is *to ordinate.* The rendering of the LXX., κατὰ τὴν τάξιν, and that of our English versions, *after the order*, is scrupulously correct and adequate.

I suppose the meaning to be not very recondite. The Messiah, as David's son, must be a king. To fulfil all the express promises and vague expectations concerning Him, He must be a priest also. Such a one as He in grand purpose was to be in the future, had appeared in small, yet typical, effect in the past: Melchizedek, a king and a priest. In such an order, rather than in the order of the Aaronic priesthood, was the Messiah to be placed.

v. 5. The position of the verb in relation to its object is here so unusual that it is impossible to avoid the suspicion of some disturbance of the text. I take it, however, as it stands.

v. 6. It is a well-known peculiarity of Hebrew poetry, that of two words that usually stand together in close connection, the one is sometimes placed alone in a former clause, and the other alone in a second clause.* See, *e.g.*, cv. 18.

In the text before us, but never elsewhere, the verb דין is followed by ב. This unusual construction warrants the assumption here of the poetical usage mentioned above. I assume, therefore, that in the words

ידין בגוים מלא גויות

the word מלא in the second clause is to be understood also in connection with ידין in the former. That is to say, that ידין stands for ימלא דין, *he fully executeth judgment.* So in Job xxxvi. 17, ודין רשע מלאת. And since there is clearly a play intended upon the words גוים and גויות, this understanding of מלא in the former clause seems necessary to give effect to that play.†

v. 7. This last verse, taken by itself, or in connection with its immediate context, presents to my mind no meaning whatever. Assuming that the Psalm, as we have it, is a collection of

---

* Very much akin to this usage is that *dislocated construction* which I have noted under Ps. lxviii. 24.

† Into this play upon words enters a quotation from Gen. xlviii. 19,—(See also Rom. xi. 25). מלא גוים appears as מלא גויות :—*fulness of the Gentiles* becomes *fulness of corpses.*

dislocated fragments, we may well believe that, if a reconstruction were possible, the meaning of this verse would immediately appear. As it is, we must link it on to the other fragments as best we may; and, of course, conjecturally.— What is the *river* here spoken of? In Ps. xxxvi. 9, God is represented as giving His people to drink of the *river of pleasure*; and this is mentioned in the next verse as the *well-spring of life*. Now since the hero of this Psalm, in v. 3, enters upon His career with the dew of youth still upon Him, it is conceivable that His continued strength is here spoken of as derived from the same well-spring of life.

Psalm CXI.

An acrostic Psalm, probably of late date, presenting no conspicuous points either of interest or of difficulty. The faithfulness of the covenant God is its main theme.

Psalm CXII.

This is closely akin to the preceding Psalm. Its antithetical relation to its predecessor is obvious. The theme of that is God in covenant with man: of this, man as in covenant with God: the saint of God. The reciprocity of this relation is closely pressed in the phrase *His righteousness endureth for ever*, which is applied to God in the former Psalm and to God's saint in the latter. Compare also the use of זכר, as of God's memorial, in cxi. 4, with the same word used of the saint's memorial in cxii. 6. Compare also the epithets הנון and רחום as applied to God in cxi. 4,—to the saint in cxii. 4.

v. 4. זרח. See note on Ps. xcvii. 11.

Psalm CXIII.

For the liturgical use of this and of the following Psalms, up to Ps. cxix, see Delitzsch. Ewald supposes this and the next Psalm to be one composition, divided into two for some imagined liturgical purpose. But for this he gives no warrant; and, on the contrary, the liturgical break that he supposes, occurs, in the actual passover celebrations of the Jews, *after* Ps. cxiv., instead of before it.

v. 2. *Blessed* (מברך) *be the Name of Jehovah &c.*

v. 3. *Praised* (מהלל) *be the Name of Jehovah &c.*

If the same verb (ברך or הלל) had been used in both verses we might be warranted in varying the mood, thus :—*Blessed be the Name of Jehovah : The Name of Jehovah is blessed.* As it is, we find two verbs of distinctly different meanings, and are therefore under no inducement to create variety by varying the moods.

v. 5. המגביהי. With regard to this word and the four others that follow in the same form,—it seems unlikely that they have anything in common with the archaic appearance of the *status constructus* in such combinations as *Abi-melech,* or *Melchi-zedek.* They look more like an affectation of archaism, such as we are sadly familiar with in modern English writing. But there may also have been some euphonic considerations which we cannot now appreciate.

v. 9. *Who maketh the barren woman to keep house, and to be a joyful mother of children.*

The allusion here, as throughout the Psalm, to the song of Hannah, and to the circumstances of that song, is very clear. But, apart from any such allusions, the meaning of the verse is so obvious and so inevitable that it can be rejected only by those whose morbid appetite loathes the plain and the straightforward, and craves intensely the paradoxical. Ewald's rendering of this place is: *Who causes the unfaithful of the house to rule as rejoicing mothers of children.*

Psalm CXIV.

v. 1. *When Israel came out of Egypt: the house of Jacob from the barbarous people,—* מעם לעז.

I use the word *barbarous* in its original meaning, because it exactly corresponds with the Hebrew expression. It is only recent times that have produced the cosmopolitan appreciation of other languages than our own. Ignorant and brutal people still are found to laugh at foreigners talking in their own language. The Hebrew word לעז, here used, is equivalent to לגנ, (see Isaiah xxviii. 11; xxxiii. 19), and to

לוֹץ. They all have the meanings (1) of *speaking in a foreign tongue*, and (2) of *ridiculing*. We may therefore suppose that the people who spoke an unknown language were always regarded as ridiculous. This feeling of contempt, it must be acknowledged, was always reciprocal.

With the text compare Ps. lxxxi. 6.

v. 2. *Judah became His saint: Israel His sacred dominion.*

It is evident that the *dominion* (Heb. ממשלות) of the latter clause must be supposed to imply somewhat of the peculiar sacredness that is expressed in the former. We need not make any assumption here, since the word משל is elsewhere used distinctively of the rule wherewith God specially ruled His chosen people. See, for example, Isaiah lxiii. 19,—*Thou never barest rule* (משלת) *over them* (sc. the heathen): *they were not called by Thy Name*. It is, of course, certain that in one sense God did and does rule over all nations; and in this sense this same verb is used in Ps. ciii. 19,— *His kingdom ruleth over all.* But it is equally certain, from the passage above cited from

Isaiah, that there was another and more restricted sense in which this word was used, viz. of that direct, or rather directly manifested, rule which God exercised over Israel. For this meaning see also Judges viii. 23, and Ps. lix. 14.

For my rendering of לקדשׁו in the text, see note on Ps. lxxvii. 14.

Psalm CXV.

v. 1. *To Thy Name give glory.* That is, of course, *Let glory be given.* See note on Ps. viii. 2.

v. 2. *Why do the heathen say, Where now is their God?*

v. 3. *Our God is indeed in heaven: He hath accomplished all that He purposed,* sc. upon earth.

A reason is here given for the cessation of God's miraculously manifested interest in Israel. A reply also to the taunt of the infidel, Where is the God that used to do such wonderful things for you? Why does not He go on doing such things? The reply is sufficient for Israel and for us:—Because God has accomplished the purpose of such miraculous manifestations.

vv. 4-7. The taunt is then turned back upon the heathen:—Our God is in heaven; but your gods are upon the earth, and are the most helpless of all earthly things.

The argument is certainly urged more directly against idolatry than against the worship of unreal gods. But practically the latter always implies and induces the former. No surer test of the unreality of an object or of a mode of worship can be proposed than this, viz. its tendency to idolatry. The reason is obvious. Things that are not must be represented by things that are: idols of silver and gold, &c. Things that are do not need any such substitutes. The more sensuous the accessories of worship, the more unreal is either the object of worship or the worship itself.

v. 7. The words ידיהם and רגליהם stand for ידים להם and רגלים להם,—unwarrantably, however, and through the carelessness either of the author of the Psalm or of a copyist.

vv. 9, 10, 11. *Israel, Aaron, and they that fear the Lord.* Observe the repeated mention of these three in verses 12 and 23; and see note on Ps. xxii. 24.

v. 16. *The heavens are Jehovah's heavens, and the earth He hath given to the sons of men.*

There is no such antithesis here as is usually supposed; as if heaven was God's place, and earth man's place. The two clauses are continuous in meaning, thus:—*The heavens are God's heavens, and the earth is God's gift to men.* Both alike are God's.

v. 17. *It is not the dead that praise Thee, &c.*

v. 18. *But it is we who bless the Lord, &c.*

It is not here intended to assert the inability of the dead to praise God. The meaning intended seems rather that which is expressed by our Saviour when He says,—*God is not the God of the dead, but of the living; for all live to Him.* They who live the life of faith in Him can never die; nor can the function of that life, which is His praise, ever fail.

We may trace a connection between this sentiment and that of verses 4—8. There the unreality of idol worship is the result of the unreality of the objects of worship. Here the worship is real, because the object of worship is real. He who is the Life itself receives worthy worship from the living : from them who live by Him, in Him, and for Him.

Psalm CXVI.

v. 1. *Fervently did I desire that Jehovah would hear the voice of my supplication.*

v. 2. *Yea,—He hath inclined His ear to me, even in the day that I called.*

This rendering of the words אהבתי כי ישמע seems to me the least open to objection of all possible renderings. The primary meaning of אהב is certainly that of *longing for, lusting after*. This is probably true of all verbs of loving, in all languages. The actual use of this verb in this sense is not frequent; but it is to be recognized with certainty in Jer. v. 31; Amos iv. 5; and with great probability in some other places. So far there is no difficulty. With regard to the construction of this verb with כי, —this might be illustrated by the usage of other verbs. But in the case of verbs of *desiring*, there is a special reason that might be urged against the presumption of this usage. It is this, viz. that the simple and natural character of the Hebrew language requires that the object of desire should be expressed directly and actually. The Hebrew desire is, not *that God would do a thing*, but *God's doing the thing* :— not *ut Deus faciat*, but *Deum facere*; or, even more directly, *factum Dei*.

To this objection I allow due weight. It happens, however, that the language does not readily bend itself to this direct expression of desire in all cases; and, occasionally, where the object of desire is the action of a third person, it is almost necessary to use כי, as in the text. A sufficient example of the two usages occurs in Ps. xxvii. 4, 5, 6,—*One thing have I desired of the Lord: it do I seek;—that I may dwell* (שבתי) *in the house of the Lord, &c.* . . . . . *that He will hide me* (כי יצפנני) *&c.* . . . . . *that He will exalt me* (ירוממני) . . . . *And now* (i.e. in compliance with the request) *is my head exalted, &c.* Occasionally, also, we find the construction with כי where the accusative with the infinitive might be expected. Thus in Isaiah i. 11, 12,—where the last two words of v. 11 are to be transferred to v. 12,—we find לא חפצתי כי הבאו,—*I have not desired that ye should come.*

I suppose the י of קולי to be the not uncommon paragogic appendage of the construct form.

Upon verse 2, it is to be noted that כי has here the same force as in Ps. lxxxv. 9. The two passages may here be compared:—

O let me listen—What is it that God is saying? Yes, indeed, He speaks peace to His people.

I longed for God to listen to the voice of my supplication:—Yes, indeed, He hath inclined His ear, &c.

With regard to the expression וביםי אקרא,—some part of the difficulty attending the usual interpretation is acknowledged by the interpreters themselves. A considerable part they have overlooked, viz. that the verb קרא denotes *a calling for help;*—not, as they assume, an utterance of praise or thanksgiving. Equally have they overlooked the obvious clue to the meaning of these words, viz. the phrase so frequently occurring, ביום אקרא,—*in the day that I call.* See Ps. xx. 10; lvi. 10; cii. 3; and cxxxviii. 3.

The Syriac translator seems to have found, or recognised, in his reading, this common phrase, ביום אקרא. Adopting this meaning, I by no means propose to prune the word ובימי so as to reduce it to the normal ביום. The initial ו is represented in the rendering given above. The final י is probably of the same character as the final י of קולי in the preceding verse. For although in the phrase ביום אקרא the construction is not grammatically that of the *status constructus*, yet logically and actually the words stand in this relation to one another. This, however, I do not contend for. My main object is to show that the words of the text, ובימי אקרא, are either a purposed modification, or an accidental corruption, of the expression ביום אקרא, which is precisely that which the context requires, and which is often found elsewhere in similar context.

v. 6. דלותי. See notes on Ps. xxx. 2.

vv. 10, 11. *It is because I have believed that I speak* (sc. of God's being gracious and just, as above). *I myself was sore troubled. I myself said in my distrust, The whole humanity is a failure.*

No attempt to interpret these two verses will be successful without a recognition of the antithesis, which is obvious enough, between the expression of *confidence* in v. 10, and the expression of *diffidence* in v. 11. The former expression is

האמנתי כי אדבר.

The latter is

אמרתי בחפזי.

The word חפז, in all its forms, invariably denotes *diffidence*. It is placed as the opposite of בטח in Job xl. 23. It is here placed as the opposite of אמת.

What is intended by this antithesis? Is it the contrast between God's faithfulness and man's unfaithfulness? I think not. It is rather a subjective antithesis: a contrast between the Psalmist's trust in God's providence at one time and his distrust at another time. I therefore take the words which express the distrust, viz. כל האדם כזב, to mean,—not *All men are liars*, but *The whole human race is vanity.*

The meaning of the whole passage may be thus put:—

It is through trust in God that I thus speak (as above, viz. of God being gracious and righteous, and of His preserving the souls of the

simple). *It was not always so. Once, in distrust, I thought that God did not care for man, and that the whole humanity was a failure.*

The antithesis may be expressed by Solomon's saying, *All is vanity*, as contrasted with St. Paul's, *Not in vain in the Lord.*

For the meaning which I have here assigned to כזב, see Isaiah lviii. 11, *A spring of water, whose waters fail not*,—לא יכזבו. See also Job xli. 9 ; and compare the use of כחש.

The construction of *(a)* האמנתי כי אדבר is remarkable. We may compare *(b)* Ps. cxviii. 10, and *(c)* cxxviii. 2. In all these places the כי seems misplaced. We expect

(*a*) *Because I have believed, I speak.*

(*b*) *For in the name of the Lord I will destroy them.*

(*c*) *For thou shalt eat the labour of thy hands.*

But in all these places the position of כי is determined by the intention of emphasizing the preceding words : thus—

(*a*) *It is because I have believed that I thus speak.*

(b) *It is in the name of the Lord that I shall destroy them.*

(c) *It is the labour of thine own hands that thou shalt eat**

v. 12. The תגמולוהי of this verse answers to the גמל of v. 7. This is one reason, amongst others, why the Psalm should not be cut in two at v. 10, where the LXX. have divided it.

v. 13. *The cup of salvation* must mean the *drink offering* of thankfulness for *saving* mercies.

v. 15. *Precious in Jehovah's estimation is death to His beloved.*

We have here two propositions in the form of one:—a construction upon which I have re-

---

* This Hebrew usage is an occasion of some difficulty in the Greek text of Luke vii. 47, which is thus literally translated in E.V. *Her sins which are many are forgiven, for she loved much; but to whom little is forgiven, the same loveth little.* The inconsistency between the two clauses of this verse is obvious. In the former, forgiveness is the reward of love: in the latter, love is the return for forgiveness. The difficulty is completely removed by a recognition of the Hebraism, according to which the proper rendering will be, *It is because her many sins are forgiven that she loveth much; but to whom little is forgiven the same loveth little.*

marked under Ps. xiii. 2. The first is that in God's estimation the death of His beloved is no light matter, but a precious thing. This sentiment is identical with that of Ps. lxxii. 14; and is expressed in the same words. The other is, that to God's beloved death is a prize. This sentiment is identical with that of Ps. lxiii. 4, viz. that *God's love is better than life*:—the *love*, חסד, of this place answering to the *beloved*, חסיד, of the text. To the same effect is St. Paul's saying, *For me to live is Christ and to die is gain* (Philipp. i. 21).

It is not only for the sake of illustration that I cite here these words of St. Paul. It is because they suggest to me the only satisfactory answer to the question,—Why this abrupt mention in this Psalm of the *death* of God's beloved? The one purpose of the Psalm seems to be thanksgiving for deliverance from death: the one subject for thanksgiving seems to be that the Psalmist could still walk before God in the land of the living. Then why this mention of death?

The answer seems to be that the Psalmist, considering perhaps that to be delivered from one form of death is only to be handed over to another form, realizes the truth that God's love to us is not quelled by that which seems to quell our love and our hope and ourselves too: that His love to our souls survives the death of our bodies: that it is only by death that our spirits can be brought into closest communion with the Father of our spirits. All these considerations the Psalmist expresses parenthetically and antithetically.

St. Paul's saying,—*To me to live is Christ, and to die is gain*—suggests this explanation of these words of the Psalm, and was perhaps suggested by them. The Apostle, recognizing the blessedness of the life which we now live by *faith* in the Son of God, anticipates the fuller blessedness of that state to which the death of the body shall introduce us, and wherein Christ who is our life shall appear.

v. 16. The אנה with which this verse begins is a sort of pathetic address which we can hardly reproduce otherwise than by a verb of beseeching.

(*Remember*) *Lord, how that I am Thy servant:—I am Thy servant, the son of Thine handmaid : Thou hast broken my bonds asunder.*

From these words we may assume that the *status* of the writer was the same as that of the writer of Ps. lxxxvi. 16.

Psalm CXVII.

As the former Psalm, and some others, so also this seems to be the composition of one who from among the heathen had been privileged to call himself by the name of Israel's God. This seems a necessary inference from the עלינו of v. 2. It is not easy to see why any Israelite should expect the heathen to praise God for His loving-kindness to Israel. It is because that loving-kindness has been extended even to *us* heathen, that they are exhorted to this acknowledgment. The writer therefore classes himself with the heathen.

The expression in v. 2, גבר עלינו חסדו, occurs also in Ps. ciii. 11. It is an intensified form of the expression עשה חסד על, as this is used in 1 Sam. xx. 8. That which God does in an ordinary way is here represented with the addition of the idea of *power*. For an example of this usage, which may be described as the extinction of the original verb by its adverb, see note on Ps. lxviii. 32.

Psalm CXVIII.

It is generally admitted that this Psalm was intended to be used in the celebration of the Feast of Booths :–perhaps on some special occasion of such celebration.

In my notes I shall indicate some tokens of this intention that have usually escaped notice. For the main points to be kept in view in the observation of such tokens, I refer the reader to notes on Ps. lxxxi.

v. 5. With this verse compare Ps. xviii. 20. It seems certain that the allusion in both places is to the deliverance from Egypt. The antithesis of מצר to מרחב is often elsewhere marked.

v. 10. *It is in the name of the Lord that I destroy them.* So in the next two verses. For the construction see note on Ps. cxvi. 10.

v. 12. *They surrounded me as bees (surround the wax).*

The word *wax* ($\kappa\eta\rho\iota\text{ó}\nu$) is supplied by the

LXX. It is possible that their reading contained the word דונג, and that this word has fallen out in consequence of its resemblance to the following word דעכו.

id. They are extinct as a fire of thorns. A fire of thorns is extinct when it is *burnt out.* This seems to have been the idea of the LXX. who give ἐξεκαύθησαν, and are followed by the Latin Vulgate with *exarserunt.*

v. 14. *My Strength and my Song.* See note on Ps. lix. 18.

v. 15. *The voice of joyous shouting* (רנה) *and of salvation, is in the tents* (אהלי) *of the righteous.*

Of these two Hebrew words, the former is almost appropriated to the joy of the *Feast of Booths.* See at the end of note on Ps. lxxxi. 4, (II. p. 102). With regard to the latter, I have elsewhere observed that the *dwelling in tents* (אהלים) was not the occasion of the festival, but the *dwelling in Succoth,* and the events connected with that dwelling. I do not therefore attach any special significance to the word אהלים here. It may be intended to denote poetically habitations in general. On the other hand, it is possible, and perhaps probable, that this mention of *tents* is intended to denote the *commemorative custom* of dwelling in *booths*.

v. 19. *The gates of righteousness* are what we should call *means of grace:* religious observances ordained of God. Compare the expression *Sacrifices of righteousness;* for which see Proleg. § 22.

v. 20. *This is the gate that Jehovah has appointed.* This Feast of Booths is such a medium of grace as is spoken of in the preceding verse. For this meaning of ליהוה see note on Ps. lxxxix. 19.

v. 22. *The stone which the builders rejected.*

Israel is the rejected stone. By *the builders* we may certainly suppose the Egyptians to be denoted. We know enough of them and of their works to warrant this designation. The Hebrews knew more, and experienced more, in their toil amongst the bricks and mortar. No designation of the Egyptians seems more appropriate in the mouth of the Hebrews than this:— *The Builders.*

v. 24. *This is the day that Jehovah hath made.*

In connection with v. 27, I suppose that the *day* here spoken of is created by the *light* there spoken of: the miraculous light from the pillar of cloud and of fire. This seems to me a probable explanation, since the commemoration of that sheltering, guiding, canopy was the occasion of the Feast of Booths, and that the Psalm seems certainly intended for the celebration of that Feast. If, however, this interpretation of the text should seem far-fetched, we may adopt the alternative rendering, *This* (sc. this Feast-Day) *is the day that Jehovah has appointed. We will rejoice and be glad in it.*

The last words go to confirm the supposition that the Psalm was intended to be used at the Feast of Booths, since joy and gladness were associated with this Feast more than with any other.

v. 27. *God is Jehovah, and hath given us light;* in allusion, probably, to the *light by night* that proceeded from the cloud, or canopy.

Deck the victim with boughs, right up to the horns of the altar.

The word חג, which I here render by *victim*, properly denotes a *festival*, and the

Feast of Booths almost exclusively. See note on Ps. xlii. 5. Here, however, it seems necessary to understand it to mean the *sacrificial victim* of that festival. And so it seems to be used in Isaiah xxix. 1. For the rest, (viz. for the rendering here given of אסרו and עבתים), I quote from Dean Perowne, to avail myself of his concise statement, as follows:—

> Luther has "Deck the feast with garlands (or boughs)," following the LXX. συστήσασθε ἑορτὴν ἐν τοῖς πυκάζουσιν. Symm. has συνδήσατε ἐν πανηγύρει πυκάσματα; and Jerome *Frequentate solemnitatem in frondosis*,—all renderings which imply a belief that the Psalm was intended for the Feast of Tabernacles. As regards this rendering, the word translated in the text *cords* may mean *thick boughs*, πυκάσματα (See Ezek. xix. 11; xxxi. 3, 4). But the verb *bind* cannot mean *deck* or *wreathe*.

To the last sentence I must object that in Hebrew, as well as in other languages, verbs of *binding* have often a primary idea of *twisting, intertwining, wreathing;* and that nothing more than this is intended by the word *deck*. *To bind garlands* is a good old English use; and the similar use of Lat. *vincire* is equally familiar.

The rendering of עד by the words *right up to* (the horns of the altar) is literal, and obviates the objection that the horns of the altar were certainly too sacred to be used as mere tying-posts. The idea seems to be that right up to the place where the victim was to be sacrificed it was to be led with such wreathing of foliage as was appropriate to the occasion. In the prescribed directions concerning such sacrifice we find nothing to warrant this. But it is impossible to avoid the consideration that our blessed Saviour, on His way to the place of His Sacrifice, was met with the Hosannas of this Psalm: was greeted with the words *Blessed be He that cometh in the Name of the Lord,* from this Psalm; and had His way strowed with branches of trees quite in correspondence with the representation of this 27th verse of the Psalm. Whether we believe that the Psalm did in this particular prophetically correspond with the event; or whether, with the easy and flippant method of unbelief, we conclude that the event was made to correspond with the Psalm;—in either case, the correspondence is obvious; and thus the authority of the Gospel histories is given to the interpretation of the text which I have adopted.

Psalm CXIX.

This long composition is an elaborately varied description of God's Word in relation to God's servant. The expression *Word of God* must, however, be taken in its widest meaning, as including every kind of communication, or of influence, as from God to man, of which the Hebrew mind had any cognizance. The changes are rung upon the following words: viz. — מצות — הקים — פקדים יי — עדות — תורה — ארחת — דרכים — אמרת — דבר — משפטים נפלאות. It is only in v. 90 and v. 122 that we fail to find an expression denoting God's Word or God's Way.

v. 9. *How shall a young man so purify his way as to keep* (לשמר) *it according to Thy Word?*

No answer is given, since the Psalmist suggests here τὸ ἀδύνατον τοῦ νόμου.

To render the Hebrew *by taking heed*, is quite unwarrantable, so far as I am able to judge.

v. 10. If not with a life of perfect purity, yet *with all my heart* have I sought Thee. The spirit was willing, though the flesh was weak.

v. 17. The verb גמל is used here in reference to deliverance from death (אחיה) just as it is in Ps. cxvi. 7, 8. So also in Ps. xiii. (v. 6, in connection with v. 4).

v. 20. The verb גרס is found only here (Kal) and in Lam. iii. 16 (Hiph). From its use in the latter place it would seem to be akin and equivalent to ערס (whence עריכה, *ground corn*, i.e. *meal*). Accordingly this verse is usually rendered, *My soul is broken for the longing that it hath, &c.* But this is very unsatisfactory. Both the LXX. and the Syr. take the verb here as expressing *desire*, and it is remarkable that the same word is used in the Targum for the שגה of Prov. v. 19, 20,—a word for which our English Version gives *being ravished*, sc. with love.

From these considerations it seems not unwarrantable to give some such meaning of the text as this :—

My soul is ravished with the love that I bear to Thy judgments at all times.

v. 21. *Thou hast rebuked the presumptuous sinners : Cursed are they that do err from Thy commandments.*

v. 24. *Princes also did speak insidiously against me.* For this meaning of דבר in conjunction with ישב, see note on Ps. l. 20. To this meaning the Niphal form of the verb is appropriate:—*they talked together.*

v. 29. הורתך חנני. The construction assumed by the LXX. (τῷ νόμῳ σου ἐλέησόν με) seems to be the right one. The meaning is, *Be favourable to me in, or by means of, or according to, Thy law,* which is in keeping with the rest of the Psalm.

v. 30. *Thy judgments have I considered,*—שויתי, "as in Isaiah xxxviii. 13." *Ewald.*

v. 42. דבר, The promise of God, which the Psalmist here opposes to the reproach of his enemies, is the *word* in which, according to this verse, he trusts: in which, according to v. 49, God had caused him to hope. In verse 43, he prays that God will not take this word, this promise, this argument against his enemies, out of his mouth.

v. 69. *The proud have patched up* (טפלו) *a lie against me.* The verb occurs only here, in Job xiii. 4, and Job xiv. 17.

v. 70. טפש כחלב, LXX. ἐτυρώθη ὡς γάλα. The verb occurs, in Hebrew, only here.

The heart is frequently said *to flow*, sc. with emotions of fear or of tenderness. A hard heart, or, as it is here expressed, a coagulated or curdled heart, is one that is devoid of sensibility.

v. 91. *They continue this day according to Thy commandments.* The preposition ל is used sometimes " as applied to a rule or standard, *according to.*" Gesenius, *sub v.* Ewald thinks that the word והלילה has fallen out of the text, and supplies it after היום, so that he is enabled to give *Morning and night wait on Thy judgments.* Since the text as it stands gives a meaning that is not only sufficient but very beautiful, we can hardly find here an occasion for such a hardy conjecture, or a " *dignus vindice nodus.*" Not to mention that the rendering thus arrived at conveys no meaning that I can fathom.

v. 96. *I have seen an end of all that is (apparently) complete; but Thy commandment is extended exceedingly ;* sc. beyond that worldly perfection. See note on xc. 10.

v. 113. *I hate them-that-halt-between-two-opinions.* I render the verse thus, in conformity with 1 Kings xviii. 21, because the word סעפים occurs only in these two places. Here it denotes those who are divided, i.e. undecided, in thought. There, with a different punctuation, it denotes the divided thoughts themselves. Much the same idea is conveyed by the Greek μεριμνᾶν, as the verb is used in Matt. vi., frequently. It is there first used in immediate connection with the saying—*Ye cannot serve God and Mammon. Therefore* μὴ μεριμνᾶτε &c. We may hence gather that this Greek verb was intended to denote a dividing of one's heart and mind:— one part being given to God, and the rest devoted to worldly cares. God, who claims all our love, and bids us cast all our care too upon Him, hates such a divided heart; and the Psalmist in this verse expresses the same hatred. See note on ci. 3.

v. 118. *Thou hast despised all who do err from Thy statutes.*

The verb סלה, or סלא, is in Syriac constantly used to denote *despising* and *rejecting*. In Psalm v. 7, it stands for the Hebrew תעב.

q

The Hebrew verb itself occurs in the same sense in Lam. i. 15. In two other places, viz. Job xxviii. 16, and Lam. iv. 2, it seems to be equivalent to סלל, *to make level,* whence the meaning of *equalizing values* may perhaps be derived. To meet the difficulty that arises from the fact of the same word being used to denote (1) *rejecting as worthless,* and (2) *setting a value upon* a thing, the proximate method of explanation is this, viz. to assume originally different meanings to one and the same root,—i.e. to assume independent roots under one form. This, in any case, seems unsatisfactory, and I have always tried to discover the general meaning that underlies the divergent denotations of the one expression. In this case, I think it not unlikely that, from the habit of depreciating that which one wishes to buy,* the word for *depreciating* may come to be used for *estimating* or *valuing.* That is to say, that the verb סלה, or סלא, primarily meaning *vilipendere,* comes to mean, more generally, *pendere.*

---

* *It is naught, It is naught, saith the buyer; but when he is gone his way, then he boasteth* (sc. of his purchase). Prov. xx. 14.

v. 119. *Thou hast removed* (השבת) *all the ungodly of the earth as dross.*

For this meaning of the verb the places cited by Gesenius give sufficient warrant. Otherwise the reading of the LXX. (חשבתי) would seem very plausible. The LXX. moreover applied the term סיגים to *men, departing from and rebelling against God,* according to the common usage of the verb סוג, in Kal and Niphal. See Ps. xxxv. 4; xl. 15; xliv. 19; liii. 4; and lxxx. 19. Their rendering is, παραβαίνοντας ἐλογισάμην πάντας τοὺς ἁμαρτωλοὺς τῆς γῆς,—a sentiment with which we may compare 1 John iii. 4,—πᾶς ὁ ποιῶν τὴν ἁμαρτίαν καὶ τὴν ἀνομίαν ποιεῖ.

Although I by no means propose the substitution of the Greek reading for that of the present Hebrew text, it is to be objected against the latter that God has *not yet* done what He is here said to have done. The separation of the dross from the pure metal: of the chaff from the wheat,—is an operation that is everywhere spoken of as reserved for the great day of judgment.

A slighter modification of the Hebrew text,

viz. the reading of חשבת for השבת, would give a meaning both suitable in itself and very consistent with that of the preceding verse, thus:—

v. 118. *Thou hast lightly esteemed all who do err, &c.*

v. 119. *Thou hast counted as dross all the ungodly, &c.*

Ewald adopts the reading of the LXX. in this 119th verse, and gives *Profligates are, thought I, all dross.*

v. 120. *My flesh shudders at the terror of Thee.* The verb סמר is applicable properly to the *hair* of the flesh. It denotes the *standing on end*, or *bristling up*, of such hair. From the notion of the bristling up of prickly points comes the word that denotes a *nail*, מסמר, and Chald. סמר, Pa. *to fasten with nails.* Hence the LXX. give καθήλωσον ἐκ τοῦ φόβου σου τὰς σάρκας μου. So also the Latin Vulgate, *Confige timore tuo carnes meas.* Symmachus gives rightly ὀρθοτριχεῖ.

v. 128. *Therefore by all Thy precepts* (or *according to all Thy precepts*: LXX. πρὸς πάσας τὰς ἐντολάς σου) *I correct everything: every false way do I hate.*

The English Version is,—*Therefore I esteem all Thy precepts concerning everything to be right;*—and this is followed by most modern commentators. Yet the Pi. of ישר never has this meaning; but, together with the Hiphil form, always denotes a *making straight*, sc. of a way or path. It would therefore seem certain that the *path* (ארח), of the second clause of this verse, is to be understood as the object of the verb, יִשַּׁרְתִּי, of the first clause.

The only textual change thus required is the reading פקודיך; and the necessity for this has been admitted very generally.

In accordance with what I have said above respecting the power of the Pi. verb ישר, my literal rendering, *I correct everything,* must be taken to mean *I correct every crooked way of mine.* The natural bent of a man's way is crooked. It is corrected, straightened, according to the standard of God's commandments.

v. 131. *I opened my mouth and panted, because I longed for Thy commandments.*

v. 132. *As Thou usest to do* (כמשפט) *to them that love Thy Name.* See note on Ps. xlviii. 12.

v. 136. עַל לֹא שָׁמְרוּ. See note on **Ps. lvi. 3.**

v. 137. *Righteous art Thou, O Lord, and upright in Thy judgments* (which) *Thou hast commanded.* I take into this verse צִוִּיתָ from the next.

v. 138. *Thy testimonies are righteous, and faithful to the uttermost.* The difficulty that attends the construction of this verse, as it stands in the received text, is entirely removed by the slight alteration which I here propose. I am the more induced to connect the צִוִּיתָ of v. 138 with the מִשְׁפָּטֶיךָ of v. 137, from a consideration of the expression מִשְׁפָּט צִוִּיתָ of Ps. vii. 7. See also Deut. vi. 1, and 20; vii. 11; viii. 11.

With regard to v. 138, as I now leave it, the construction is homogeneous throughout. Whereas, as the text stands, צֶדֶק must be taken in stat. constr. with the following word; whilst its correspondent, אֱמוּנָה, in the parallel clause, stands in no connecting construction whatever.

Moreover the division that I here propose will make the former clause of this 138th verse precisely identical with the former clause of v. 144.

v. 140. *Thine oracle is thoroughly proved, or attested, and Thy servant loveth it.*

For this meaning of צרופה, see notes on Ps. xvii. 3, 4, where I have observed that צרף, often found in connection with verbs that denote *trying and testing*, does itself denote the result of such trying and testing, viz., actual *purgation*.

Under Ps. cv. 19, I have also noted a remarkable connection between this verb and the word אמרה, for which I have in both places given *oracle*.

v. 144. *Thy testimonies are righteous for ever, &c.* The same words, in the same construction, as in v. 138.

v. 147. *I rose early in the twilight &c.*

The construction, with ב, does not, perhaps, admit of the same interpretation of קדם here as in the next verse, where the meaning seems to be, *Mine eyes prevent the night-watches;*—i.e. Mine eyes awake before the due time of watching.

v. 149. כמשפטיך חיני, *Quicken me as Thou art wont.* This, which is the rendering of the

Prayer-Book Version, is preferable to that of the Authorized Version,—*Quicken me according to Thy judgment.* Of the latter I will not say that it is sheer nonsense, but that it conveys no meaning to my mind. For the meaning here assigned to משפט, see note on Ps. xlviii. 12.

v. 150. There seems here an intentional antithesis of קרב to רחק.

v. 152. *I have long had knowledge from Thy testimonies, for Thou hast founded them of old.*

The second clause accounts for the קדם of the first. If the testimonies had not been founded of old, the Psalmist could not have acquired knowledge from them of old. It is not, of course, meant that his experience was commensurate with the age of the testimonies. It is rather as if he should say—*This knowledge of mine is no new thing, nor is it derived from recent sources. I acquired it long ago from those testimonies that God long ago established.*

For the use of the preposition מן in this sense, compare Ps. xciv. 12, מתורתך תלמדנו, *Thou teachest him out of Thy law.* For ידע used absolutely, of being wise, or acquiring wisdom, the reader will easily recall other examples.

v. 160. ראש דברך אמת, *The sum of Thy Word is faithfulness.* Comp. Prov. i. 7,—*The fear of the Lord is the summing up of knowledge.*

v. 161. *Princes have persecuted me without a cause ; but it was of Thy words* (not of theirs) *that my heart was afraid.*

The three Hebrew children before Nebuchadnezzar, and Peter and John before the chief priest and his council, afford illustrations.

v. 165. *Great is the peace of them that love Thy law, and to whom it is no stumbling-block.*

St. Peter (Ep. 1, ii. 8), seems thus to understand these words. He considers the case of some to whom even the *Word of God* is a stone of stumbling and a rock of offence.

Psalm CXX.

This Psalm, and the fourteen that follow, have a peculiar title, viz. שיר המעלות, or למעלות. The most probable explanation of this title seems to be that which refers this series of Psalms to the occasions of *going up* to the Temple at the great festivals. It is, however, certain that they were not composed for such occasions;—excepting, perhaps, the 122nd. This is sufficiently proved by a glance at their subjects, which are these:—

120. Deliverance from personal enemies.
121. Trust in God's providential care.
122. Going up to Jerusalem restored.
123. Trust in God in time of persecution.
124. The same.
125. General trust in God.
126. Congratulation upon deliverance.
127. Recognition of God in domestic affairs.
128. The same.
129. Confidence in God with defiance of the enemy.
130. Supplication under a sense of sin.
131. Childlike submission to God's will.
132. The considerations that led to the building of a Temple to Jehovah.

133. God's choice of Zion.

134. A short anthem apparently for the use of the night watchers in the Temple.

It will hardly be pretended that these Psalms, as a collection, were composed for any one special occasion. They may have been collected, partly for their brevity, for the use of the pilgrim trains; but that their collection, for any purpose, was made almost at random, seems beyond doubt.

cxx. 3. *What can be added to thee, or what can surpass thee, thou false tongue?*

v. 4. *Can the sharpened arrows of the warrior, or the missile brands?*

For יסף, in the sense of *surpassing*, see 1 Kings x. 7, and 2 Chron. ix. 6.

The comparison of the slanderous tongue with an envenomed arrow is common enough. For its being likened to a *burning* arrow see James iii. 6.

The גבור, of v. 4, denotes a warrior skilled especially in the use of the bow, as I have observed upon Ps. lii. 3. See also cxx. 4. The last words of this verse I have translated so as to give the true meaning; to which it matters nothing whether רתמים means *juniper* or *genista*. The word probably denotes something that was supposed to retain incandescence, or heat, in an extraordinary degree. Such incandescent missiles were showered upon the enemy as arrows. See Ps. xi. 6. In Ps. cxl. where the slanderous tongue is deprecated, *burning coals* are spoken of, as here, as showered upon the head of the enemy, and as being a due and fit return of calumny.

v. 5. *Meshech* and *Kedar* are usually understood as typical of the cruel people amongst whom the Psalmist found himself:—Not that he actually dwelt with Meshech and Kedar. The LXX. render these words ἡ παροικία μου ἐμακρύνθη; taking משך to denote extension of time. Conversely, as Delitzsch observes, in Isaiah lxvi. 19, they take the word משכי, of the expression משכי קשת, as the name of the people *Meshech*, whom they call Μοσόχ.

Psalm CXXI.

If any of this series of Psalms were composed specially for the occasion of *going up* to Jerusalem, this and the next may perhaps claim the distinction. This, because of the expression in the first verse, *I lift up mine eyes to the hills, &c.*, the rest of the Psalm being in this respect colourless.

v. 6. The *lux maligna* of the moon has been suspected, and expressed, very generally.

Psalm CXXII.

v. 1. *I rejoiced with them that said* (באמרים) *to me, Let us go, &c.* If we would render "I rejoiced *when they said*," &c., we must read באמרם.

v. 2. עמדות היו רגלינו,—A construction indicative of the late origin of the Psalm.

v. 3. *O Jerusalem! rebuilt as a city that was utterly ruined,*—literally, *as a city to whom was utter ruin* (חרבה instead of חברה).

For עיר in connection with הרבה, see Lev. xxvi. 31, 33; Jer. xxvii. 17, xliv. 2, 6 (specially of Jerusalem); and Ezek. xxxv. 4.

For the expression בנה חרבה, *to build up ruins*, see Isaiah lviii. 12; lxi. 4; Ezek. xxxvi. 10, 33. Mal. i. 4.

For יחדיו, or יחד, in the sense of *altogether, completely, utterly*, see Job xxxiv. 15; xl. 13; Ps. xiv. 3; xix. 9; xxxv. 26; xxxvii. 38; xl. 14; liii. 3; lxii. 9; lxxiv. 6, 8; cxli. 10; Isaiah xlii. 14; xlv. 16; Jer. v. 5.

The reading and the interpretation here proposed, being thus warranted, might claim consideration even if brought into competition with a reading that would yield a meaning of some sort. In competition with a reading from which no allowable meaning has yet been derived, it may claim preference. The usual rendering,—*a city that is united in itself*,—or, *compact within itself*, cannot be got out of the words as they stand. The verb חבר denotes always the bringing together of two or more things, an idea quite foreign to that of essential unity. Moreover, the construction is full of difficulty.

But even if these objections be overlooked, —What is the import of the usual interpretation? That Jerusalem was a compact city. Is this a circumstance to be expressed in such an ejaculation of love and wonder? It is not even a peculiarity of Jerusalem. Most ancient cities must have been so compact. No straggling suburbs could exist in the old days of continual warfare. A city was usually a walled town, or at least a knot of dwellings and fortifications drawn together as straitly as was compatible with life and locomotion. To say, then, that Jerusalem was so built was to say nothing worth saying.

Delitzsch, who takes בנויה, in the first clause, to mean *rebuilt*, admits that there is nothing correspondent to this in the second clause. But this admitted requirement is satisfied by my proposed reading.

v. 4. עדות is here used in the same sense as חק and משפט in Ps. lxxxi. 5.

Psalm CXXIII.

v. 3. *Be gracious to us, O Jehovah, Be gracious to us ; for we are filled full with contempt.*

v. 4. *O let our desire be filled full* (i.e. satisfied) *with the same scorn to the wealthy, with the same contempt to the proud.*

For this rendering I adopt a reading which differs almost imperceptibly from that of the received text, viz. in v. 4, — — — — —
רב תשבעה לה נפשנו הלעג לשאננים הבוז לגאיונים.
The division of the first two words of this verse I assimilate to the division of the same two words in the preceding verse. The only textual alteration is the substitution of ל for ה as the prefix of שאננים. This alteration is sanctioned by the LXX., and is demanded by the most stringent of all the rules of Hebrew grammar, viz. that a word in the construct state cannot have the definite article. Now we must retain the definite article of לעג in conformity with that of בוז. Therefore the prefix of the following word cannot be ה. I suppose it to be ל,—לשאננים, in conformity with the לגאיונים at the end of the verse. This was the reading of the LXX., who

give τὸ ὄνειδος τοῖς εὐθηνοῦσι καὶ ἡ ἐξουδένωσις τοῖς ὑπερηφάνοις.

Let it be considered, further, that the word נפש is very commonly used in the sense of *desire*, and that it is *invariably* used in this sense when it appears in connection with the verb שׂבע. The expression שׂבעה נפשׁי can have no other meaning than that *my desire is gratified*. In the case before us, therefore, we are driven to the absurd rendering, *Our desire of scorn and contempt is fully gratified.* The absurdity is obviated by the slight change here proposed.

I have rendered the words הלעג and הבוז, *the same scorn .... the same contempt.* So also Delitzsch, who well observes that the article of these words is "retrospectively demonstrative." This is sufficiently emphasized by the LXX.

In favour of a rendering which seems to me not merely preferable but inevitable, I will add only that in a Psalm of which the penultimate verse is an acknowledgment of insult received, we may be well pleased to find that the last verse conveys not a mere repetition of that humiliating acknowledgment, but a spirited purpose of retaliation.

With regard to the awkward word באיינם, I have only to say that the small difficulty it presents is not removed by the division of the word suggested by the *Keri*. Its meaning is plain enough, and is adequately reproduced by the LXX.

Psalm CXXIV.

In view of some more recent deliverance, this Psalm borrows its images from the overthrow of the Egyptians, and the deliverance of Israel, at the Red Sea. I have observed, upon Ps. lxxvi., that " the resources of Hebrew poetry seem to have been so far exhausted by the triumphal songs of that great occasion, that the language appropriate to that occasion is constantly re-echoed whenever in after times a similar strain of triumph is required." To the same effect Dean Perowne says here, " We know how constantly both Prophets and Psalmists are in the habit of comparing the return from Babylon to the deliverance from Egypt."

The return from Babylon is usually conjectured to be the subject of this Psalm; but the language would serve as well for any other such occasion.

v. 5. זידונים is to be compared, in point of structure, with באיונים in the 4th verse of the preceding Psalm.

Psalm CXXV.

v. 3. "Not for a continuance shall the sceptre of heathen tyranny rest upon the holy land. God will not suffer that; so that the righteous may not at length, through the power which pressure and use exercise over men, also participate in the prevailing ungodly doings." *Delitzsch.*

Psalm CXXVI.

v. 1. *When Jehovah turned the captivity of Zion, we were like them that are recovered from sickness* (בחלמים).

This is the rendering of the Chaldee. The same Hebrew word is used to express Hezekiah's restoration from sickness in Isaiah xxxviii. 16. The LXX. there give παρακληθείς. Here they give παρακεκλημένοι, from which it appears that here also they understood the same restoration. In Syriac the word denotes, in Aph. *to restore to health,* in Ethpe. *to be so restored.*

The usual modern rendering, *we were like them that dream,* implies a figure far-fetched, and much less natural and less appropriate than that which I have here adopted. Jerome, however, gives *quasi somniantes;* and it is to be admitted that in Hebrew this is by far the most usual meaning of the word.

The figure of sick men restored to health is parallel with that of dry land refreshed with water, in v. 4.

In the poetry of all languages the joy of restoration to health is described as exquisite. Who has not had some taste of it?

v. 4. *Turn our captivity, O Jehovah, as streams in a dry land.*

This is the primary meaning of the root נגב in Hebrew, and the usual meaning in Syriac. The primary meaning is surely intended in Judges i. 15.

v. 6. משך הזרע may be translated *the sow-*

ing of seed, that is, so much as may be required for one sowing. See the same expression in Amos ix. 13. How the verb which denotes *drawing* became applied to this special meaning, it may be impossible to discover.

Psalm CXXVII.

v. 2. *In vain do ye rise up early, and take rest late, and eat the bread of anxious toil:— Surely He giveth sleep to His beloved?*

The preceding verse tells how vain are human precautions, without God. This verse tells how vain, without God, are human toils and cares; and, moreover, how unnecessary. Surely God's beloved ones may find some interval of cessation from care and turmoil; some rest in Him! *Casting all your care upon Him, for He careth for you,*—this seems to convey the meaning of these two verses.

The remainder of the Psalm seems specially intended to obviate anxious care with regard to children.

v. 3. *Behold children are a possession granted by Jehovah: the fruit of the womb is His gift.*

נחלת יהוה, says Gesenius, "is— *(a)* the especial possession of Jehovah, i.e. Israel, for whom Jehovah cared and watched, as being His own,—*(b)* a possession granted by Jehovah." For the latter meaning he cites only this place.

v. 4. *As arrows in the hand of the warrior* (גבור) *so are the children of young persons.*

For גבור in this connection see note on cxx. 3.

The expression בני הנעורים is equivalent to ראשית אונים, for which see Ps. lxxviii. 51.

v. 5. The usual translation of this verse is admissible:—*They shall not be ashamed when they speak* (i.e. plead their cause) *with the enemies in the gate.* But there is much to be said in favour of that which Gesenius proposed, viz. *Blessed is the man that hath his quiver full of them* (sc. the *arrows* mentioned in the preceding verse). *They shall not be discomfited, but shall destroy their enemies in the gate.*

It is certain that at least in one place (2 Chron. xxii. 10,) the verb דבר has this meaning. It was so understood by the LXX., who give ἀπώλεσε ; and, in the corresponding passage in 2 Kings xi. 1, the expression is varied by the use of the verb אבד. It is equally certain that we must assume such a meaning of the verb in order to account for the noun-substantive דבר, *destruction*, specially by *pestilence*. Now since, as I have observed in my note on Ps. lxxvi. 4, it is usual to liken an attack of pestilence to a discharge of arrows, we may herein detect a reason for this uncommon use of the verb דבר in this place, viz. in its association with *arrows*.

It will be admitted that the similitude loses its point, according to the usual translation. To say that a man's sons are like arrows: to go on further to say that a man is blessed who has his quiver full of such arrows; and then to represent these arrows as speaking for their father against his enemies,—seems somewhat absurd. On the other hand, to liken them to arrows, and to represent their father as using them as arrows, viz. by destroying the enemies,—this is to employ a well-sustained metaphor with a consistent meaning.

If it be thought that the preceding verb, יבשו, is more in keeping with the idea of pleading one's cause than with that of destroying enemies; let it be remembered that this verb is very often used to denote *discomfiture before one's enemies.* I suppose the meaning here to be that the sons will not be so discomfited before their enemies, but will rather destroy them.

Psalm CXXVIII.

v. 2. יגיע כפיך כי תאכל, *For it is the labour of thine own hands that thou shalt eat.*

For the construction see note on Ps. cxvi. 10.

v. 3. *Thy wife, as a fruitful vine, in the inner chambers of thy house, &c.*

Since, in Psalm xlviii. 3, I have rendered ירכתי צפון *the inner recesses of the Sanctuary,* I can have no hesitation in putting the same meaning upon the word ירכתי in the text. So also Ewald and others. See the same expression in Amos vi. 10. The English Version, *by the sides of thy house,* is plausible, because we look for a vine on the outer walls, not in the inner chambers. It should be considered that the locality mentioned is not that of the vine but that of the wife; just as in the next clause the locality is not that of the olive branches but that of the children. As we find the children (who are like olive branches) round about the table, so we find the wife (who is like a fruitful vine) inside the house;—which is *comme il faut.*

v. 4. The position of כי in this verse is to be explained by the supposition of a considerable pause after הנה,—a pause which seems almost requisite under the circumstances, and which certainly serves to display the beautiful picture of the Psalm, before the lesson of the picture is taught. *Behold!—Look upon this picture!—For thus shall the man be blessed who feareth the Lord!*

The transition from the optative to the imperative is very natural. *God* is the subject of the former: *Thou* art the subject of the latter:—*May God bless thee* . . . . *Do thou enjoy the blessing.*

Psalm CXXIX.

v. 6. *Let them be as grass on the roofs, which withers before it is grown up.*

The use of שלף in the sense here required is unexampled. On the other hand, חלף is precisely the word that the occasion requires. One feels strongly tempted to substitute this latter word:—a change that obviously suggested itself to my own mind before I was aware that it had been proposed by others. That this was the reading of Aquila seems certain, since he gives ἀνέθαλεν, for the precise correspondence of which with חלף see my notes on Ps. xc. 5 and 6.*

He took the verb in its primary meaning; but this is unnecessary here; for although it properly denotes *substitution*, sc. of new for old, that is, *renovation*, and therefore is very appropriate to designate the *revival* of withered plants, it is also quite appropriately used to denote those successive changes of a plant which we call *growth*. And this must be the meaning of the word here, if it be admitted in the place of שלף.

---

* In Ps. xc. 5, 6, we find connected mention of חציר, חלף, and יבש, just as we should find them in the text according to the proposed emendation.

Those who are contented with the שלף of the text are yet constrained to translate it as if it were חלף. They fancy some resemblance between the drawing of a sword from its sheath, or of a foot from a shoe, which is the proper meaning of שלף, and the development of buds or blossoms. Accordingly, in some copies of the Septuagint Version, ἐξανθῆσαι takes the place of ἐκσπασθῆναι.

v. 7. *Wherewith the reaper filleth not his hand, nor he that pileth up* (the sheaves) *his bosom, or lap.*

The meaning of the verb עמר requires to be carefully distinguished. It does not, in Hebrew or in any of the cognate languages, mean *to bind*, as has been usually assumed. The assumption was probably made in order to account for the nouns substantive עמיר and עמר. It was supposed that these words denoted *bundles* from the idea of *binding*. But in truth they denote *heaps* from the idea of *accumulating*. This might have been surmised from the fact that the word *Omer* is used as a measure of capacity, of things that could not be bound or bundled up.

From the idea of *heaping up* comes that of

the Hithpael, viz. to *heap up oneself, to exalt oneself, to be boastful, to lord oneself*,—concerning which see my note on Ps. xciv. 4.

Closely cognate with עמר is גמר, which has the two apparently opposite meanings of (1) *to complete, to finish*, and (2) *to leave off, to fail.* I quote here the meanings given by Gesenius. The paradox is explained by the consideration that men desist from that which is finished:— that the *leaving off* or *ceasing*, which this verb denotes, is consequent upon completion* :—that at least this is the proper meaning of the word, the primary idea of which is probably the same as that of עמר, viz. *to pile up, heap up.* We find the same transition from *heaping up* to *completing* in the same uses of the Latin *culmen*, and of its derivatives *cumulus, cumulo.*

---

* Under Ps. xlix. 9, I have remarked that *cessation upon completion* is the proper idea of חדל also.

Psalm CXXX.

v. 4. כי עמך הסליחה למען תורא.

For with Thee is forgiveness, to the intent that Thou mayest be feared, viz. by the heathen.

The LXX. render the last two words of the Hebrew, ἕνεκεν τοῦ ὀνόματός σου. Since in Isaiah xlii. 4, they give ὄνομα for תורה, and in Jer. xxiii. 27, νόμος for שם,—concerning which see note on Ps. lix. 12,—it is quite possible that they here took תורא as meant for תורה, that they represented this reading by the proper word νόμος, and that the ὄνομα is only a corruption of their Greek text. This seems the more probable since Symmachus gives ἕνεκεν τοῦ νόμου.

There is another explanation which, though not so ready to hand, is yet, I think, preferable. It is possible that the LXX., with the same reading and pointing as in the received text, paraphrased the last two words, so as to give the same meaning in the more familiar expression למען שמך. Under Ps. xxv. 11, I have pointed out what seems a conventional association of this expression with the verb סלח. We consider, further, that by the *Name of Jehovah* is intended very frequently, His fame or reputation amongst the heathen; that this fame is often mentioned as bringing with it fear; and that this fear was dependent upon, and commensurate with, the continuance of God's favour to His people by the continual forgiveness of their sins. The reader will easily call to mind passages in confirmation of these statements. I quote the first that occurs to my own mind, from Ps. cii. 16, &c.—*The heathen shall fear the Name of Jehovah, and all the kings of the earth Thy glory, When Jehovah shall build up Zion . . . . . When He turneth to the prayer of the destitute, &c.*

If then the Septuagint rendering is not an intentional paraphrase, it is due to a most extraordinary accident that it represents perfectly, and in the most appropriate terms, the meaning of the Hebrew as we find it.

I must add that we are by no means bound to follow the editors in their separation of the words ἕνεκεν τοῦ ὀνόματός σου from this 4th verse and joining them to the next. This is clearly a mistake.

It is usually supposed that these words,

There is forgiveness with Thee that Thou mayest be feared, mean that God pardons men in order that they (the pardoned ones) may fear Him the more. This may be a true statement; but I do not think it is the statement here intended.

Psalm CXXXI.

v. 1. *O Lord, my heart is not haughty, nor are mine eyes lifted up ; and I do not exercise myself with things that are too great and too hard for me.*

v. 2. *But I have brought my soul into the likeness and similitude of a weaned child, the suckling of its mother. Like a weaned suckling is my soul.*

v. 3. *Wait, O Israel, for the Lord, henceforth and for ever.*

Upon v. 2, it is to be observed that the verb דוממתי is taken as equivalent to דמירי, *(Piel).* Since דמה certainly has sometimes the same meaning as דמם, it is no great matter to assume that the latter has sometimes the same meaning as the former. This assumption is not gratuitous. The two verbs, שוה and דמה, both meaning *to be like,* are so often found together that we are almost compelled to recognize the same two verbs, in the same conjunction, in the text. For examples of this conjunction see Isaiah xl. 25; xlvi. 5; and Lam. ii. 13.

In the same verse, עלי in both clauses is the noun substantive עול, *a sucking child.* In the former clause it has the appended י as the poetic form of the construct state. In the second clause, the same י is appended without any such reason, as it is often elsewhere found. See note on cxiii. 5.

Against the usual interpretations, as for example that of Ewald,—*I have soothed and quieted my soul, like a child weaned from his mother,*—or that of Dean Perowne,—*I have stilled and hushed my soul, as a child that is weaned of his mother,*—it may be observed that the preposition על cannot mean *of* or *from.* Moreover, that it is contrary to ordinary experience to represent a newly-weaned child as hushing its soul.

The Psalmist likens himself, and Israel in general, to a child weaned from its mother's breast, solely in respect of that *craving* that each feels. In the preceding Psalm those who wait with longing impatience for the redemption of Israel are likened to those who watch for the morning. *Wait, Israel, for Jehovah,* is the exhortation that immediately follows this comparison. In this Psalm the same waiting and wanting ones are likened to a newly-weaned child; and here again the comparison is followed by the same note of encouragement:—*Wait, Israel, for Jehovah.*

Taking the Psalm as a whole, it expresses the merging of all ambition and of all aspiration in the waiting and longing for God.

Psalm CXXXII.

It is generally admitted that this Psalm was composed by some one of David's descendants. In my opinion we are almost compelled to assign it to Solomon. Not to insist unduly upon the fact that verses 8, 9, 10, are Solomon's own words, used appropriately by him upon the occasion of the dedication of the temple, and appropriate to no other occasion,—I consider that no subsequent prince of David's house, nor even Solomon himself on any subsequent occasion, could have dwelt so exclusively upon the pleasing aspect of Israel's relations towards God. Here we find a pleading of God's promise that if David's children should keep His covenant, &c. they should sit upon David's throne. There is no mention of any other conduct resulting in God's displeasure : no deprecation of that displeasure : no mingled tones of trust in God and distrust of themselves, such as we find in all the later Psalms that have an historical basis.* To the truth of this remark, v. 10 supplies no exception. *Turn not away the face of Thine anointed*, is not directly a deprecation of God's anger. It is a citation and pleading of His express promise.

A peculiarity of this Psalm that requires to be observed, in order to the development of its meaning, is the strongly marked expression of reciprocity between the house of David and God. If David proposes one thing, God proposes an-

---

* For a contrast, see Ps. lxxxix. " It is hardly probable," says Dr. Perowne, against the supposition of a later date for this Psalm, " that there should be no lamentation over the fallen fortunes of David's house, as in Ps. lxxxix."

other in the same words. If God's action in respect of David is expressed by a certain word, that word is used to express David's action in respect of God. The same expressions are used to denote the action of both parties. The fundamental occasion of this peculiarity is to be found in the history, as it is given in 2 Sam. vii., or 1 Chron. xvii. There we find David, on the one hand, purposing to build a house for God: God, on the other hand, purposing to build a house for David. Now although it is evident that these two purposes are different in kind,—that is, totally different,—they are expressed in the same words. By almost a play upon the words, God's purpose is represented as reciprocal to David's purpose. In the Psalm the expressions are somewhat forced, in order to keep up this exaggerated and fanciful idea of reciprocity. Not to mention that David's oath to God, in v. 2, finds its counterpart in God's oath to David, in v. 11,—it is particularly to be observed that David's purpose, in v. 1, is reciprocated by God's purpose in v. 6; but that this is so expressed as to obscure the distinction of the parties engaged. It is not easy to see, at first sight, whether it was the purpose of God towards David, or that of David towards God, that was heard at Ephratah, in the plains of Jaar. Again, the expression מצאנוה of v. 6, would seem strange, did we not see that it is suggested on David's part as the reciprocal of God's saying as recorded in Ps. lxxxix. 21,—*I have found* (מצאתי) *David my servant: with my holy oil have I anointed him:*—the two sayings,—the one on David's part, and the other on God's part,—having a distinctly expressed reference to some transaction at Bethlehem. Since, according to the one saying, this transaction was the anointing of David by Samuel, we can hardly doubt that the reference of the other saying is to the same event.

v. 1. *Remember, O Lord, for David's sake, all his solemn purpose* (כל ענותו),

v. 2. *How he sware, &c.*

For the construction of the first verse, compare the prayer of Nehemiah (v. 19),

זכרה לי · · · כל אשר עשיתי.

For the meaning which I have given to ענותו, it is necessary to observe a power of the verb ענה, and of its derivatives, which has not been duly recognized. The verb, which denotes in general to *pronounce, declare,* has the special meaning of *declaring a purpose* in Gen. xli. 16, and Deut. xx. 11.

Of the derivatives, the same word as in the text occurs in Ps. xviii. 36,—*Thy purpose hath made me great.* The usual interpretation of this verse puts a meaning upon the word which it never elsewhere bears, and which is glaringly inconsistent with the context. The submissive meekness of man towards God is intelligible. The assertion of such submissive meekness of God towards man savours of profanity.*

The same word, with probably the same meaning, is found in Ps. xxii. 25. *He hath not despised the purpose of the poor man.*

Akin and equivalent is the word מענה, as it occurs in Prov. xvi. 1 and 4. In the latter verse there can be no doubt as to its meaning, viz.—*The Lord hath made all things for His own purpose* (למענהו).

Add to this, that the meaning of *purpose,*

---

* On the other hand, the assertion that David's greatness was the result of God's express purpose with regard to him, is one that is consistent with the context and worthy of the occasion.

intent, is assigned by Gesenius to the noun substantive מֲעַן which supplies the very common expression לְמַעַן, *to the intent, in order that.*

It is to be observed, further, that the עֲנוֹת of the text is equivalent to the עֲנִי of 1 Chron. xxii. 14, which appears thus in the English Version :—*Behold in my trouble* (בְעָנְיִי; LXX. κατὰ τὴν πτωχείαν μου) *I have prepared for the house of the Lord.* I feel warranted in assuming that these two words are equivalent, as well as akin, since in both places they denote some state or condition on David's part immediately antecedent to his preparations for the building of the Temple. If, then, the word means *trouble*, or *poverty*, in the one place, it must have the same meaning in the other place. Now it is certain that David was neither in trouble nor in poverty when he made such preparation. He had attained the very summit of wealth and prosperity. We must therefore exclude the meaning of *trouble* from both places. And then the Psalm indicates a meaning which we can hardly avoid. It does not mention any difficulty which David had in his preparation, but distinctly and fully calls to God's remembrance the oath that he sware and the vow that he made. It is therefore in the highest degree probable, if not certain, that the words in both places denote *purpose* or *intent*. The rendering of 1 Chron. xxii. 14, will thus be, *Behold in my purpose I have prepared, &c.**

v. 6. *Behold, we heard it* (sc. God's purpose towards David) *at Ephratah* (Bethlehem) *we discerned it in the fields of Jaar* (Bethlehem).

The obvious reference of Ephratah is to Bethlehem; and this is very generally admitted upon grounds quite independent of those which I have occupied in my preliminary observations. As a result of those observations it would appear that Bethlehem is precisely the place of which we should expect mention to be made in a Psalm which describes the communication of God's purposes to David; since it was at Bethlehem

---

* The LXX. indirectly sanction this rendering. For they certainly read כעניי instead of בעניי. But this reading makes nonsense if we take עני to mean *trouble*. David could not make preparation *according to, or in respect of, his trouble*. But that he should make preparation *according to his purpose* is precisely that which the occasion requires, and which, as I think, the words mean.

that God called him from tending sheep and anointed him to be king over Israel.

If this be established, it follows with almost equal certainty that Bethlehem is also intended by the expression שְׂדֵי יָעַר :—that this latter expression is a poetical varying of the denotation. Examples without number might be adduced of this usage, viz. the denoting of one and the same object by one expression in the former clause, and by a varied expression in the latter clause, of the same sentence. To go no farther than this Psalm :—we find, in vv. 2 and 5, *Jehovah* in the former clause, and the *Mighty One of Jacob* in the latter. These are identical. In v. 4, we find *sleep to one's eyes* in the former: *slumber to one's eyelids* in the latter. These are identical. In v. 5, we find *a place* for God in the former : *habitations* for God in the latter. These too are identical. The Hebrew scholar does not need to be told that these are only examples of a widely prevalent rule of Hebrew poetry; and he will not think that it is upon the warrant of these only that I assert the identity of שְׂדֵי יָעַר with אֶפְרָתָה in this 6th verse.*

---

* It may perhaps be impossible to account for this

Of the somewhat unexpected use of the verb מצא I have given an account in my preliminary observations. This use, however, is not so strange as it may appear at first sight. The verb, in its ordinary use, denotes *finding*, not only as the result of active search, but as a passive experience.

The meaning of this 6th verse seems to be that the house of David,—not David personally and individually; for the verbs are both plural,— heard and discovered God's purposes for the first time at Bethlehem. This we know to be historically true.

The fem. suffix of both verbs is in agreement with the fem. noun עבות *purpose*, in v. 1.

v. 8. In this and the following verses we

---

designation of Bethlehem as שדי יער. Amongst some other conjectures, it may be observed that the word יער denotes *honey*. Perhaps the neighbourhood may have been remarkable for its honey. Modern travellers state that almost every house in Bethlehem is provided with an apiary on the roof. In a land that is described as flowing with milk and honey, it should not surprise us to find some place that derives its name from the latter product. Any such conjecture, however, I refrain from putting in the text, lest it should tend only to weaken my argument.

seem to have Solomon's own words, as they are recorded in 2 Chron. vi. 41, 42. It is not necessary to suppose that the writer of the history copied the words of this Psalm. The Psalm does not seem intended for public use,—though it may have been so used. If Solomon composed the Psalm at the same time that he uttered the dedication prayer, nothing is more likely than that he would use the same expressions in both.

One thing seems to me certain, that there was no occasion subsequent to the dedication of the Temple upon which these words could be appropriately used,—no occasion to which they would apply with any meaning whatever. They are not words that could be used—as many other popular expressions — at random, and upon almost any occasion. Their meaning is exhausted by the one special occasion to which they refer, and cannot be utilized for any more general purpose.

Psalm CXXXIII.

1. *Behold what a good and pleasant thing it is for brethren to dwell all-together;*—(sc. not actually upon Zion, but with Zion as their common rallying-point: their centre of national life, as it is expressed at the end of the Psalm).

2. *As the good oil upon the head, descending to the beard,—I mean Aaron's beard,—which descended even to the collar of his robes,*

3. *So is the dew of Hermon, that descendeth upon the hills of Zion.*

For there (sc. in Zion) *Jehovah ordained the blessing: life for evermore.*

The subject of this Psalm is not the blessedness of unity. It is rather God's choice of Zion. Does it seem strange that this comparatively low hill should be chosen? Let it be considered that with God there is no respect of high and low. The lower things are, equally with the higher, partakers of the gifts of God's grace. The consecrating oil affected not Aaron's head alone, but it descended to his beard; yea, even lower down, to his garments. So the same dew that falls upon the sublime peaks of Hermon falls equally upon the lowly hill of Zion.

This aspect of the Psalm,—a very obvious one,—relieves us of many difficulties. I never could understand in what respect the oil upon Aaron's head, descending to his beard, &c., or the dew of Hermon descending upon Zion, could be emblematic of unity. Neither could I, or any-one else, understand how the dew of Hermon could descend upon Zion.

v. 1. The יחד here is equivalent to אחד, and the expression גם יחד corresponds to גם שנים, for which see Gen. xxvii. 45; Prov. xvii. 15; xx. 10, 12; and 1 Sam. iv. 17. This latter expression denotes a unified two,— *tous deux*, as the French say. The גם of the text serves to intensify the unity which is already denoted by יחד, so that the expression means *all-one*, or *all-together*.

Delitzsch and Perowne take גם here to mean *also*,—*i.e.* as superinducing unity upon the natural ties of kindred. The former says: —" Good and delightful it is when brethren, united by blood and heart, also (corresponding to this their brotherly nature) dwell together." But it is most certain that the Hebrew will not bear this meaning; and since the usage of the text is so perfectly explained by the usage of the places cited above, it is unnecessary to seek for a more recondite meaning than that which is usually given, and which I have adopted.

v. 2. It would serve the purpose of the illustration somewhat better if we were to take the expression פי מדותיו to denote the lower, rather than the upper, parts of the vestments. Otherwise, the *mouth* of a garment surely means the upper rather than the lower opening.

v. 3. The כ of this verse, corresponding to the כ of v. 2, stands for כן, as in Ps. cxxvii. 4.

Psalm CXXXIV.

1. *Behold, bless ye Jehovah, all ye servants of Jehovah: ye that stand in the house of Jehovah by night.*

2. *Lift ye your hands in holiness, and bless Jehovah.*

3. *May Jehovah bless thee out of Zion, even He that made heaven and earth.*

The opinion that we have here a greeting of the priest-hood by the laity, and a responsive blessing by the priest-hood, seems to require no demonstration. Ewald, however, puts the whole Psalm in the mouth of a layman.

v. 2. I take קֹדֶשׁ as used adverbially :— *in holiness.* Comp. St. Paul's words in 1 Tim. ii. 8,—ἐπαίροντας ὁσίους χεῖρας. The priests cannot be exhorted to lift up their hands *towards the sanctuary,* according to the meaning of these words in Ps. xxviii. 2, where the expression is used by one outside, and perhaps far away from, the sanctuary. Here the priests are within the sacred walls.

Psalm CXXXV.

This is a medley. It is not easy to discover in it either homogeneous structure or continuous thought.

v. 2. *Ye that stand in the house of Jehovah, &c.* Comp. Ps. cxxii. 2. To stand in the Lord's house, or within its gates, is an expression of covenant *status.* Correspondingly, the Hallelujah of this Psalm is a covenant privilege. See Prolegom. § 23. This verse, then, is not necessarily addressed to the priests alone; although it seems framed upon the first verse of the preceding Psalm, which is so exclusively addressed.

v. 5. *For I know.* This looks like an expression of personal experience, branching off from the general experience of Israel mentioned in the preceding verse. But the thought is pursued no further. The writer reverts immediately to the more general theme.

vv. 6, 7. These verses are taken from Jer. x. 11, 12, 13, where they certainly represent certain stages of the Creation of the World. We can therefore hardly avoid taking the expression of the text, מעלה נשאים מקצה הארץ, as equivalent to ואד יעלה מן הארץ in Gen. ii. 6: —both referring to the mists that served instead of rain, before that God had caused it to rain upon the earth.* But the Psalmist goes on to mention the gift of actual rain; and he connects this new phenomenon with lightning. See

---

* If it be objected that נשיא denotes a *cloud* rather than a mist, and that it cannot, therefore, be identified with the אד of Gen. ii. 6; let it be considered that there is no sharp distinction between the two things; and that, for the words, this very word אד re-appears as עננא in the Targum of Onkelos.

1 Sam. xii. 17, and Zech. x. i.* In both these places rain at harvest-time is spoken of,— that is, extraordinary or unexpected rain:—in both

---

* Zech. x. i. *Ask ye of the Lord rain in the time of harvest* (מלקוש), *and the Lord will make lightnings, and give them showers of rain.*

This is mentioned as an illustration, or test, of God's power and good-will. I render מלקוש by *harvest*, because this is undoubtedly its proper meaning, although by custom it came to denote the *rain* that usually fell just before harvest-time. But it is certain that the rain here spoken of was not the usual rain. A test put to God always takes the form of a request for something strange, unexpected, παράδοξον. To say that if His people ask for rain He will send it to them in the time of rain, is sufficiently absurd. On the other hand, nothing was regarded as more strange than rain at harvest-time. In Prov. xxvi. 1, it is said to be as extraordinary as snow in summer. Accordingly Samuel puts this as a test whereby his integrity should be divinely and supernaturally vindicated: —this calling for rain at the time of wheat-harvest. The extraordinary request was granted, but by means of thunder and lightning. It is very likely that Zechariah had this history in view when he proposed the same test to the Israelites of his day:—Ask ye anything whatsoever of the Lord, as a test of His superiority to vain idols. Ask snow in summer. *Ask rain at harvest time. For the rain He will make lightnings.* Nothing is too hard for the Lord.

places it is brought about by lightning. And I suppose that it is because the first rain that God caused to fall on the earth was regarded as extraordinary, that it is attributed by the Psalmist to the immediate agency of lightning. Accordingly I render

v. 7. *Causing mists to arise from the surface of the earth: making lightnings for the rain: bringing forth wind from His stores.*

It is not unlikely that some reference to this notion is to be found in Ps. civ. 4,—*He maketh the winds His messengers, and the flaming fire His ministers:*—that is to say, in both this Psalm and that, *lightning* and *wind* are mentioned as the agents of God's extraordinary manifestations of His power and purpose.

The thought is continued from the history of the Creation to the history of the deliverance from Egypt (v. 9); *He sent signs and tokens into the midst of thee, O Egypt.*

v. 11. לסיחון &c. The construction of this verse is very remarkable. The verse itself is taken from verses 19 and 20 of the next Psalm. There, by a strange oversight, the ל with which many other verses begin, and which is dependent upon the verb הודו at the beginning of the Psalm, is prefixed to clauses which have no such dependence. The compiler of this Psalm transferred the blunder to his own compilation, and this without any excuse whatever. The הודו, which accounts for the inadvertent prefixing of ל to verses 19 and 20 of the following Psalm, is here altogether wanting.

v. 13. See Ex. iii. 15.

v. 14. See Deut. xxxii. 36.

v. 15-20. See Ps. cxv. 4-11.

v. 21. *The Lord, who dwelleth at Jerusalem, be blessed out of Zion.* The construction is the same as that of the last verse of the preceding Psalm. The difference between the two is that, in the one God gives, in the other God receives, blessing out of Zion.

Psalm CXXXVI.

As usual in a retrospection of God's dealings with His people, this Psalm goes back to the Creation of the World. It commences with expressions which are intended to exhaust all possibilities of power and authority in order to confer them upon Jehovah.

In the refrain, כי לעולם חסדו, the peculiar meaning of חסד must be borne in mind. Properly denoting *covenant goodness*, "it is so intimately connected with *covenant faithfulness* (אמת) that it partakes somewhat of the meaning of the latter." *Proleg.* § 20.

v. 7. אורים *luces*, for מארות *lumina*, is, says Delitzsch, without precedent. Many such nice distinctions become obliterated in the corruption of all languages.

v. 15. נער. The same word that is used in the original account, Exod. xiv. 27.

vv. 19, 20. See note on v. 11 of the preceding Psalm.

Psalm CXXXVII.

This beautiful composition presents very few points of difficulty. It was probably written after the return from Babylon. This is indicated not only by the past tenses, but in a more demonstrative manner by the שם of verses 1 and 3.

v. 2. ערב, *a willow.* The root is probably akin to ארב, *to interweave,* and the tree so called from the uses to which it is applied, viz. the making of baskets, booths, &c. It is mentioned as one of the trees to be used for the construction of the booths at the Feast of Booths; Lev. xxiii. 40.

v. 3. The כי introduces the reason why they hung up their harps. It was because their heathen masters asked them to sing and play upon their harps when they were in no mood for such merriment.

For there they that had led us away into captivity asked us to sing our own songs (Heb. our particular songs, i.e. the songs of Zion); *and they that had made us howl asked for merriment.*

For this meaning of דברי שיר see note on Ps. cv. 27.

For the meaning I have assigned to תוללינו, —standing as it does in connection with שיר,— compare Amos viii. 3, והילילו שירות היכל,— "*and they shall howl the songs of the temple,*" i.e. the songs shall be turned into howling. The antitheses here intended appear with more distinctness subsequently. Why should the songs of Zion be sung in the land of the alien, in the land of our captivity? Why should we afford merriment to those who have made us howl with sorrow and indignation?

It does not devolve upon me, in consequence of my interpretation, to account for the causative power of the form תוללינו, since this power has been assumed for the form (by Gesenius and others) with a view to a different interpretation.* It ought, however, to be observed that a verbal substantive in such a form denotes the abstract rather than the concrete:—the *cause* of wailing rather than the *causer*.

It has been thought that the LXX. regarded the initial ת of this word as the Aramaic equiva-

---

*Delitzsch, inclining to the opinion that the word is causative of ילל, adduces הושב and תלמיד as examples. But neither of these words has causative power.

lent of שׁ; and that their rendering, ἀπαγαγόντες, shows that they took the word as if it were שׁוֹלְלֵינוּ. And this, according to poetical custom, would be a very suitable synonym to correspond with the preceding שׁוֹבֵינוּ. There is, however, no known Aramaic הלל answering to the Hebrew שלל; and this Hebrew word is no-where else represented by this Greek word.

v. 5. *If I forget thee, O Jerusalem, let my right hand forget* (sc. its musical skill).

This seems the most appropriate way of filling up the poetical ellipsis.

v. 7. The ill-will of Edom, manifested in the day of Israel's distress, is mentioned in Obadiah, 10-14.

id. ערו appears as גלו in the Syriac; so that this place is identified with Micah i. 6.

id. עד היסוד בה. It is certain that the meaning is, *unto the foundation;* but the construction has not yet been satisfactorily explained. The LXX. probably had a different reading. In view of the difficulty of the construction, I am inclined to think that the last word בה has been carelessly inserted by a copyist who had the next word בת in his eye, and was perhaps even further confused by the following בבל.

v. 8. *O daughter of Babylon, thou wasted one.* The word שדודה may be so regarded as prophetical. Yet it is allowable, also, to render it *Thou that art to be wasted.* See remarks on the passive participle in Prolegomena, § 20. (Vol. I. p. 66).

The daughter of Babylon denotes only the Babylonians. This usage is very common.

Psalm CXXXVIII.

For a conjecture as to the author, see note on v. 7.

v. 1. *I will praise Thee with all my heart, before the mighty will I play upon the harp to Thee.*

In view of v. 4, there seems little room to doubt that this is the meaning intended. Here the Psalmist praises God in the presence of the mighty. There the mighty themselves (the kings of the earth) praise God.

v. 2. *I will worship towards Thy holy temple.*

This attitude of worship is assumed with the view of directing the mighty towards the object of worship.

id. For Thou hast magnified Thy Word above all Thy reputation.

See note upon Ps. xlviii. 11.

v. 3. *When I called, then Thou answeredst me; and at my desire Thou didst mightily encourage me.*

The expression בנפשי in the second clause corresponds to ביום קראתי in the former. In this second clause I take the verb as it stands in the received text; although many considerations would lead us to prefer רחב to רהב. Taking the word as it stands, and with the meaning usually assigned to it, I regard עז as used adverbially.

v. 4. Here again I refer the reader to my note on Ps. xlviii. 11.

v. 5. *Yea, they shall sing in the ways of Jehovah that great is the glory of Jehovah.*

It is now customary to give,—*They shall sing of the ways of Jehovah.* There is, however, no warrant whatever for this construction of שיר

with ב. Whereas, on the other hand, בדרך invariably means, *in the way*. What, then, is the meaning of this assertion, or prophecy, that the kings of the earth shall sing in the ways of Jehovah that great is the glory of Jehovah? The answer may perhaps be found in the consideration that none can in any degree recognize or acknowledge the glory of God, until in some degree, they have been induced to walk in His ways.

v. 6. This verse confirms the view that I have taken of the preceding verse. God's praise is worthily uttered from the mouth of babes and sucklings. How can the kings of the earth worthily utter His praise? Only in His ways: in child-like modesty and humility:— *For though Jehovah be high, yet it is the lowly that He regards: the lofty he knows from afar.*

v. 7. Am I worthy to sing His praise? If a qualification is lowliness, then I may plead lowliness. *Though I walk in the midst of trouble, Thou keepest me alive.*

It might almost be conjectured that the Psalmist was one who could rank with the kings of the earth: as one, moreover, who had learned the lesson of humility from misfortune. He would hardly have turned the thought from the kings of the earth, who can find God's way only from adversity, to himself as pleading adversity, if he had not been a co-ordinate in royalty as well as in adversity.

v. 8. *Jehovah perfecteth for me. Jehovah, Thy goodness is for ever: The work of Thy hands, O leave it not unfinished.*

The antithesis between גמר, *to complete*, and רפה *to leave off, desist from, a work*, ought to be observed, and in a translation well marked. For the former, see notes on Ps. xlix. 9, and cxxix. 7. For the latter, see Nehem. vi. 3; Prov. iv. 13; and Ps. xlvi. 11. The Psalmist's meaning seems to be that God, who had begun a good work in him, or by him, was expected to perfect and accomplish the same.

Psalm CXXXIX.

Here the leading and pervading thought is, that God, who knows our bodily frame, (Comp. ciii. 14), knows also the thoughts and intents of the hearts. As in v. 1, He is said to *search and know* the former, so, in v. 23, He is requested to *search and know* the latter.

There is also what may be called a tentative thought, to this effect, viz. that God who knew all about us before our active and independent and conscious life began, will still know us when all this seems to be past.

v. 2. רע denotes not *thought* in general; but, subjectively, *desire*, as in this verse; and, objectively, *favourable regard*, as in v. 17. It is thus equivalent, in both senses, to רצון, to which it is also akin :—רעה being the Aramaic form of רצה.

v. 3. *Thou art familiar with my path and my couch, and Thou art acquainted with all my ways.*

The verb זרית, of the former clause, is to be explained by regarding it as parallel to the verb, הסכנתה, of the latter. As this latter denotes acquaintance derived from living together,—סכן being equivalent and akin to שכן—so I suppose זרה to be equivalent and akin to זור and דור, with the meanings of (1) to turn aside to lodge, (2) thus to be a stranger, (3) then to be a guest. As a guest, living in the same house, and having a common livelihood, with his host, is thus familiar; so is God represented as intimately acquainted with a man's habit of life. The Greek ξένος and ξενόω correspond with the Hebrew throughout all this usage.

v. 5. *Thou hast shut me in behind and before, and hast laid Thy hand upon me.*

Man is surrounded by God in space; and this space is here described in detail, as of three dimensions: *behind, before, above.*

But for צרתני the LXX. read יצרתני.

v. 6. *This knowledge is too wonderful for me.*

For this meaning we must read הדעת, which expression Gesenius says is used κατ' ἐξοχὴν of *the knowledge of God.* Compare דעת אלהים in Hos. iv. 1; vi. 6, with הדעת in Hos. iv. 6. I incline to the supposition that this is the right reading of the text:—the initial

PSALM CXXXIX.

ה being confounded with the final ה of the preceding word, and then omitted, *de more.* The LXX. read דעתך,—ἡ γνῶσίς σου.

v. 8. אסק. It has been disputed whether to assume נסק or סלק as the root of this word. Since neither of these appears in existing Hebrew, we are restricted to Aramaic usage,—(the Arabic being here unrepresented). In this usage we find some forms of practically one and the same verb belonging to the former, and some to the latter, root. Castell assumes one root only, viz. סלק; and supposes the ל to fall out in some inflections; just as, in verbs with an initial נ, this consonant falls away in obedience to certain euphonic laws. But it ought to be considered that to this case such laws of euphony are not applicable. Nothing is gained, in this respect, by the omission or absorption of the ל of סלק. Or, even if there had been any such gain, it would have been available as well for the one as for the other class of Aramaic forms. Moreover, the proposed omission of ל from כלק is unexampled. Delitzsch can hardly be in earnest when he adduces, as an example, the abbreviation of יבבב to יסב.

By the modern school-boy, who sees that the first Latin verb he has to learn,—*esse, sum, fui,*—is formed from two or three distinct roots, the solution of the difficulty is found in the assumption of two distinct roots in this case. So J. D. Michælis, criticizing Castell, says—

Quod de Lamed excidente habet noster, plane contra linguarum Orientalium morem est Duo potius sunt ascendendi verba, סלק et נסק. Ex his סלק Syris, Chaldæis, Samaritanis usitatum, ignotum Hebræis Arabibusque, in solo præterito ac participio Peal, ac conjugatione Ethpaal, ponitur ; at in futuro, imperat, et infin. Kal, totaque conjugatione Aphel, נסק usitatum, quod et Hebraico legis Ps. cxxxix. 8.

v. 11. *If I should say, Surely darkness will stamp me out; then is night light about me.*

For ישופני it has been proposed to read יצופני See Job xi. 17. תעפה כבקר תהיה,—*darkness shall be as the morning;* or, as Renan gives it, *Les tenèbres du present deviendront un matin.* But, although this conjecture is ingenious and plausible, it is counterbalanced by the authority of the LXX., who render the Hebrew word here by the same word (καταπατέω) wherewith they reproduce the שאף of Ps. lvi. 2 and 3, and Ps. lvii. 4. Since then the existing text contains a difficult reading, which was also the reading of the LXX., it is the safest plan to accept it, and make the best we can of it.

I accept not only the reading but also the rendering of the LXX. *If I say, Surely darkness shall tread me down, &c.* For I consider that the word *darkness* is often elsewhere used to denote *death, the grave, the under-world.* To such a meaning the idea of *treading-down* is appropriate. See the connection of דכא with מחשכים in Ps. cxliii. 3.

For this meaning of the verb שאף, which with the LXX. I identify with the שוף of the text, see my note on Ps. lvi. 2.

The suggestion of this 11th verse is, that perhaps darkness—the darkness of the grave—may hide the human soul from its divine origin. It must be carefully observed that the following verses, up to v. 17, are occupied with a *reductio ad absurdum* of this suggestion. As in Ps. xciv. 9, the question is asked,—*He that formed the eye, shall He not see?* &c., so here it is considered sufficient to assume that the darkness that follows death can no more hide us than the darkness that preceded birth;—*when we were formed secretly, and fashioned in the lower parts of the earth* (v. 15); that is, in obscurity and mystery. God saw us, knew us, then. He will see us, and know us, in the darkness and mystery of death.

To this consideration verses 13-16 are subordinate.

v. 13. *For it is Thou who hast begotten my soul:*—

So I translate כליותי; since it is acknowledged that this word denotes the seat of the *affections &c.*

Thou who hast overshadowed me in my mother's womb.

So I translate תסכני; since this word is in other places represented by ἐπισκιάζω in the Septuagint Version; though not here. The peculiar meaning of this Greek word will appear from Luke i. 35,—δύναμις ὑψίστου ἐπισκιάσει σοι. The meaning in both places is that *procreation is God's creation*. In the Psalm this is only the expression of the general truth, Τοῦ γὰρ καὶ γένος ἐσμέν;—but in the Gospel the intention of something extraordinary is unmistakeable.

v. 14. *I praise Thee for that I was wonderfully separated* (or *consecrated*)—sc. from my mother's womb. See Ps. xxii. 10, and lxxi. 6, —*Marvellous are Thy works, and especially this soul of mine that knoweth (them).*

The construction does not allow the usual rendering of נוראות נפליתי, viz. *I am fearfully and wonderfully made.* The former word is used adverbially (as in Ps. xlv. 5, and lxv. 6); and, with regard to the latter, we must consider that פלה, or פלא, denotes first *separation*, then *separation for a purpose*,—that is, *consecration.* To the Greek of St. Paul (Gal. i. 15), ὁ θεὸς ὁ ἀφορίσας με ἐκ κοιλίας μητρός μου, the same equivocal meanings, mechanical and moral, are rightly attributed. The word denotes both the natural *separation* from the mother, and the moral *consecration, setting apart,* to God. Since the word may denote either of these, it seems to have been chosen, certainly by St. Paul, and perhaps by the Psalmist, to denote both.

The fact of the two words, נפליתי and נכפלאים, being thus brought into juxtaposition, is sufficient to suggest that they are used in two different senses. This was the conceit, or humour, of the age,—to put in juxtaposition similar forms with diverse meanings. It is what we call *punning*. See note, and foot-note, upon Ps. cvi. 28. Now since נפלאים, in connection with מעשיך, must mean *distinguished*, in the sense of being *extraordinary*, we must take the previous word נפליתי in the other sense, viz. of being *separated*.

For my rendering of the latter part of this verse, I suppose the Psalmist's meaning to be that the separation from the mother, which is individualization, is the introduction to conscious life, to the knowledge of God and of His works. And that this surely signalizes man as the most wonderful of God's works, viz. this faculty or potentiality of *knowing* all His other works.

v. 15. *Not hidden from Thee was my own self* (עצמי) *which was made in a hidden place, and was fashioned in the lower parts of the earth.*

I adopt this meaning of עצם because it enables me to link on this verse more easily and consistently to the preceding verse. It denotes just that to which the preceding verse has introduced us, *the conscious, reflective, self.* At the same time, the usual concrete meaning of the word (*my bone*) may be accepted as sufficient for the occasion.

v. 16. *Thine eyes did see my compacted folds* (גלמי); *and in Thy book were recorded all the days wherein they were formed, when as yet there was none of them*, (sc. *of those days*).

The meaning is that God knows, from the first, the development, and the days wherein that development should take place, even from the first day, i.e. the day of conception, unto the day of birth. I can find no other meaning than this; but I admit that the thought is a commonplace one, and is expressed in too ample verbiage.

The word גלם denotes that which is compactly involved, as a cloak folded up, or as the parts of anything as yet undeveloped: a leaf or flower in the bud: a *fœtus* in the womb.*

---

* The aptness of this expression will be recognized by the most casual observer. The condition of undeveloped organisms is that of being wrapped or folded together. The words *development* and *evolution* denote the unfolding, or unrolling, of that which before has been folded or rolled up.

verb is found only in 2 Kings ii. 8, where it denotes the folding of a cloak. The noun substantive גלום, *a cloak*, occurs in Ezek. xxvii. 24; and גלם, *a fœtus*, only here. The root is probably akin to גלל.

In my translation of the words ולא אחד בהם I have been guided by Ps. xc. 10,— בהם in both places having the same meaning: —*As for the days of our years, there are seventy years of them;* compared with the text, *When there was none of them.*

v. 17. *And to me, O how precious were Thy favourable regards,*—i.e. as soon as I became conscious of them—*O God;—How great the sum of them!*

v. 18. *Should I reckon them, they are more numerous than the sand. I awoke, and I was still with Thee.*

The thought is here continued in the straight line. As God knew my processes of development before my birth, so, at my birth, He manifested His good purposes towards me: purposes which thenceforward became reciprocal. The emphatic ולי, with which the 17th verse begins, marks the response of the soul that awakens to independent life, and to the consciousness of God's love. The more definite expression of this thought is reserved to the close of v. 18,—*I awoke* (from the unconsciousness and darkness of the womb) *and I was still with Thee.* The loving care that tended those days of unconscious existence was manifested to my consciousness when I awoke to life.*

v. 19. At this point it is customary to find a paradox. How strange to descend from such sublime thoughts, of humanity affiliated to Deity,—of God's eternal love being as it were complemented by man's love to God,—to bloodthirsty expressions, such as are supposed to be found in this and the following verses. I cannot see the paradox. Man awakes to the consciousness of two things, viz. of good and of evil:

---

* Our birth is but a sleep and a forgetting:
The soul that rises with us, our life's star,
   Hath had elsewhere its setting,
   And cometh from afar.
Not in entire forgetfulness,
And not in utter nakedness,
But trailing clouds of glory do we come
   From God who is our home.
Heaven lies about us in our infancy.
    Wordsworth: Intimations of Immortality.

—of God and of that which is opposed to God. In proportion to the sincerity of his love to God appears the sincerity and the intensity of his hatred of all that is opposed to God. Most assuredly, our love towards God is to be measured by the intensity of our hatred of God's enemies. *Ye that love the Lord, See that ye hate the thing that is evil.*

The expressions of blood-thirst are not to be taken literally. On the other hand, they are not to be smoothly obliterated. Is there not still a conflict between God and that which is not of God? If there is,—Are we to falter between the two? Will not the soul that awakens to the love of God awaken simultaneously to hatred and active opposition of all that is not of God? Will not God's enemies become our own, personal, irreconcileable, enemies? To these questions there can be but one answer; and this answer is given here and in the sequel.

אם תקטל אלוה רשע. This word אם sometimes introduces the *protasis* of an imprecation, whereof the *apodosis* is omitted. Such a usage is commonly assumed here; but, I think, without warrant. There is nothing to be supposed or imagined that would supply the ellipsis.

The same objection lies against the more common meaning of the word: *If Thou slayest the wicked,*—What then?

I propose a slight change in the division of the words, thus:—

אמת קטל אלוה רשע.

It is in faithfulness that God destroys the wicked. Compare liv. 7. *Destroy Thou them in Thy faithfulness.* To exterminate wickedness is a duty towards God that man has undertaken. It is a reciprocal obligation; and therefore the Psalmist hastens to give the assurance of his part:—

It is in faithfulness towards me that God destroys the wicked. So now, on my part, in faithfulness towards my God, I charge you blood-thirsty men that ye depart from me.

v. 21. See above under v. 19.

v. 23. See above, introductory note.

Psalm CXL.

A comparison of this Psalm with the sixty-fourth shows a correspondence that can hardly be accidental. *The slanderous tongue* is the subject of both.

v. 8. *O Jehovah, my Lord, Thou strength of my salvation, in the day of arming Thou hast provided a covering for my head.*

Perhaps St. Paul had this in mind when, describing the Christian armour, he spoke of *the hope of salvation as a helmet.* Compare also Isaiah lix. 17.

v. 9. *Grant not, O Jehovah, the desires of the wicked man: further not his plot for his exaltation.*

The last word of this verse I take to be לרומו, instead of the ירומו of the text. The LXX. seem to have read, or conjectured, בל ירומו. If this was a conjecture it would be suggested rather by the reading that I propose than by that which we find.

v. 10. The construction of this verse will appear strange, unless we connect it with v. 8, —a connection that seems plainly to be intended. As there the Psalmist says—*Thou hast provided a covering for my head, &c.,* so here he continues,—

As for the head of them that compass me about (sc. with lying words, as in cix. 3,) *let the mischief of their own lips cover them.*

In exact composition we should expect "*it*" (sc. *the head*) instead of "*them.*" But this is precisely the inexactitude that is to be looked for in a Hebrew composition.

v. 11. *Let it* (sc. עמל) *bring even upon themselves* (ימיט ועליהם) *coals of fire: let it cast them into pits so that they rise no more.*

The division of the words ימיט ועליהם which I propose brings a two-fold advantage. It enables us to regard עמל as the continuous subject of the verbs, and it gives just that emphasis to עליהם which the occasion requires.

For the meaning of ימיט see Ps. lv. 4. It seems a strange use of the verb; but we need not defend it here. The two examples are sufficient to establish it as a recognized expression to denote the bringing of evil upon any-one.

It surely does not admit of any doubt that

the words בָּאֵשׁ גֶּחָלִים are to be taken together. See note on cxx. 4.

Psalm CXLI.

This seems to be the evening prayer of one who exercised judicial functions: who sought to administer judgment in justice; but who had to compete with, and to defend himself against, others who procured to themselves advantage and applause by perverting judgment. He prays that no such temptation may prevail over him (v. 3, 4,). In v. 5, he defends his own impartial conduct on the grounds, not of justice only, but of kindness; and he tests the principle of his conduct by applying it to himself. If, says he, a righteous man should smite me, it were a kindness. If he should convict me (יֹכַח, a judicial term) it would be an anointing of my head, that I hope my head would not refuse or resent, &c. The sixth and seventh verses are occupied with imprecations of God's wrath upon the unrighteous judges; and the Psalm ends with a prayer for guidance under circumstances of special perplexity, and for deliverance from circumstances of special danger.

The following translation will perhaps enable the reader to follow the main thought throughout.

1. Jehovah, I have called upon Thee: haste Thee to me: hear my voice when I cry unto Thee.

2. Let my prayer ascend as incense before Thee, let the lifting up of my hands be an evening offering.

3. Set a watch, O Jehovah, upon my mouth; guard Thou the door of my lips.

4. Let not my heart incline to any evil thing, to invent pretexts wickedly with men who are workers of iniquity; and let me not taste of their dainties.

5. Should a righteous man smite me, it were a kindness. Should he convict me, it would be an anointing of my head that I hope my head would not refuse. Nay, but my intercession should still be (made for them) in their misfortunes.

6. Smashed by the rock be their judges, so that they (sc. the people) may hear my words that they are acceptable.

7. As when one plougheth and splitteth up the earth, so let their bones be scattered at the mouth of the grave.

8. But to Thee, O Jehovah my Lord, are mine eyes directed; in Thee have I trusted, bare not Thou my soul.

9. Preserve me from the power of the snare that they have laid for me, and from the traps of them that work iniquity.

10. Let them fall into their own nets; let me only pass quite over them.

v. 2. *Let my prayer ascend,* תכון. It is, literally, Let my prayer be *erected.* The phenomenon of a perpendicularly ascending cloud of smoke is here indicated. See note on Ps. xx. 4.

id. *Let the lifting up* (משאת) *of my hands be an evening offering* (מנחה).

In view of the common expression, נשא ידים, it would be unwarrantable to say that משאת here denotes *an offering.* On the other hand, it is not unlikely that the word may have been chosen here as a *double entendre,* to include the idea of such an *offering* as should be complementary to the *incense* of the preceding clause.

With regard to the *Minchah,* as here mentioned,—In the service of the tabernacle (Numb. xxviii. 3, &c.), the whole burnt-offering of both morning and evening was to be followed by a *Minchah.* One feature of this offering, viz. the *incense,* is here associated with the morning; whilst the *Minchah* itself is mentioned in connection with the evening. It is an example of *hendiadys,* which, in other words, is a poetical distinction without any real difference. It is probable that the *Minchah* is thus mentioned in connection with the evening service because it was the closing ceremony of the day; although it was equally the closing ceremony of the morning service. And the reason why the evening service is here specially mentioned is that the prayer of the Psalm is an evening prayer. This is sufficiently indicated by the figurative language of the next verse.

v. 3. As watches and guards were set at the close of the day, the language of the text, although used figuratively, characterizes the Psalm as an evening prayer. The figurative use is to the effect that it is more important to guard the door of one's lips, than the door of one's house; just as, more actively, it is said in Prov. xvi. 32, *He that ruleth his spirit is better than he that taketh a city.*

v. 4. להתעולל עללות. I take this expression to mean *to make pretences* or *to feign occasions*, as an unjust judge may do. So the LXX., τοῦ προφασίζεσθαι προφάσεις, and Latin Vulgate,—*Ad excusandas excusationes*. But the Syriac gives the more usual, and the more empty, meaning of *doing deeds;*—and this notwithstanding that the Syriac עלא, עללהא, denotes *an occasion,* and specially *a feigned occasion.* So also the Chaldee, as in Dan. vi. 4, 5. Both our English Versions adopt what I call the empty meaning. So also Ewald and others. "*To commit deeds,*" says Ewald. Yet such a simple idea would hardly be expressed so clumsily, and with such exuberance of emptiness. Surely something more than this must be intended.

id. *Let me not taste of their dainties,* (במנעיהם).

I understand this of such popular favour as an unjust judge seeks and gains. To this I have been led by a comparison of Prov. xxiv. 23, 24, 25,—

It is not good to have respect of persons in judgment. He that saith unto the wicked, Thou art righteous, him shall the people curse, nations shall abhor him. But to them that rebuke shall be favour,—למוכיחים ינעם.

The *favour* (נעם) of the last verse is that which a worthy judge may claim of the worthy. It is so claimed by the worthy judge in v. 6, of this Psalm, where we find the same word נעם.

That which an unjust judge obtains by iniquity the Psalmist abhors: *Let me not taste of it.* But the same thing obtained by equity is acceptable, and desirable.

v. 5. I have above described יכח (Hiph.) as a judicial term. It is used as synonymous with שפט in Isaiah ii. 4; xi. 3 and 4. See also Gen. xxxi. 37; Job ix. 33; and the above-quoted Prov. xxiv. 25.

v. 6. נשמטו בידי סלע, *Smashed by the rock.* I take the word בידי merely as a preposition, as in v. 9.

id. *That they* (the people who had had experience of unjust judges) *may hear my words, for they are acceptable,* נעמו. See the latter part of note on v. 4.

v. 7. This verse describes, by a comparison, the scattering of the bones of the unrighteous judges, who are supposed to be hurled from the top of a rock. This is likened to the scattering of clods of earth by the plough. As here the earth is cleft (בקע) and dislocated, so in 2 Chron. xxv. 12, where we read of a number of Edomites being hurled from the top of a rock (סלע), it is added, *And all of them were broken in pieces,* וכלם נבקעו. Taking this place into consideration we can hardly avoid referring the expression בקע - - - עצמים to the breaking of the bones of the wicked judges who in the preceding verse are precipitated down the rock. But to obtain this meaning we ought to read עצמיהם instead of the עצמינו of the text. And this, according to the Codex Alexandr., was the reading of the LXX.; as it was also that of the Syriac translator. The exigency of the case would suggest and enforce this reading, even without such warrant.

vv. 8, 9. With the sentiment of these two verses, compare that of Ps. xxv. 15,—*Mine eyes are ever looking unto Jehovah, for it is He that plucketh my feet out of the net.*

Psalm CXLII.

Taking this Psalm by itself I feel disposed to give credit to its title, which attributes it to David. But Ewald and others, with some show of probability, take this in connection with the two which immediately precede; assigning them to one and the same author. Now the small considerations which might be adduced against the Davidic authorship of this Psalm are increased at least three-fold in our estimate of the triplet.

Ewald says that the language of these three Psalms is devoid of any trace of an imitation of older songs. Yet this Psalm contains a very close imitation of an acknowledged composition by David. Compare the following consecutive expressions here, viz.—

v. 7.✱ הצילני · · · · · כי אמצו ממני

v. 8. הוציאה

id. תגמל עלי

with the consecutive expressions of Ps. xviii., viz.—

v. 18. יצילני · · · · · כי אמצו ממני

v. 20. ויוציאני

v. 21. יגמלני

These points of resemblance indicate either an intentional copying of another's work, or a reiteration of sentiment in the same language by one and the same writer; just as we find St. Paul repeating the same sentiments in the same expressions in different epistles. This latter supposition would confirm the representation of the title of this Psalm. If it was really composed by *David in the cave*, it is easy to understand how the same turns of thought, expressed in the same words, would be found here and in Ps. xviii.

v. 5. The imperatives in the verse are plainly rhetorical. They import no difficulty into the construction.

id. *There is none that looketh after my soul*, sc. for good. The verb here used is דרש. When the expression occurs, *To seek after one's soul for evil*, the verb is usually Pi. of בקש.

v. 7. For דלותי see note on xxx. 2.

v. 8. *Bring forth my soul out of prison to praise Thy Name. The righteous are waiting on my account, till Thou shalt revive me.*

I have followed the LXX. in my rendering

of the words בי יכתרו, ἐμὲ ὑπομενοῦσι. They give the same rendering of the same verb in Job xxxvi. 2. The word has this meaning more commonly in the Aramaic dialects. The Syriac translator, for example, uses it to represent the ἐὰν μείνητε of St. John's Gospel, viii. 31.

The peculiar usage of גמל which I have pointed out in my note on Ps. cxix. 17, is to be observed here; since the Psalmist writes under apprehension of death. The word is used specially of deliverance from death. In addition to the places referred to under Ps. cxix. 17, I cite here the use of גמול in Ps. ciii. 2, in connection with the deliverance of life from the grave in v. 4; and of הגמול in Ps. cxvi. 12, in connection with verses 7 and 8 of the same Psalm.

Psalm CXLIII.

Regarding this Psalm as a late composition, and as consisting to a great extent of reminiscences of earlier Psalms, I take from Ewald the following indications of these earlier sources.

With v. 1 comp. lxv. 6; cxviii. 5. Ver. 2 from Job xiv. 3, 4, &c. Ver. 3 from lxxxviii. 6, or rather immediately from Lam. iii. 6. Ver. 4 from cxlii. 4; lxi. 3; lxxvii. 4. Ver. 5 from lxxvii. 6. Ver. 6 from lxiii. 2. Ver. 7 from xxviii. 1. Verses 8, 10, 11, from li. 10-13; v. 9; xxv. 1.

v. 1. באמנתך ענני בצדקתך. *In Thy faithfulness hear me: in Thy righteousness.*

This somewhat peculiar construction compels our observance of the distinction (thus evidently intended) between these two words. There are abundant grounds, as I have elsewhere shown, for the supposition that the former of these terms denotes God's faithfulness, generally, to all His creatures; and the latter His specially covenanted favour to His chosen people. The former, indeed, may be regarded as covenanted faithfulness, in consideration of the terms of the covenant made with Noah; but the latter has reference exclusively to the Abrahamic covenant. The Psalmist pleads both in one breath. See note on lxxiv. 20.

v. 9. אליך כסיתי. *(Fleeing) unto Thee I hide myself.* For this pregnant construction see note on Ps. lix. 10. The LXX. have allowed the idea of *fleeing*, which is necessarily understood, to supplant that of *covering*, or *hiding*, which is expressed. They give, πρός σε κατέφυγον. The words are wanting in the Syriac.

Psalm CXLIV.

Like some other of the later Psalms, and more conspicuously than any other, this consists of extracts from earlier compositions. Unlike some others,—as, for example, Ps. cxxxv.,—this compilation presents an appearance of homogeneous structure, as far as verse 12. At this point we find not only an abrupt change of matter and of style, but also the introduction of a passage which is found no-where else, and which is plainly of a much earlier date than the compilation itself. This passage, moreover, is followed up by a verse in the later style. We cannot, therefore, assume that the compiler, having built up the former part of the Psalm with borrowed materials, here introduces something of his own. Like the curiously interpolated bit of antiquity found in Numb. xxi. 14, 15,—concerning which see my note on Ps. lxviii. 19,—it is as conspicuously incongruous as a Roman tile in a mediæval building. Ewald places it among the songs of David's time; but, considering that the conditions of happy contentment which it describes must have been the result of a long and honourable peace, and that these conditions can hardly be found before the reign of Solomon, he says there is no reason for doubting that it is really of Solomon's time. His more specific assignment of the date to the first half of Solomon's reign is founded upon an erroneous interpretation (as I think) of v. 12; and is very fanciful, even on the assumption that his interpretation is correct.

I subjoin a translation of this interesting fragment.

v. 12. *(We) whose sons are as plants reproductive in their youth: whose daughters are as gar-*

ners fashioned in the likeness of a treasure-house:

v. 13. *Our garners full, supplying (provision) of every kind: our sheep bringing forth thousands and ten thousands in our fields:*

v. 14. *Our chiefs exalted:—no invasion: —no going forth* (sc. into captivity) *:—no wailing in our streets.*

As a mere setting, so to speak, of this older portion, Ewald would reject the initial אשר of v. 12, as well as the whole of v. 15. The rejection of the former seems unnecessary.

Upon v. 12, it is to be observed that I take מגדלים as the Piel participle. No-where else is the verb found in Pual. In Piel it means *to rear, to bring up,* as plants, or as children. For the latter see 2 Kings x. 6; Isaiah i. 2; xxiii. 4; xlix. 21; li. 18; Hos. ix. 12. The word נטע denotes a *young* plant, from which growth and increase may be expected. In Job xiv. 9, it is used specially in reference to its capability of growth and reproduction, in contrast with an old and dried up tree. The usual interpretation of the text, according to which the sons are likened to plants reared in their youth is somewhat inane.

As in Ps. cxxvii. 4, a blessing is associated with the children that are brought forth in youth,—בני הנעורים,—so here they are counted happy who rear children while they themselves are yet young,—בנעוריהם.

The daughters are likened to excavated store-houses. There can, surely, be no difficulty in understanding the זוית of this verse as identical in meaning, as in substance, with the מזוים of the next verse. And the word מחטבות, which I have rendered *fashioned*, properly means *hewn out*, or *hollowed out, excavated*. The root is closely akin to חצב, which has much the same meaning. The comparison, which may appear gross to us, was obvious and natural to those who (with the same idea) used the word נקבה to denote a woman, or a female in general. Following the suggestion of this word, it is worth while to observe the connection of חצב, *to hew out*, with מקבת, *an excavated stone pit*, in Isaiah li. 1; and to bear in mind that both these words are figuratively used to express the origin of the Israelitish nation from Abraham and Sarah, who are mentioned in the next verse.

I suppose היכל here to mean a treasure-house, as in Ps. xlv. 9, for the reasons there given.

With regard to the words אלופינו מסבלים, which I render *Our chiefs are exalted*, against the usual opinion according to which אלוף is identified with אלף, *an ox*,—I observe that this word always elsewhere has the meaning which I have assigned to it. Further,—that if these words had been intended to denote *pregnant and gravid cattle*, as is usually supposed, they would hardly appear, as they do, in the masculine gender. Lastly,—that if the verb סבל meant simply and solely *to bear, or carry*, sc. a burden, then its passive must mean *to be borne or carried*,—a meaning which is not suitable to any interpretation of the passage. But if, as there is reason to suppose, this verb has a primary meaning of *lifting up*, from which there is an easy transition to that of *bearing*, or *carrying*, then its passive meaning is that of *being lifted up*, or *exalted*, which is that which I have adopted.*

---

* The close and almost inevitable connection between the idea of *lifting up* and that of *carrying* is exemplified by the Latin *fero, to bear*, which borrows some of its most important forms from *tollo, to lift up*.

This last consideration has the more weight because the Pual form of this verb is found nowhere else, so that there is the more temptation to assign to it an arbitrary meaning, as Gesenius does. Putting aside the Chaldee Poal of Ezra vi. 3, the only other form of the verb that has a passive meaning is the Hithpa. of Eccl. xii. 5, *The grass-hopper becomes a burden*, יסתבל ; —that is, even such a light thing as a grasshopper is carried with difficulty. There is thus absolutely no warrant whatever for putting the sense of *being burdened* upon the passive form of a verb whose active form denotes *bearing*.

That this verb סבל is used in the sense of *lifting up* in Isaiah liii. 11, appears from the rendering of the LXX., τὰς ἁμαρτίας αὐτῶν αὐτὸς ἀνοίσει. And St. Peter, referring to this place, is careful to use the same word;—the more so, as he interprets the passage to denote Christ's lifting up of our sins upon the cross. His words are, (Ep. 1, ii. 24),— ὃς τὰς ἁμαρτίας ἡμῶν αὐτὸς ἀνήνεγκεν ἐν τῷ σώματι αὐτοῦ ἐπὶ τὸ ξύλον.

Upon the whole passage Kimchi remarks that it expresses a fulfilment of the three-fold promise given in Deut. xxviii. 4, viz. of a blessing upon "*the fruit of thy body, and the fruit of thy ground, and the fruit of thy cattle.*" I suppose this to be true; but its truth depends entirely upon the interpretation which I have given to verse 12.

In the Preface to this work I have remarked, in reference to the received versions of the Psalter, that "reverence, love, and familiarity, accumulating through many ages, have combined to hide their blemishes, or to transform them into beauties." Surely no more striking illustration of this truth can be adduced than that which is furnished by the current interpretations of this twelfth verse. When the sons and daughters of a nation are the subject of a poetical description, we must look for a reciprocal relationship between the figures employed corresponding to that which exists in nature. But,—not to mention that it would seem more suitable to liken the young men, rather than the maidens, to the corner-stones of temples or palaces,—What reciprocity, what relationship, what correspondence, is there between young plants and corner-stones?—whether these corner stones be inside or outside, whether they be sculptured into human forms or not.

Psalm CXLV.

When the youthful geologist, Hugh Miller, found fossil fishes embedded in flag-stones, he was not allowed to jump to the conclusion that these fishes had ever lived. There was an orthodox alternative, viz. that God had made them of stone originally, and had put them in the flag-stones to try our faith. With much the same sort of orthodox indignation are we forbidden to suppose that this alphabetical Psalm, which lacks the *Nun* verse, ever had a *Nun* verse. The Psalmist purposely omitted it.

Yet the difficulty which we find in trying to ascertain this purpose :—in trying to discover why a man who set himself to write an alphabetical Psalm should omit an important consonant,—is greater than the difficulty which attends the supposition that a verse has been accidentally dropped. The LXX. and the Syriac translators supply the want. Did they find a gap, and fill it up as best they could? I think not. The LXX., as a rule, followed their text in a most servile manner. It is doubtful whether they would even perceive an alphabetical arrangement in the Hebrew. But to my mind it is certain that they would not trouble themselves to supply any deficiency of their text in accordance with such an arrangement. I conclude, therefore, that they found no such deficiency.

The verse, in much the same form in which the LXX. &c. found it, is found also in one MS. of Kennicott, thus :—

נאמן יהוה בכל דרכיו וחסיד בכל מעשיו.

For דרכיו the LXX. read דבריו; and this is preferable. Their rendering of the whole verse is,—πιστὸς κύριος ἐν τοῖς λόγοις αὐτοῦ, καί ὅσιος ἐν πᾶσι τοῖς ἔργοις αὐτοῦ.

To discredit this supplement it is thought sufficient to say that it is mainly a repetition of v. 17. But it seems unlikely that those who wished to invent a supplement could not have invented a sentiment *de novo*. One may reasonably suppose that they would not profess to fill up a gap by merely copying a verse that follows almost immediately. Is it likely that those who have to restore a series *a, b, c, d, e, &c.*, if they find the term *b* wanting, will fill its place by a repetition of the term *d*? I think not. The fact that the verse which is supplied in the Greek text is found, with some variations, a little further on in the Hebrew, is, I think, a strong warrant of its being genuine. And then, as if to clench the matter, we may assume that this repetition is the very cause of the omission. What more likely occasion of omitting a verse, than the fact that the same verse is repeated almost immediately, and almost *ipsissimis verbis*?

But the variation that is found in the repetition is not without significance. In v. 10, we find a distinction that is observed throughout the Psalm:—*All Thy works acknowledge Thee, Jehovah; and Thy saints bless Thee.* In accordance with this distinction we find in verses 14, 15, 16, mention of God's goodness to all living creatures. This is guaranteed to them by His general *faithfulness* (אמונה). In verses 18, 19, 20, we find mention of His specially covenanted goodness to His saints:—to them that call upon Him: to them that fear Him: to them that love Him. This is guaranteed to them by His specially covenanted *right-*

eousness (צדקה). For, as I have observed in my Prolegomena, § 22, "The word צדק denotes a constant characteristic and manifestation of a state of covenant relationship." And again (upon the use of these two words in Ps. lxxxv. 12), that they denote respectively God's faithfulness in nature and in grace. See also note upon Ps. cxliii. 1.

It is, then, quite in accordance with this distinction that we find verses 14, 15, 16, headed with the general sentiment *The Lord is faithful &c.* (נאמן); and verses 18, 19, 20, introduced with the more special assertion *The Lord is righteous &c.* (צדיק).

v. 5. דברי נפלאתיך אשיחה, *The particular details of Thy wonders let me speak.*

The Psalmist begins to tell of these in v. 14. At this verse Delitzsch says,—"The poet now celebrates in detail the deeds of the gracious King." For this use of דברי see notes on cv. 27, and cxxxvii. 3.

v. 14. זקף *to lift up.* This word, which in Hebrew occurs only here and in the next Psalm (v. 8), has in the Aramaic dialects the more specific meaning of *lifting up upon a pole, crucifying*, sc. a criminal. See Ezra vi. 11, for the Chaldee usage; and, for the Syriac, Matt. xxviii. 5; Mark xv. 27, 32; and John xix. 20, 32. If we suppose, what is by no means improbable, that this is the word which our Lord used in giving His disciples an intimation of the manner of His death (John iii. 14; xii. 32, 33), then that intimation would be more plainly significant than it appears in the Greek.

v. 16. *Opening Thy hand, and satisfying the desire of every living thing.*

Psalm CXLVI.

v. 5. *Blessed is he who regards the God of Jacob as his help* (בעזרו) *: whose hope is in Jehovah his* (sc. Jacob's) *God.*

I have elsewhere remarked upon this use of ב, that it much resembles the use of the French *en*.

v. 6. *Who made the heavens and the earth, the sea, and all that is in them : who observeth faithfulness* (אמת) *for ever.*

In the eighth verse God's goodness towards His people is mentioned. They are there spoken of as צדיקים; and as regards them God's צדקה is pledged by implication. For we may certainly regard the אהב צדיקים of v. 8, as equivalent to the expression אהב צדקה of Ps. xxxiii. 5. We therefore find here the observance of the same distinction as in cxliii. 1, and in the *Nun* and *Tsadde* verses of cxlv.

Psalm CXLVII.

In this Psalm, as in the later Psalms generally, we find the unqualified expression of a truth which only by degrees dawned upon the mind of the Hebrews, viz. that Jehovah, the God of their gracious dispensation, was the one God of nature. See notes upon Ps. xciii. 4, 5. God's Word is here represented (viz. in verses 15, 18, 19,) as the one *fiat* of all that is done in nature and in grace.* Comp. Ps. xxxiii. 4 and 6.

---

* I take this opportunity of observing that, although these later Psalms rank below those of earlier date in respect of natural beauty, yet in other respects they are most valuable. They mark the development of religious thought, and the progress of religious knowledge. Not that this development and progress are to be regarded as

The connection between these two Psalms (the 147th and the 33rd) is obvious. Ewald puts them close together. But the 147th is so distinctly framed upon the pattern of the 33rd that we are induced to put a considerable interval between them. Men do not usually imitate that which is of their own age.

In v. 1 of this Psalm we find an incomplete imitation of the first verse of the 33rd. In the same verse we meet with the improper construction זמרו אלהינו corresponding with the זמרו לו of the 33rd.

In v. 2 there is a beautiful adaptation to existing circumstances of xxxiii. 7. In the earlier Psalm it is said, *He gathereth together* (כנס) *the waters of the sea.* In the later Psalm we find *He gathereth together* (יכנס) *the dispersed of Israel.* We are reminded of Isaiah xl. 11, 12; where He who feeds His flock like a shepherd, gathers the lambs with His arm, and carries them in His bosom, is He who measures the waters of the sea in the hollow of His hand.

---

pure gain. In the earlier age the realm of religion is the scope of communal life. Later on it dwindles to the scope of the individual mind.

Verses 10 and 11 of this Psalm are also to be compared with xxxiii. 17, 18; and, as I have said above, verses 15, 18, and 19, with xxxiii. 4 and 6.

v. 1. *Praise the Lord, for it is good: harp (unto) our God, for it is pleasant: the Tehillah is befitting* (sc. to His saints).

In view of the use of טוב and נעים in Ps. cxxxiii. 1, it would be unwarrantable to refer these adjectives to God. Delitzsch well observes that "Ps. xcii. 2, shows that כי טוב can refer to God; but נעים said of God is contrary to the custom and spirit of the Old Testament; whereas these two words are in cxxxiii. 1, neuter predicates of a subject that is set forth in the infinitive form."

It is certainly necessary to supply, at least in thought, the class of persons to whom the *Tehillah* is befitting, just as it is supplied in Ps. xxxiii. 1,—לישרים נאוה תהלה. This is required in accordance with the usual construction; for which see Prov. xvii. 7; xix. 10; and xxvi. 1. For the sentiment, I refer the reader to note on Ps. xxxiii. 1.

v. 2. *Jehovah buildeth Jerusalem ;* that is, of course, buildeth up its ruins. See note on Ps. cxxii. 3.

v. 10. *Not in the strength of the horse does He delight, nor yet the legs of the man does He favour.*

The use of the definite article so emphatically,—*the horse* and *the man*,—is sufficient to show that the man is mentioned in connection with the horse, viz. as its rider. The mention of the man's *legs*, in this connection, is natural enough. Gesenius supposed that cavalry and infantry were intended.

v. 12. It can create no surprise to find that the LXX. make this verse the beginning of a new Psalm. Already the Psalmist has looked up from nature to nature's God, and with that God has identified Jehovah. We hardly expect a repetition of this process in the same Psalm.

However this may be, it seems to me very probable that these latter verses were suggested by some unusually severe wintry season. Otherwise, the Psalmist would hardly have restricted his view of nature to these phenomena of snow, of frost, and of thaw. It is from these phenomena exclusively that the lesson is taught. He who covers the earth with snow and binds it up with frost, and then sends His Word to melt them, (v. 18), sends the same Word to Israel.

Psalm CXLVIII.

The two main divisions of this Psalm are conspicuously marked. In the one, all things in heaven,—in the other, all things in and under the earth,—are called to praise Jehovah. The latter is again split up into two subdivisions: — the subject of the former being *man*: of the latter all other earthly agents, animate and inanimate.

A difficulty that has been only partially recognized arises from this calling upon universal nature to join with man in this work of praising God. "How," asks Delitzsch, "is this to be explained? .... Does the invitation, in the exuberance of feeling, without any clearness of conception, here overstep the boundary of that which is possible?" He adds that "the call to praise proceeds rather from the wish that all creatures, by becoming after their own manner an echo and reflection of the divine glory, may participate in the joy at the glory which God has bestowed upon His people after their deep humiliation."

But the real point of the difficulty appears only upon the consideration that the *Tehillah*, to the participation in which universal nature is here invited, is everywhere else represented as the peculiar privilege of those who had been admitted into covenant relationship with God. One would suppose, therefore, that not only physical phenomena, and all living organisms below man, would be excluded from this privilege, but also a very large proportion of the human race itself. And indeed this supposition accords with the truth of the matter. The truth of the matter, bared of the excrescences of a fervid imagination, is regained by the Psalmist, and strictly expressed, in the last verse. Let all the rest go for what it is worth, as a flight of fancy,—and undoubtedly its worth is very great,— yet, after all, the bare truth is that the *Tehillah* is the exclusive privilege *of His saints, of the children of Israel, of the people that had been brought nigh unto Him.*

Regarding thus the main part of this Psalm as a flight of the imagination, I must point out that verses 5 and 6 seem intended as a sort of *fulcrum* for this flight. Whereas the *Tehillah* is really a privilege of those who are brought into covenant relationship with God, the Psalmist here adduces that sort of covenant which God is often assumed to have made with universal nature, as a warrant for this stretch of his imagination. He gives this expressly as the grounds upon which other creatures than man can be at least poetically called to join in the Tehillah :—*Let them praise* (יהללו) *the Name of Jehovah ; for He commanded and they were created : He established them for ever and ever : He gave them an ordinance, and will not transgress it.*

For this interpretation of the 5th and 6th verses, see notes below. For the peculiar significance of the *Tehillah* I refer to my Prolegomena § 23 ; and for the covenant relationship between God and nature which is assumed, and sometimes expressed, in these later Psalms, see note below on v. 6, and compare Ps. cxlvi. 6.

v. 6. חק נתן ולא יעבור. *He hath given*

an ordinance, and will not transgress it. The word חק here seems to denote a *promise,* or *covenant,* that God has made with nature, rather than a *law imposed.* Upon Ps. cv. 10, I have observed that the word is there used as if equivalent to ברית, *a covenant.* And it is certain that elsewhere the uniformity and continuance of nature are mentioned as the fulfilment of some sort of undertaking or engagement on God's part. I need refer only to Ps. cxlvi. 6, where God is spoken of as having made the heaven and the earth, and all that is therein, and as observing faithfulness (sc. towards them) for ever.

עבר is used in connection with חק in Jer. v. 22; although Ewald says this can have no application to the usage of the text.

v. 9. *Fruit trees and all cedars* (ארזים).

v. 10. *Wild beasts* (החיה) *and all domestic cattle* (בהמה).

The distinction I have observed in the 10th verse is usually recognized. See Gesenius. The same distinction is not so obvious in the 9th verse; though it is equally intended. Upon the mention of *the cedars which God has planted*, in Ps. civ. 16, I have remarked that "these trees seem to be mentioned as of God's planting in distinction from trees, shrubs, crops, &c. of ordinary agriculture."

Psalm CXLIX.

Free from all such imaginary and poetical extensions of Israel's prerogative as characterize the preceding Psalm, this is a perfect and distinct example of the *Tehillah*. It is an expression of trustful confidence in God, and of boastful defiance of all that is not of God. But it is Israel, and Israel only, that with quiet dignity rests in the one, and proudly fulminates the other.

v. 1. *The New Song* is identified with the *Tehillah* here, in Psalm xl. 4, and Isaiah xlii. 10. For the peculiar meaning of this expression see notes on Ps. xxxiii. 1, and xcvi. 1.

Here, as everywhere else, the *Tehillah* is the privilege of the *saints* of God, חסידים. See Prolegomena § 20.

v. 3. *Let them praise His Name with a*

pipe (מחול). See note on verse 4, of the next Psalm.

id. The verb יזמרו here is appropriate to the כנור which is mentioned in connection with it, as a stringed instrument; but not to תף, which was an instrument of percussion.

vv. 7, 8, 9. *It is written, that they shall execute vengeance on the heathen, and punishments on the nations: that they shall bind their kings in chains, and their nobles in fetters of iron: that they shall execute judgment on them: —this proud privilege belongs to all His saints.*

I make all three infinitives dependent upon כתוב. See Ps. xl. 9, where, as here, this participle means *It is written*, and has the infinitive לעשות dependent upon it.

For כבלי ברזל, in v. 8, see note on cv. 18.

Psalm CL.

v. 1. *Praise God in His sanctuary : praise Him in the firmament of His power.*

" On earth, as in heaven," says Ewald.

The same distinction appears, I think, in the next verse.

v. 2. God's *mighty acts* are wrought on earth : His *excellent greatness* is in heaven.

v. 4. *Praise Him with the tabret and pipe* (מחול). This word is usually taken to mean *dancing*. I suppose it to be only another form of חליל, *a pipe or flute;* for these reasons :—

(*a*) The word occurs here amongst the names of a great number of musical instruments. There is, therefore, a presumption that it does itself denote a musical instrument.

(*b*) It is associated with תף here, and in the third verse of the preceding Psalm; also, in a fem. form, in Exod. xv. 20, and Judges xi. 34. But the word חליל, which is acknowledged to mean *a pipe*, is similarly associated with תף in 1 Sam. x. 5, and Isaiah v. 12.

(c) As here we find

נבל וכנור תף ומחול

so in 1 Sam. x. v. we find

נבל ותף וחליל וכנור.

(d) The Syriac translator identified the מחול of the text with the חליל of 1 Sam. x. 5, and Isaiah v. 12. Moreover, he gives the same translation of תפים ומחלת in Exod. xv. 20, and in Judges xi. 34. In 2 Sam. vi. 5, we find the same musical instruments mentioned as in the text, excepting that, in the place of מחול, the word מנענעים occurs. But this is rendered, in both the Syriac and the Chaldee, by the same word (רביעין) that is used by the Syriac to represent the מחול of the text, the מחלת of the places cited above, and the חליל of 1 Sam. x. 5, and Isaiah v. 12.*

---

* The Aramaic רביעא, according to the etymology, would denote some *square* instrument; and probably a *drum* or *tabret*. I have not, in the text, adduced the authority of the Syriac version to prove directly that מחול means a *pipe*, or *fife*; but to show its identity with חליל. The translator seems to have taken it to denote a square variety of the תף, which was probably circular. It is remarkable that Egyptian sculptures and paintings show both these forms of drum, or tabret, or tambourine.

I conclude that the combination of תף and מחול, here and elsewhere, is precisely that with which we ourselves are familiar, viz. that of *drum and fife.*

v. 6. *Let everything that hath breath praise Jehovah.* It is not necessary to regard this as an extension to all living creatures of Israel's peculiar privilege of the Tehillah, such as we have observed in Ps. cxlviii. Since the Psalmist has pressed into the service of Israel, for this great work of praise, every instrument of music that he can think of, we must suppose that he at last regards everything that hath breath as instrumental in the same service.

To the praise-full soul of man all nature is attuned; and the grand organ awaits only the human touch, to proclaim that

"EARTH WITH HER THOUSAND VOICES
PRAISES GOD."

INDICES.

A. Of passages from other parts of Holy Scripture, explained or illustrated.

B. Of subjects incidentally treated of.

C. Of Hebrew words explained.

A

Gen. ii. 6. ...... ii. 319.
vi. 3. ...... i. 373.
xiv. 14. ... i. 117.
xiv. 15. ... i. 353.
xv. 6. ...... i. 70.
xix. 20. ... i. 266.
xxvii. 40. ... i. 324.
xxxix. 21.... i. 133.
xli. 8. ... ii. 68.
xlix. 3. ... ii. 84.
xlix. 10. ... i. 355.
xlix. 14. ... i. 397.
Exod. vi. 3. ... ii. 114.
x. 3. ...... ii. 93.
xv. 11. i. 207, ii. 188.
xix. 21. 22. ... ii. 229.
xxiii. 31. ... i. 407.
xxxiv. 7. ... i. 73.
xxxiv. 9. ... i. 175.
Lev. iv. 2. ...... i. 46.
v. 5, 6. ... i. 8.
v. 17, ... i. 46.
vi. 1-7. ... i. 47.
xiv. 12. ... i. 50.
xxi. 6. ...... ii. 73.
xxiii. 42, 43. ii. 97.
Numb. vi. 12 ...... i. 50.
vi. 24-26... i. 383.
xi. 20 ...... ii. 81.
xvi. 5 ... i. 375.

Numb. xx. 11 ...... i. 431.
xxi. 4 ...... i. 409.
xxi. 18, 19. i. 406.
xxiv. 4 and 16. ... i. 364.
xxiv. 17, 18. i. 355, 423,
[427.
xxv. 3-5. ... i. 309.
xxv. 9 and 18. ... ii. 282.
Deut. i. 1. ...... i. 411.
ii. 1-8. ...... i. 410.
vi. 25. ...... i. 70.
x. 14. ... ii. 111.
x. 20, 21. ... i. 367.
xv. 14. ...... i. 117.
xxviii. 28, 34. ... i. 363.
xxxii. 4. ... ii. 178.
xxxii. 15. ... ii. 25.
xxxii. 18. ... ii. 159.
xxxii. 43. ... i. 380.
xxxiii. 2. ... ii. 62.
xxxiii. 12. ... i. 352.
Joshua vii. 1. .... i. 48.
Judg. v. 18. .... i. 427.
xi. 16. .... i. 412.
xiii. 25. ...ii. 69, 71.
Ruth ii. 7. .... ii. 65.
1 Sam. vi. 3. .... i. 61.
x. 2. .... ii. 221.
xii. 17. ...... ii. 320.
xiii. 14. ... i. 255.

A

1 Sam. xviii. 14....	ii. 199.	Isaiah xxiii. 18. ...	i. 88.
2 Sam. viii. 13. ...	i. 350.	xxvi. 13. ...	i. 125.
1 Kings v. 18 ...	ii. 111.	xxviii. 9. ...	i. 88.
vi. 29.	ii. 41.	xxix. 1. ...	ii. 267.
viii. 34, 36, 39.	i. 175.	xxxv. 6, 7, 8. ...	ii. 119.
xviii. 21. ...	ii. 273.	xxxviii. 11. ...	ii. 154.
1 Chron. xvi. 30...	ii. 190.	xxxviii. 11-19 ...	ii. 140.
xxii. 14. ...	ii. 310.	xxxviii. 13.	ii. 271.
2 Chron. xx. 1. ...	ii. 108.	xxxviii. 16.	ii. 191.
xxii. 10. ...	ii. 294.	xl. 4.	i. 196.
xxvi. 16-21 ...	i. 51.	xl. 31. ...	ii. 210.
Job. v. 25.	ii. 20.	xlii. 3.	ii. 184.
x. 20.	i. 299.	xlii. 4.	i. 344.
xi. 17.	ii. 334.	xlii. 12. ...	i. 381.
xv. 7.	ii. 159.	xliv. 20. ...	ii. 204.
xxxiv. 37...	i. 73.	xlv. 2.	ii. 127.
xlii. 10. ...	ii. 121.	xlv. 25. ...	i. 170.
Prov. i. 7.	ii. 281.	xlviii. 19. ...	ii. 19.
iv. 23. ...	i. 422.	l. 10.	i. 99.
vii. 20....	ii. 101.	li. 9.	ii. 148.
xvi. 4. ...	ii. 309.	liii. 2.	ii. 302.
xxiv. 23-25. ...	ii. 350.	liii. 5.	i. 103.
xxvi. 2.	ii. 115.	liii. 10. ...	i. 60, 252.
xxvii. 25 ...	ii. 176.	lvi. 11.	i. 348.
Eccl. xii. 5. ...	ii. 362.	lxiii. 19.	ii. 249.
Isaiah i. 11, 12...	ii. 254.	lxvi. 12.	i. 133.
i. 28....	i. 72.	lxvi. 19.	ii. 284.
iii. 1. ...	i. 141.	Jer. iv. 30.	i. 212.
vii. 11. ...	ii. 41.	v. 4, 5.	i. 360.
ix. 6....	ii. 150.	vii. 22, 23.	i. 29.
xiv. 13. ...	i. 286.	x. 25.	ii. 87.

Jer.	xxii. 14. ...	i. 212.	Matt	xxii. 45. ...	ii. 239.
	xxiii. 12 ...	i. 210.	Mark	xii. 37. ...	ii. 240.
	xxiii. 27...	i. 344.	Luke	i. 20-23 ...	ii. 71.
	xlii. 20. ...	i. 107.		i. 35	ii. 336.
	xlviii. 45...	i. 423.		vii. 47. ...	ii. 259.
Lam.	ii. 18.	ii. 67.		xx. 38. ...	ii. 252.
	iii. 49	ii. 67.		xx. 44. ...	ii. 239.
	iii. 53. ...	ii. 201.	John	i. 14.	ii. 124.
Ezek.	iii. 15, 16, 26, 27.	ii. 70		ii. 10	i. 217.
				iii. 14	ii. 368.
	ix. 4.	ii. 82.		xii. 32, 33,...	ii. 308.
	xx. 23	ii. 230.	Acts	iv. 25-27. ...	i. 78.
	xxxiii. 22...	ii. 70.		v. 4.	i. 49.
Dan.	ii. 1, 3. ...	ii. 69.		viii. 26. ...	ii. 54.
Hos.	ii. 20. ...	ii. 62.		x. 4.	i. 151.
	v. 2.	ii. 200.		xiii. 22. ...	i. 255.
	vi. 6.	i. 67.		xiii. 34	i. 66.
	vii. 16. ...	ii. 77.		xvii. 31. ...	ii. 50.
	ix. 9.	ii. 200.	Rom.	iii. 4.	i. 55. & 316.
	xiii. 14. ...	i. 369.		iii. 19	i. 367.
Amos	ii. 7. ...	i. 329.		v. 9.	i. 249.
	viii. 3. ...	ii. 325.		v. 13.	i. 199.
Micah	iii. 3, 4. ...	i. 121.		vii. 4.	i. 239.
Hab.	iii. 2. ...	ii. 160.		viii. 3	i. 32.
	iii. 10, 11. ...	ii. 73.		xv. 9.	i. 68.
Zeph.	iii. 7. ...	i. 120.	1 Cor.	x. 1, 2. ...	ii. 99.
Zech.	x. 1. ...	ii. 320.	Gal.	i. 10. ...	i. 116.
Matt.	vi. 25....	ii. 273.		i. 15.	ii. 337.
	xii. 41. ...	i. 78.		iii. 6-29....	i. 31, 33.
	xxi. 16. ...	i. 92.		iii. 13, 14...	i. 244.
	xxii. 32. ...	ii. 252.		iv. 4, 5. ...	i. 240.

iv.

B

Gal. iv. 25, 26	ii. 135.	Heb. x. 10.	i. 238.
Eph. ii. 12-17	i. 244.	x. 28.	i. 40.
iv. 9.	i. 419.	x. 29.	i. 250.
iv. 26.	i. 85.	James i. 15.	i. 310.
vi. 6.	i. 116.	i. 17.	i. 327.
Philipp. i. 21.	ii. 260.	1 Pet. ii. 8.	ii. 281.
Col. i. 20-22	i. 244.	ii. 22-25.	i. 249, ii.
iii. 22.	i. 116.		[362.
1 Thess. iv. 16.	i. 284.	1 John iii. 4.	i. 73.
Heb. i. 7.	ii. 211.	Rev. xiv. 3.	i. 206.
x. 2.	i. 295.	xiv. 10.	ii. 57.
x. 5-7.	i. 237.		

B

Achan, sin of	i. 48.
Ammon	ii. 108.
Ananias and Sapphira, sin of	i. 49.
ἀνθρωπάρεσκος	i. 116.
Anthropomorphism	i. 153.
ἀνομία	i. 197, 198.
Arabah, a designation of the South quarter	ii. 235.
Baal-Peor,	ii. 230.
Baca, valley of	ii. 118.
Beulah,	i. 125.
Burning arrows,	ii. 283, 284.
Burning of pastures,	i. 221, ii. 113.
Cedars of Lebanon,	ii. 213.

Crucifixion,	ii. 368.
Darkness, plague of	ii. 222, 224.
Destruction=change of form	ii. 161.
Dislocated construction,	i. 142, 143, 427.
Dumbness, upon a divine communication	ii. 68.
Eating ashes, a mark of insanity,	ii, 203, 204.
Ecstasy,	i. 363.
Elymas, conjecture as to his name,	ii. 71.
Ephratah,	ii. 311.
Gebal,	ii. 103.
Giving and Taking, equivocal,	i. 420, ii. 51.
God of the living,	ii. 252.
Hephzibah,	i. 125.
Idolatry,	ii. 251.
Jashobeam,	ii. 30.
Jaar, fields of	ii. 311.
Jehovah and Elohim, indifferent use of	ii. 12.
Jeux d'esprit,	ii. 231.
Kadesh,	i. 416.
κνίση,	i. 154.
Leper, disqualifications of	i. 50.
Leviathan,	ii. 45.
Lightning, as producing rain,	ii. 319, &c.
Liver, as a seat of emotion,	i. 126, 192.
Maledictory Psalms,	ii. 8, 237.
Mattanah	i. 402.
Melchizedek, order of	ii. 242.
μεθύω,	i. 217.
μεριμνᾷν,	ii. 273.
Minchah, ritual of	i. 151.
Minchah, daily service of	ii. 348.

C

Miracles, cessation of...	ii. 250.
New Song,	i. 205, ii. 188.
παλιγγενεσία, ...	ii. 214.
Red Sea, ...	i. 413.
Sacrifices, Levitical	i. 232.
Sacrifices of the dead	ii. 231, 232.
Samuel, his Books,	i. 253.
Sin-Offering,	i. 56.
Slave,	i. 116.
Snares,	i. 101.
Stone weapons,	ii. 153.
Succoth, ...	ii. 97 &c. and 225.
Suph, ...	i. 406.
Tabernacles, feast of	i. 263, ii. 97 &c. and 263 &c.
Tehillah,	i. 71.
Teruah = Tehillah,	ii. 150.
Trance,...	i. 364.
Trespass-Offering,...	i. 56, 57.
Video — invideo,	ii. 23.
Vocalized consonants,	i. 193.
Zoan, ...	ii. 79.
Zoar,	i. 266.

C

אהב, *to desire*	ii. 253.
אזכרה	i. 151.
אחז	ii. 68.
אשד	i. 338.
אך	i. 359.

C

אמלל	i. 87.
אפונה	ii. 143.
אשם	i. 71.
בגד	i. 19.
בחן, as distinguished from צרף	i. 127.
בכא	ii. 119.
בל	i. 128.
בעל	i. 123.
בשן	i. 402.
בשׂר	i. 372.
גבור	i. 320.
גבול	ii. 111.
גבל	ii. 108, 110.
גלגל = קשׁ	ii. 112.
גלם	ii. 339.
גמל	ii. 270, 355.
גמר	i. 295, 296.
גרס	ii. 270.
דביר	i. 186.
דבר = אבד	ii. 294.
דבר, *Hiph.*	i. 147.
דלה	i. 191.
דרור	ii. 115.
דשן, *Piel*	i. 153.
הגיון	ii. 173—175.
היכל	i. 255.
התעמר = התאמר	ii. 182, 299.
מתנה = והב	i. 406—418.
זכר	i. 155.
זקף	ii. 367.
זרע = זרח	ii. 191.

חן	i. 263 ; ii. 266.
חדל	i. 296.
חזה	i. 364.
חטאת	i. 71.
הלכה	i. 98.
חלף	ii 160, 207.
חלץ	i. 89.
חניך	i. 117.
חנמל	ii. 83.
חסד and חסיד	i. 65,
חפר	i. 208.
חק = ברית...	ii. 218 and 376.
כחש	i. 49, 146.
כמה	i. 368.
כסה = כסא, *the feast of booths*	ii. 96—101.
כסף, *the verb*	ii. 115.
כשר	i. 395.
כתר	ii. 355.
לץ	i. 76.
מאס	i. 120.
מחול	ii. 879.
מחקק	i. 855.
מסך	ii, 55,
מעל	i. 19.
מץ	i. 77.
משפט	i. 292,
משפתים	i. 398.
נדב	i. 396.
נוף	i. 286.
נטח = שפך	i. 139, 415 ; ii. 22,
נסך	i. 79,

סלק = נסק ...	ii. 333.
נפש, as distinguished from לב	i. 106.
נשק	i. 79.
סבל	ii. 361.
סוף	i. 415.
סלא = סלה	ii. 273.
עון	i. 73.
עז, *glory*	i. 93.
עמר	ii. 299.
ענה, expressing *purpose*	ii. 308.
ענק	i. 118.
ערבה	ii. 235.
ערג	i. 261.
עשב, *dried grass*	ii. 177, 212.
עתק	i. 87.
פעם, *the verb*	ii. 68, 69.
פשע	i. 71.
צדק	i. 70.
צמד	i. 309.
צער	i. 265.
צפון	i. 288.
צרף, as distinguished from בחן	i. 127; ii. 219.
קרקר and קדקד	i. 423, 424.
קרע	i. 211.
קשט	i. 351.
ראה, in an ethical sense	ii. 23.
רוד, Hiph.	i. 324.
רכסים	i. 196.
רפה = רמה	ii. 77.
רעש	ii. 19.
שׁגה	ii. 177.

שׁאף	...	...	...	...	i. 329; ii. 334.
שׁגע	...	...	...	...	i. 363.
שׁחר	...	...	...	...	i. 361.
שׁלם, *to compensate*	...	...	...	i. 47.
שׁנה	...	...	...	...	ii. 160.
שׂפתים	...	...	...	...	i. 398
שׁקט	...	...	...	...	ii. 65.
תהלה	...	...	...	...	i. 71.
תו	...	...	...	...	ii. 82.
תועפות	...	...	...	...	ii. 186.
תכן	...	...	...	...	ii. 53.
תף	...	...	...	...	ii. 380.
תרועה ...	...	...	...	...	ii. 150.

FINIS.

GEO. POWLSON, Printer, Advertiser Office, Market Gate, Warrington.

www.ingramcontent.com/pod-product-compliance
Lightning Source LLC
Chambersburg PA
CBHW032014220426
43664CB00006B/235